Global Migration, Social Change, and Cultural Transformation

Global Migration, Social Change, and Cultural Transformation

Edited by Emory Elliott, Jasmine Payne, and Patricia Ploesch

palgrave
macmillan

GLOBAL MIGRATION, SOCIAL CHANGE, AND CULTURAL TRANSFORMATION

First published in 2007 by
PALGRAVE MACMILLAN™
175 Fifth Avenue, New York, N.Y. 10010 and
Houndmills, Basingstoke, Hampshire, England RG21 6XS.
Companies and representatives throughout the world.

PALGRAVE MACMILLAN is the global academic imprint of the Palgrave Macmillan division of St. Martin's Press, LLC and of Palgrave Macmillan Ltd. Macmillan® is a registered trademark in the United States, United Kingdom and other countries. Palgrave is a registered trademark in the European Union and other countries.

ISBN-13: 978-0-2306-0054-6
ISBN-10: 0-2306-0054-9

Library of Congress Cataloging-in-Publication Data
Global migration, social change, and cultural transformation / edited by Emory Elliott, Jasmine Payne, and Patricia Ploesch.
p. cm.
Includes bibliographical references and index.
ISBN 0-230-60054-9
1. Globalization—Social aspects. 2. Globalization in literature. 3. Emigration and immigration. I. Elliott, Emory, 1942– II. Payne, Jasmine. III. Ploesch, Patricia.
JZ1318.F5167 2007
304.8—dc22 2007013676

A catalogue record of the book is available from the British Library.

Design by Scribe Inc.

First edition: December 2007

10 9 8 7 6 5 4 3 2 1

Printed in the United States of America.

Contents

Part 3 Global and Domestic Economies

Acknowledgments

In the summer of 2000, the University of California, Riverside's Center for Ideas and Society was awarded a multiyear Rockefeller Foundation Residency Site research grant for a project that focused on three pivotal areas of inquiry: migration, immigration, and social transformations; cultural diversity and the arts; and social change and cultural transformation. This generous grant created germane dialogues and points of departure for scholars, artists, and professionals traversing the humanities, social sciences, and arts. As a residency site, the University of California–Riverside (UCR) hosted internationally renowned scholars who directed small faculty seminars and workshops. This collection has developed from the conversations, debates, and teachings made possible by support from the Rockefeller Foundation, the University of California–Riverside, and the Center for Ideas and Society. We are most grateful to the following individuals within these institutions whose contributions were invaluable: the Rockefeller Foundation's Dr. Tomas Ybarra-Fausto was encouraging of this project from its inception; at the University of California–Riverside, Chancellors Raymond L. Orbach and France Cordova, Deans Carlos Valez-Ibanez and Patricia O'Brien, and Executive Director of Corporate and Foundation Relations Georgia A. Elliott offered unflagging support and institutional guidance; and the staff at the Center for Ideas and Society, Laura Lozon and Marilyn Davis, have expertly and patiently handled the logistical needs of each aspect of our programming.

Members of the UCR faculty helped to make the project a resounding success, particularly the following individuals who participated in the focused research groups enabled by this grant: Edgar Butler, Amalia Cabezas, Edward Chang, Ralph Crowder, Stephen Cullenberg, Jennifer Doyle, Tracy Fisher, Paul Gelles, Paul Green, Katherine Kinney, Tiffany Ana Lopez, Karen Pyke, Michelle Raheja, Dylan Rodriguez, Parama Roy, Anna Scott, Barbara Tinsley, Carole-Anne Tyler, and Devra Weber. We were delighted to welcome the following Rockefeller Residency Fellows whose short time at the center made a lasting contribution to the advancement of research in social change and cultural expression: Frances Hasso, Amitava Kumar, Toby Miller, Glen Mimura,

Jenny Sharpe, and Letti Volpp. The fellows, as well as the faculty and students of UCR, benefited greatly from the knowledge and expertise brought to the project by our three Resident Faculty Visitors, Professors Lisa Lowe, Toby Miller, and Leo Chavez, each of whom spent the winter and spring quarters on campus in 2001/02, 2002/03, and 2003/04, respectively.

We are grateful to Gabriella (Ella) Georgiades, Editor of African Studies, Latino and Latin American Studies, and Sociology at Palgrave Macmillan, whose confidence and guidance made this volume possible. We also thank editorial assistant Joanna Mericle for her help and patience. Jenny Sharpe's essay "Gender, Nation, and Globalization in *Dilwale Dulhania Le Jayenge* and *Moonsoon Wedding*" was originally published in the journal *Meridians: Feminism, Race, Transnationalism*; we are grateful for their permission to republish this piece.

And finally, our thanks to the reviewers of the manuscript for the press, the contributors, and the many participants in the Rockefeller Residency Site at UCR's Center for Ideas.

—*Emory Elliott, Jasmine Payne, and Patricia Ploesch*

INTRODUCTION

Global Migration, Social Change, and Cultural Production

Emory Elliott, Jasmine Payne, and Patricia Ploesch

Globalism is increasingly the subject of public discourse and national anxiety. New communication networks, global (im)migrations, and deterritorializations have made the old notion of nationally defined communities and cultures outmoded. These changes are typically represented in two simultaneous and contradictory ways. On the one hand, these shifts are characterized as a new world order that threatens to topple a once-dominant Western power, replacing its previous economic virility with vast populations of educated and inexpensive "foreign" laborers. Conversely, it offers a panacea, an emancipatory technological marvel whose advances have created a marketplace that literally delivers the world to your doorstep via keystrokes. These dichotomous views of the rapid changes in global immigration and migration patterns, changing centers of production, and shifting cultural formations too often limit this complex issue to a one-dimensional argument about capitalist economic development or decline in the new world order.

Global Migration, Social Change, and Cultural Transformation challenges this contradictory impulse in several important ways. First, the essays collected here expand the issues raised as a result of an increasingly transnational landscape, eschewing a purely economic discussion by addressing the interdependent and interpenetrating arenas of cultural production, social movements, race, and self-articulation. Second, this amplification is enabled by the scope of disciplinary backgrounds and transdisciplinary perspectives represented in the collection that challenge, push, and contest the boundaries of what are considered "global" issues, ranging from poetry, to text-messaging in the United Arab Emirates, to the U.S. prison-industrial complex. Cultural production is a central tenet of that challenge, for, as Toby Miller explains in this volume, "culture is more than textual signs or everyday practices. It also provides the legitimizing ground on which particular groups claim resources and seek inclusion in national narratives." Moreover, culture also indexes the ways in which different communities "are transformed by their contact and interaction with each other" (Rowe 2000, 25). Third, by insisting on the connection between race and the discussions of globalism, the contributors to this volume draw together the analytical strategy of U.S. multicultural critique and transnationalism. The volume probes the cultural expressions of migrants, border workers, and immigrants as they transform and are transformed by life in a new land. In a time of increasing transnational flows of culture, people, and capital, "home" has become a borderland where cultural traditions, values, and ways of life come together, clash, meld, and are transfigured. And in this way, it represents, takes part in, and is a part of the new internationalist and comparative movement in American Studies.

Throughout this volume we have operated on the assumption that thinking about the questions raised by transnationalism must be answered through an interdisciplinary reading of social struggle, cultural production, the migration of communities, and capital throughout the globe. While not diminishing the impact of shifting capitalist forces, *Global Migration, Social Change, and Cultural Transformation* attempts to heighten understandings of a changing world by separating "globalization" from strictly economic considerations through a demonstration of the multiple ways in which communities "produce and rearticulate new kinds of localizing discourses and modes of cultural production and consumption" (Lenz 2002, 464) and how those are refracted in terms of race, gender, sexuality, the nation, violence, and economics. The questions raised by the new global order require a complex, nuanced approach, but one that is also cognizant of and responsive to the enlarged context raised by a more integrated global context. Likewise, this critical approach also engenders a new form, one that is interdisciplinary rather than intradisciplinary.

Previous critical work on globalization has provided important theoretical frameworks through which the deconstruction of dichotomous language and modes of analysis surrounding theories of "the global" could be explored. While some authors have concerned themselves with identifying an enriched approach to the topic of globalization, one that does not engage, but rather rejects a binaried model of globalization, others have considered the impact of growing technology on both the theory and praxis of globalizing processes. Frederic Jameson warns of the flattening effect and homogenizing potentiality of theorizing globalization (*1998*, xii), while Jan Nederveen Pieterse and J. K. Gibson-Graham address the reciprocating roles of capitalism and technology in the proliferation of globalization, and how these relationships impact shifts in cultural and national agencies that arise both in resistance to and in tandem with globalization (Pieterse 2003, 10; Gibson-Graham 2006 14–15). Likewise, Arjun Appadurai's work on globalization foregrounds the plasticity of the imagination as an antidote to those theories that locate the globalizing process as a stable, immutable entity (*1996*). What arises out of these critical social-science approaches to globalization is that it cannot nor should not be approached as a monolithic system that develops polarities. Rather, it functions as a highly malleable series of processes and theories that in turn represent and impact multivalenced communities of people.

Furthermore, authors such as Lisa Lowe, David Lloyd, and Leslie Sklair have considered the impact of globalization at both a micro and macro level, and therefore have examined its affect on cultural production (Lowe and Lloyd 1997; Sklair 1998, 293). Lowe and Lloyd's and Sklair's respective work, as well as the work of Roseann Gonzales, Carol Gould, Henry Giroux, Anthony Giddens, David Harvey, Paul Jay, Roland Robertson, Raymond Williams, Stuart Hall, Janet Woolf, Janet Abu-Lughori, and Barara Abou-el-Hai[1] have taken to task definitions of globalization that limit their theoretical scope and, in turn, ignore marginalized and local communities and do not include the transnational and international, which often make up the most nuanced facets of what we consider global. Likewise, the *PMLA* 2001 special session "Globalizing Literary Studies" presented a rich reading of globalization's impact on literary studies as a crucial element of cultural production, and situated this import of these conversations within a specific discipline.

Global Migration, Social Change, and Cultural Transformation's contribution to these important sets of arguments about globalization can be considered both thematically and structurally. It arranges its critical framework across disciplines, rather than within the social sciences or the humanities, and is structured by thematic similarity rather than disciplinary familiarity. In so doing, it poses a challenge to a university system that is often impeded by disciplinary organizational structures. We have organized contributions to *Global Migration, Social Change, and Cultural Transformation* into three major thematic areas that address and intersect with the larger goals of rethinking race, class, and economics and revisioning cultural production: global and domestic economics, U.S. immigration and cultural production, and transnational narratives. As transnationalism is an organizing principle behind this volume, the nation is a foremost concern for our contributors, and its presence in these contributions permeates the terms of race, gender, orientalism, sexuality, and violence. The thematic organization of this book also allows for very specific readings from a wide variety of fields, but it has also benefited from the more telescopic work that effectively identifies and defines the broad terrain that the more specific pieces explore.

By considering the role of transnational narratives in this volume, patterns develop around definitions of "nation" and "tradition" as they form and reform the theoretical contours of globalization, and their impact on networks of cultural production and social change. In Part 1: "Transnational Narratives," the work of Grace Kyungwon Hong, Jenny Sharpe, and Frances S. Hasso grapples with these definitions along the lines of culture and technology, and considers economics as tangential rather than integral to expressions of subjectivity within and between communities.

In "'Most Overrated Western Virtue': The Politics of Knowledge in Zadie Smith's *White Teeth*" (Chapter 1), Hong reveals how multiculturalism posits itself as a postcolonial process, yet this "multicultural celebration of difference" actually flattens the differences the novel seeks to highlight as antithetical to colonialism. Therefore, multiculturalism functions as a neo-, rather than a post-, colonial ideological practice. Furthermore, Hong points out how any reading of White's novel as a multicultural text not only runs counter to the novel's politic goals and import, but also positions the novel as a global product, since multiculturalism, she remarks, is marketable. In contrast, Hong argues, Smith's novel offers a "postneocolonial" argument that locates the novel's investment in irrationality as a countermeasure to both colonial and neocolonial ideologies. The novel's "irrationality," Hong argues, involves a refusal of static categories of identity (both personal and inter/national) and therefore the "inevitable" global paradigm inherent to multiculturalism.

While Hong's essay considers how global networks impact literary as well as theoretical forms between cultures, and in turn highlights the dangers of cultural marketability; Jenny Sharpe's "Gender, Nation, and Globalization in *Dilwale Dulhania Le Jayenge and Monsoon Wedding*" (Chapter 2) considers globalization's impact intraculturally. Sharpe contends that advances in technology in India, which are in turn represented in Bollywood films, change the contours of what is considered traditional in relation to Indian nationalism. She argues that global changes push not only the definition but also the boundaries of what is considered traditional and, therefore, necessitates a revision in feminist approaches to "tradition" in this context. Bollywood films, she asserts, and the cultural types they seek to represent, both enact and are enacted upon by tensions surrounding globalization in such a way that both reveals and renders invisible economic, cultural, and gender gaps in Indian culture.

Frances Hasso's essay "Comparing Emirati and Egyptian Narratives On Marriage, Sexuality, and the Body" (Chapter 3) works through the impact of technology as a result of globalization and considers alterations to gendered juridical and national categories. Technologies, such as text-messaging and

Instant Messenger, she argues, have impacted gender relations within and between Emirati and Egyptian men and women by creating a space of agency for women who have access to such technologies. The challenges new technologies pose to gender relations, Hasso contends, therefore also impact juridical approaches to gender dynamics and, therefore, press the boundaries of citizenship and culture in both Emirati and Egyptian societies.

Though these essays demonstrate how economics impacts cultural expressions, Hong, Sharpe, and Hasso are also concerned with the dangers of cultural conflation, and facile multiculturalism. Their work thus proves cultural productions and representations that result from immigration and migration both within and between national, religious, juridical, and political boundaries. These essays clearly demonstrate Amy Kaplan's argument that "the notions of the domestic and the foreign" are mutually constitutive and, as such, demonstrate the permeability of (inter)national and cultural identities that are invested in rapidly shifting personal and social demographies (2005, 4).

In the thematic section "U.S. Immigration and Culture" (Part 2), the essays by Cynthia Young, Karen Pyke, Steven Gould Axelrod, and Tiffany Lopez grapple with what it means to "belong" in a given culture, and how inclusion in and exclusion from conceptions of nation and citizen affect the expressive forms of cultural belonging, as they resonate both personally and within communities. Through examinations of changes in literary form and iconography, these essays address the role of internalized racism, sexism, and xenophobia brought about by immigration and migration as it relates to the development of cultural identities within the United States.

From the Third World Newsreel, to Charles Reznikoff's contributions to avant-garde poetic form, to questions surrounding internalized racism in African American communities, to the role of religious and gendered iconography in the development of Chicana identities, these essays present forms of cultural production that envelop, actively revise, and resist hegemonic aesthetic, political, and social paradigms. Cynthia Young's essay "Third World Cinema Newsreel: Third Cinema Practice in the United States" (Chapter 4) discusses Third World Newsreel's (TWN) investment in creating what Young describes as a "radical Third World subject and a radical Third World public capable of transcending" racialized, classed, ethnic, or national identities. Though Young points to the TWN's important contribution to filmic practices that consider the global as well as the local and, therefore, "forged transnational forms of solidarity and support," problems arise, she states, with the rhetorical engagement of "transcendence." "Transcendence," she contends, assumes a concrete and static paradigm that "face[s] many of the self-same structures underpinning colonialism."

In "Charles Reznikoff: Poetry and Cultural Change" (Chapter 6), Steven Gould Axelrod looks to shifts in American poetic form as not only the representation of changes in cultural production as a result of immigration, but also the catalyst to global change. Axelrod notes Reznikoff's affect on U.S. as well as world poetic forms, and he elucidates Reznikoff's incorporation of other immigrant and migrant poetic voices into his own expressions of cultural subjectivity. As such, poetry itself is situated not only as a site where globalism becomes evident, but it is also the crucible for social and political change. Both Young's and Axelrod's essays consider the power of literary and visual projects in developing ties intra- and internationally, and they create spaces for agency outside the rubrics available through dominant discourse. At the same time, Young, Axelrod, Pyke, and Lopez present the nuanced complications that arise in this process of development. Pyke's essay on internalized racism (Chapter 5), and Lopez's essay on the Virgen de Guadalupe's integral function in reconceptualizing Chicana identification and activism (Chapter 7), poignantly reveal how communities respond to the often-suppressive ramifications of globalization on immigrant and migrant identities. While Pyke's essay "Defying the Taboo on the Study of Internalized Racial Oppression" engages the racist implications of investments in colorblind racism. Lopez's essay "Veneration and Violence: The Pedagogical Force of Virgin Iconography in Chicana Literature and Visual Art" presents the Virgen de Guadalupe as a synthesis of cultures that functions as an icon of transnationalism who instructs as much as she represents Chicana cultural identity.

Economic shifts are a primary component of the transformations taking place on a global level, but they are not the sole aspect that should be considered when delineating the impact of globalism. By drawing attention to "economics," this project does not seek to replicate scholarship that examines globalism in terms of wealth, capital, production, and consumption. Rather, the thematic organization of "Global and Domestic Economies" (Part 3), seeks to realign and amplify the conversation about economics in relation to transnationalism. Conceptualized economics more broadly and metaphorically, here economics emerges as a tool for describing, identifying, exploring, and challenging systems of object and property relations and networks of meanings and exchange. This resonates particularly in terms of race and immigration, two issues that are inseparable from one another and that permeate each contribution to the volume. Moreover, as Anjan Chakrabarti, Stephen Cullenberg, and Anup Dhar observe, the terms economics and economic development have a history, and need to be thoroughly investigated as problems in and of themselves. By examining the tangled constellations of global and domestic exchange, these authors reveal and challenge the consequences of increased global inequities and interpenetrations. Miller, Margaret Gray, Dylan Rodriguez, Chakrabarti, Cullenberg, and Dhar are united in their commitment to questioning the exchange between culture and politics, between the immobile and the mobile, between the exploited and those who seek to speak on their behalf, and between the third world and global capital.

Toby Miller's "Culture, Dislocation, and Citizenship" (Chapter 8) provides an overview of major changes in immigration since the 1960s and offers an analysis of what these shifts mean in terms of culture. A consequence of increased immigration, he suggests, is that culture is progressively a marker of difference rather than of collective identity. Moreover, the change wrought by transnationalism's movement of communities is that culture has become crucial to economic development for both emerging and advanced economies. Central to Miller's discussion is what the effect of immigration has been on culture and how political enfranchisement and its economic opposite are mediated through cultural difference. While debates about globalism and transnationalism often idealize the mobility and movement of goods and people, Dylan Rodriguez's essay "Toward a Theorization of the U.S. 'Prison Regime': White Supremacy, Bodily Immobilization, and the 'Society Structured in Dominance'"(Chapter 9) provides a counternarrative to that tendency by examining the immobility and violence enacted against the prisoner's body in the United States. For Rodriguez, the carceral system is fundamental to American identity, and indeed is central to its self-articulation in the global context. The growth of state-sanctioned violence and militarized punishment of racialized communities domestically has informed America's position in the global community as what Rodriguez calls in his essay "a global antisocial formation" that underlies the signification of "America" as a signifier of both occupation and juridical force. The nation-state harnesses the immobility of the prisoner to constitute the mobility of free citizens both domestically and internationally.

One of the fundamental catalysts for immigration is economic necessity, and the effect of increased noncitizen laborers both in the United States and worldwide is palpable. Noncitizen workers are often excluded from basic labor protections, and as a consequence, they occupy tenuous economic positions that do not allow them to voice their objections to labor conditions, pay, or treatment. In her essay about the relationship between this class of workers and those who advocate on their behalf, "The Mechanics of Empowerment: Migrant Farmworker Advocacy" (Chapter 10), Gray demonstrates the complexities of this affiliation, elucidating the vexed structure in which advocates attempt to use their own power to affect change on behalf of the nonimmigrant workers. While Gray's analysis focuses on a particular region and group of workers in the United States, her analysis of the constitution of power at play in this multifaceted issue has wide-reaching ramifications for noncitizen labor in a much broader context. In "Orientalism and the New Global: The Example of India" (Chapter 11), Chakrabarti, Cullenberg, and Dhar offer a counternarrative to the "depoliticized" discourse of development. By treating development as discourse, the authors contextualize India's models of economic growth and expansion within the historical framework of colonialism. They argue that, in fact, the models of development that have been debated in India have been molded along the Orientalist ideology of the good and bad "Other." Orientalism, they suggest, has not disappeared, but has shifted into new patterns and locations. The neoliberal celebration of global capital, they argue, necessitates that those who are made invisible and immobile, who exist outside the reach of global capital, are, in fact, most affected by it.

Because of the increasingly diverse student populations of American universities and colleges, those of us who teach in the humanities and social sciences are especially well-positioned to begin the work of charting innovative and creative ways of conceptualizing what the so-called new world order means. Questioning our fields, terminologies, and methodologies for thinking about relationships between and among communities and cultures is required as we attempt to understand and explain the complexities of transnationalism. The approaches that emerge from this volume and others like it will better equip scholars, teachers, and students to study how the global and the local are intertwined, and how transnational capitalism transforms and is transformed by local societies and cultures.

Notes

1. Thank you to our readers whose suggestions for further reading demonstrate how complex and varied the critical work about globalization both within the humanities and social sciences has been, and continues to be.

References

Appadurai, Arjun. 1996. *Modernity at large: Cultural dimensions of globalization.* Minneapolis: University of Minneapolis Press.

Jameson, Fredric. 1998. Preface to *The cultures of globalization*, eds. Fredric Jameson and Masao Miyoshi. Durham, NC: Duke University Press.

Kaplan, Amy. 2005. *The anarchy of empire in the making of U.S. culture*. Durham, NC: Duke University Press.

Lenz, Gunter H. 2002. Toward a dialogics of international American cultural studies: Transnationality, border discourses, and public culture(s). In *The futures of American studies*, ed. Donald Pease and Robyn Wiegman. Durham, NC: Duke University Press.

Lowe, Lisa, and David Lloyd. 1997. *The politics of culture in the shadow of capital: Post-contemporary interventions.* Durham, NC: Duke University Press.

Rowe, John Carlos. 2000. Post-nationalism, globalism, and the new American studies. In *Post-nationalist American studies*, ed. John Carlos Rowe. Berkeley: University of California Press.

Sklair, Leslie. 1998. Social movements and global capitalism. In *The cultures of globalization*, eds. Fredric Jameson and Masao Miyoshi. Durham, NC: Duke University Press.

PART 1

Transnational Narratives

CHAPTER 1

"Most Overrated Western Virtue": The Politics of Knowledge in Zadie Smith's *White Teeth*

Grace Kyungwon Hong

Archie Jones, one of the many hapless "heroes" of Zadie Smith's novel *White Teeth* (2000)[1], faces a decision of epic proportions. As a seventeen-year-old English soldier during World War II, he finds himself alone in the Bulgarian woods with perhaps the most iconic representation of twentieth-century evil: a Nazi collaborationist doctor whose expertise in genetics and whose participation in the "internal German matters" regarding "the sterilization program" and the "euthanasia policy" (*WT*, 90), hints at the darkest and most horrifying kinds of human experimentation. Should Archie kill this man, this representative of the amoral nadir of human existence, a man who routinely and casually decided who should live and who should die? Yet in so doing, Archie would become *the very thing* he is destroying. Should he let him go, and allow this man to further perpetuate his kind of eugenicist science, in fact, allow him to turn a strain of eugenics into the defining science of the twentieth century? One might think that this decision upon which, one could argue, the fate of the world hangs, would be difficult, if not nearly impossible to make. But it is not so very hard for Archie, or at least, it is not so hard for long. Because unlike you or me, Archie does not worry himself with any of these grand ideas. Instead, to make this decision on which, one could argue, the entire fate of the twentieth century hinges, Archie flips a coin. And he flips it badly.

How could someone possibly entrust such a decision to the vagaries of a coin toss? That is so irrational, so absurd. How could the loyal—if admittedly somewhat simple—subject of the once-greatest empire on earth, an empire that prided itself on order, rationality, *the proper way of doing things*, toss a coin to decide a man's fate, a country's fate, a world's fate? And, come to think of it, how does someone flip a coin *badly*?

As a matter of fact, it is perfectly possible to flip a coin badly, if what that means is to flip it over your head, causing you to go scrambling after it in the aforementioned Bulgarian woods, leaving said Nazi collaborationist doctor open to grab your pistol and shoot you in the leg. And that is exactly what happens to poor Archie Jones.

Because Archie allows Dr. Marc-Pierre Perret to live, Dr. Perret goes on to mentor a brilliant young scientist, Marcus Chalfen. Chalfen figures out a way to control the genetic code of mice so as to be able to predetermine, with pinpoint accuracy, how they will live, what diseases they will and will not have, and when they will die. He does this in order to eventually do the same with humans so as to save us from our own diseased, random, irrational bodies, "for illness was, to Marcus, nothing more than bad logic on the part of the genome" (*WT*, 260). Marcus Chalfen also fathers a boy who ends up being Irie Jones's classmate at school. Irie just happens to be the half-Jamaican daughter of Archie who, in marrying and conceiving a child with Irie's Afro-Caribbean mother Clara, is doing some genetic manipulation of his own, but of the far more usual kind.

This is, however, many years after the fateful moment in the Bulgarian forest, when the young man in charge of this momentous decision has turned into a washed-up middle-aged Brit—one who makes his living deciding where the perforations go in direct-mail advertising, and for whom the words "ineffectual" and "insignificant" might be generous descriptions. The war, not to mention Archie's actions during it, has become completely irrelevant at this point: "Nothing he did *then* mattered *now*" (*WT*, 12; italics in original). His war stories have become the boring prattling of an old man reliving his glory days; the bullet in his leg is not a sign of heroism but rather an odd deformity that creates awkward silences in conversation. And when a story sets up one of its main characters in this way, there really is nothing one can do but read this character as an allegory of postwar English masculinity, which is, of course, an allegory for England itself. It is a familiar story to us now: the once-powerful empire is dealt its final blow during World War II, after which it becomes all too clear that the Marshall Plan, the Bretton Woods institutions, and decolonization movements have turned England back into the small, rather insignificant island in the North Atlantic it once was, an island whose main industry now consists of selling off pieces of an invented heritage in the shape of Buckingham Palace snowglobes and Big Ben commemorative plates.

This essay advances the idea that to describe the waning of the British Empire is to invoke the new geopolitical order that supplanted it. This contemporary neocolonial "new world order" sees the United States perched, somewhat precariously, on top. As I will argue, neocolonialism is importantly an episteme, a "structure of feeling" as Raymond Williams might call it. This epistemological formation is different from that of colonialism, marked by the smug Western belief in its own superior rationality, modernity, and civility. Yet, as I will go on to argue, it is also different from the postcolonial moment that exposed this rationality as a falsehood by articulating the "return" of the histories of violence and savagery upon which colonialism depended but for which it could not fully account. *White Teeth*, in contrast, can be read as a text that addresses the neocolonial moment, insofar as it takes the postcolonial critique for granted and makes it mundane and ordinary. This essay advances the idea that *White Teeth* reveals the erasures and the epistemological repressions of the neocolonial moment. In other words, it is not so much postcolonial as it is postneocolonial.

A brief contextualization of this transition from the era of colonialism, during which the British Empire was the pre-eminent geopolitical power, to the era of neocolonialism and globalization, characterized by the (somewhat shaky) ascendancy of the United States, is instructive here. World War II marked the turning point, described by Giovanni Arrighi as comprised of "decisive moments in the redistribution of assets from Britain to the United States which hastened the change in leadership in systemic processes of capital accumulation" (1994, 17). Of course, this moment depended upon centuries of colonial history. In the post–World War II era, the United States took advantage of the colonial holdings of a war-torn Europe to achieve power and an unprecedented global influence (albeit one that has been steadily declining ever since).[2] In exchange for badly needed U.S. technology and consumer goods, Europe bartered the only asset it had left: economic access to its colonial territories. Phillip McMichael writes, "An ingenious triangular trade was established to enable Europe to finance imported American technology and consumer goods. This arrangement also provided the United States access to raw materials from European colonial territories, paying in dollars deposited in European accounts in London banks. From these accounts, European states could finance imports from the United States" (2004, 42). In other words, England financed its rebuilding efforts by transferring to the United States the economic benefits of its colonial power.

Weakened by World War II, the imperialist nations of postwar Europe found that they were not in any position to contest the many decolonization movements that arose to challenge centuries of European domination. A series of independent nation-states were established, and, for a moment, with the establishment of the Non-Aligned Movement and the historical gathering of postcolonial nations at the 1955 Bandung Conference, it seemed like it might be possible for the so-called third world to have some real autonomy. As Cedric Robinson has observed, the struggle over whether the United States or the Soviet Union would emerge as the new global hegemon at the moment when Europe's power seemed to be receding was exactly what was at stake in the Cold War. Robinson writes, "While the official world contestation, the Cold War, has been taken to have subsumed all other conflicts, it is now possible to cast the competition between the two imperial hegemons, the United States and the Soviet Union, as a historical sidebar to the struggles to obtain or vanquish racial domination" (1997, 134). That is to say, the supposed struggle between capitalism and communism provided "an ideological machine with which to preserve imperial and colonial 'adventures' among darker peoples and to suppress democratic movements at home" (Robinson 1997, 135).

In retrospect, we can see how the contemporary geopolitical order became organized around U.S.-led transnational capitalism. In the 1970s and 1980s, nationally organized economic development was the leading strategy. The notion of "development" posited that each postcolonial nation-state could replicate the development process of the United States and Europe through nationally organized economic growth based on the importation of Western technologies and industrialization (McMichael 2004, 71). Yet by the 1980s, as it became clear that postcolonial states had become more impoverished rather than less, the development project was declared a failure, and the era of "globalization" began.[3] Rather than imagining the world economy as a set of linked, equivalent nation-states with their own discrete economies, the globalization project imagines each nation-state occupying a particular niche in a globally integrated world economy. Through the structure of international debt, managed through the International Monetary Fund (IMF) and the World Bank, the formerly colonized nations of the world are forced to open their markets and economies to transnational capital by instituting structural adjustment policies that devalue currency, undercut social programs, and open their economies to foreign investment. Thus, the shift into neoliberalism in the last twenty years has marked what some have called a new imperialism,[4] based on the United States' ability to dictate the terms of the world economy through World Bank and IMF policies of structural adjustment and debt, and backed by U.S. militarism.

While Arrighi defines the "long twentieth century" as the era in which the United States became the center of capitalist development, superceding Britain, the actual U.S. nation-state does not dominate the world in the same way as the previous imperialist power. Indeed, Richard Barnet notes, writing about the post–World War II alliance of the United States, Britain, and Japan that made the United States the foremost power in the world, "America's [post-war] moment of global supremacy turned out to be puzzlingly brief. Even as the alliance that symbolized America grew, the extraordinary power of the United States was slipping away" (1983, 12). Some have even argued that the United States' current dependency on militarism and force may be less a sign of its global dominance as it is an indication of its inability to wield economic or political hegemony.[5]

In this essay, I examine the ways in which certain aspects of *White Teeth* are symptomatic of the contemporary geopolitical order. Yet in so doing, I want to avoid reifying the power of the U.S. nation-state. Rather than assuming that U.S. global hegemony is inevitable and totalizing, I suggest that the U.S. nation-state's place in the contemporary geopolitical order is foremost as a trademark or brand name signifying "dominance." As such, this essay examines the ways in which U.S. global hegemony articulates what Raymond Williams might call a "structure of feeling."[6] By reading *White Teeth*—a text set in England and its colonial holdings and written by a non-American—as symptomatic of the contemporary geopolitical order organized around U.S. dominance, I contend that this order does not imply the literal territorial or economic dominance of the United States, but rather calls up a structure of feeling that is the mark of a U.S.-centered form of capitalism. This form of capitalism need not be *literally* bound to representations of the United States nor written by "Americans."

In particular, the contemporary structure of feeling is marked by the ironic displacement of the metanarratives of the previous era. Certainly, there are moments in *White Teeth* that literally describe English decline and U.S. ascendancy. For example, it is certainly significant that this narrative is so fixated on World War II—that moment when the old imperial regime was supplanted by the new neocolonial one. And, again, it "remembers" the waning of the British empire when it imagines the great Kingston earthquake of 1907, and Captain Charlie Dunham's "strange feeling, the powerlessness; to discover there is another country more equipped to save this little island than the English" (*WT*, 300). That country, of course, was the United States, sending ships full of provisions down from Cuba to assuage the suffering of the Jamaicans. Turning the ships away, as Dunham's superior officer does, is not going to do much to preserve the empire either. Nothing makes an empire look worse than thousands of starving and dying colonized subjects about whom they can do nothing. And the damage is done already by the Americans even thinking of Jamaica as their responsibility to help in the first place. In these and other ways, *White Teeth* does represent in very literal ways the emergence of the United States as the global hegemon of the twentieth century.

Yet even with these literal descriptions of U.S. ascendancy, this text's main gesture to the new geopolitical order lies in its ironic recounting of the breakdown of the epistemological structures of the old. That is, *White Teeth* truly marks the demise of the British Empire exactly by mocking it, by making the hapless Archie into the personification of the British Empire. In other words, *White Teeth* cannot take British imperialism seriously enough to critique it. In contrast, postcolonial scholarship takes these narratives of British colonialism seriously enough to center it in its critique. Colonialism was based upon the generally held notion, at least on the part of the English, that the effect of colonization on the colonized was to modernize their economies as it "civilized" their political and cultural institutions. Of course, as colonialism was making Britain wealthier than anyone could have possibly imagined, such a narrative of progress explained away the violence and exploitation associated with the accumulation of that wealth as a necessary means of correcting the backward and primitive colonized subjects themselves. Postcolonial revisionist histories represented colonialism not as an organized system that spread order and civilization to the savage and primitive parts of the world, but rather as a complex and ultimately random confluence of competing interests and contradictory desires.

In this regard, the trajectories of postcolonial scholarship that deal with the production of knowledge have very helpfully addressed what cannot be known by the rationalized epistemology of the West, and post colonial scholars have noted how difficult it is to recover and to narrate the irrational and the nonsecular. Edward Said has famously argued, for example, that the study of the "Orient" by the "West" produces the Orient as the mysterious, passive, constitutive "other" to the West, through which the West defines itself as having agency, as rational, and as scientific, and upon which a mode of colonial administration and exploitation was based: "Orientalism as a Western style for dominating, restructuring and having authority over the Orient" (1979, 3). Given that Western epistemology has neither the means nor the inclination to understand its colonized territories as anything beyond its "other," as that which exists to give the West meaning and definition, the project of narrating a non-Western history becomes very complex. Dipesh Chakrabarty notes, "'Europe' remains the sovereign theoretical subject of all histories" (2000, 27) "through a procedure that subordinates these narratives to the rules of evidence and to the secular, limited calendar that the writing of 'history' must follow" (2000, 41).

In particular, postcolonial scholarship reveals that the modern represses the conditions of its own making by relegating the "nonmodern" to the irrational and the nonsecular. Historical time is secular, homogeneous, and forces a diversity of events to conform to a unitary and linear temporality as follows: "The secular code of historical and humanist time—that is, a time bereft [of] gods and spirits—is one such universal. . . . Although the sameness of our sciences can be guaranteed all the world over, the sameness of our gods and spirits could not be proved in the same objective manner. . . . So it could be said that although the sciences signify some kind of sameness in our understanding of the world across cultures, the gods signify differences" (Chakrabarty 2000, 76). These forms of knowledge—history and the social sciences—that we have inherited privilege rationality and secularity; irrationality and nonsecularity must be translated to support secular rationales, or else belong to the sphere of the unknowable. This being the case, to narrate irrationality through the language of rationality is to perform a violent act that erases as much as it records. Following these invaluable insights offered by postcolonial studies, scholars have assumed that the nonsecular and the antirational stood in for all that could not be narrated through the institutions of modernity, and that they constituted what Chakrabarty calls "what the modern represses in order to be" (2000, 46).

In distinction, *White Teeth* seems to say that, actually, the irrational and the nonsecular are *not* that difficult to know, and in fact, they are quite easily apprehended. At one point in the book, Archie's best friend Samad proclaims, "Rationality! Most overrated Western virtue!" (*WT*, 195). And, indeed, *White Teeth* seems to say that rationality is indeed overrated—overproduced and overemphasized—in the histories of imperialist epistemology. Thus, my purpose is not to argue that *White Teeth* simply exposes the irrationality of British colonialism. For this text, apprehending the erased otherness of colonial modernity—irrationality and nonsecularity, in particular—is not a complex maneuver but a rather transparent one. If the metanarrative driving the *previous* geopolitical order—as represented by British colonialism—is that of Western rationality meeting and correcting the irrationality of the non-West, and the metanarrative of postcoloniality is the return of that repressed irrationality, *White Teeth* is less concerned with remembering British colonialism as it is with remembering the moment of breakdown, the moment of epiphany that came with the postcolonial critique of British colonialism. That sense of epiphany is what *White Teeth* gently mocks.

In this way, *White Teeth* is symptomatic of the geopolitical order that supplanted colonialism, one marked by the recognition of difference and diversity rather than linear progress toward a universal goal. Under British colonialism, that goal was embodied by the ostensibly superior civilization of the English. Narratives that take recourse to order and rationality cannot describe today's geopolitical realities, and instead, scholars have shifted toward an analytic of difference and diversification to understand them. Mike Davis (2004), for example, observes that while urban economies in such places as

Lagos, Nigeria, actually cannot sustain any more people, people keep migrating to these urban areas anyway, creating enormous "slum corridors" stretching thousands of miles. These slums are absolutely unsustainable, and yet somehow they not only sustain themselves, but they also grow. In fact, in many of these largest cities in the world, informal economies outpace formal ones, to the extent that formal economies are absolutely dependent on informal ones.[7] It is through industries that do not self-sustain or reproduce but rather emerge only to immediately fall apart and then sprout up again that we apprehend our new geopolitical order. In this context, the recognition of difference is important. Yet "difference," too, becomes another totalizing narrative. If there is anything that *White Teeth* reveals, it is that difference and diversification are themselves inadequate as analytical categories.

The work of J. K. Gibson-Graham demonstrates the simultaneous importance and limitation of difference as an analytic. They argue compellingly for why we must develop an analytic that can recognize informality and difference by noting that the most well-intentioned of Marxists ascribe to capitalism a unity, singularity, and totality against which it is difficult to imagine any effectual transformation. In contrast, Gibson-Graham suggest that what we call "capitalism" is in reality "a set of different practices scattered over the landscape that are (for convenience and in violation of difference) often lumped into the same category" (1993, 18). In this case, anticapitalist or noncapitalist modes of living are not merely possible, but they are also as common and inevitable as capitalism seems to be. As helpful as this analysis is, I feel that it does not adequately account for the difficulty of an epistemological break. Gibson-Graham presuppose too much of a transparency to the strategy of reading and identifying differentiation and diversification. In other words, why are we *now* able to notice differentiation and proliferation when some very smart people were unable to do so previously? Is it that we just happen to be smarter now?

I would suggest that we are able to recognize differentiation because, currently, the dominant narrative is the very narrative of difference, proliferation, and unevenness. In other words, currently, if the cultural logic of the previous era of British colonialism was a developmental narrative toward the supposedly universal goal of civilization, the dominant structure of feeling of the current order is differentiation. Contemporary transnational capital no longer accrues profit only through rational, organized means, but rather, and as important, through all sorts of practices that any scholars (including Gibson-Graham) might have once considered outside the purview of capitalistic accumulation. These practices encompass those that Gibson-Graham marks as noncapitalistic. In fact, their description as follows of the variety of forms of labor exploitation, which they argue are not completely subsumable under the "capitalism" category, are actually uncannily similar to how others describe how capitalism now works: "Independent forms in which a self-employed producer appropriates her own surplus labor, capitalist forms in which surplus-value is appropriated from wage labor; collective or communal forms in which producers jointly appropriate surplus labor; slave forms in which surplus labor is appropriated from workers who do not have freedom of contract" (1993, 20). Certainly those of us who study contemporary capitalism need to recognize that a variety of economic practices exist—some formal, regulated by legal and social constraints, and others informal. But is recognition enough when the largest corporations in the world are dependent on these very small family-run sweatshops, on child labor, and on prison labor—that is, on labor that is not protected by the notion of "freedom of contract?"[8] Can we say that these corporations are somehow *not* capitalist in nature?

I use Gibson-Graham's arguments to illustrate a larger point about both the promise and limitations of the recognition of difference. It is important to be able to know how processes of exploitation work. It is imperative that we understand all the complexities of the differentiated modes of labor, and it is very important to understand that not all of them are necessarily incorporated into global capital as totalizing. However, in the end, claiming to be able to recognize effortlessly all these proliferating forms of difference only reproduces a totalizing sense that we can know and see everything. A part of the project must be to consider, again, what we do not, and cannot, know.

Such a project is crucial because of the ways in which texts like *White Teeth* have been mobilized as evidence of a multiculturalist resolution to the violent histories of colonialism. It has been noted previously that novels like *White Teeth* are "post-postcolonial" texts (Moss, 2003, 11). Laura Moss defines this term in relation to *White Teeth* by noting that these texts take hybridity casually—representing "hybridity . . . as a practice of everyday life," as Moss has called it (2003, 11). Moss takes as her example the novel's representation of literal racial mixing—the easy and unself-conscious hybridity of a character like Irie Jones. *White Teeth* proposes that the racialized, migrant, postcolonial subject—such as Irie Jones—is not only knowable, but also is already so much a part of a radically heterogeneous England that the notion of integration or assimilation is moot.

Unlike postcolonial writers like V. S. Naipaul, whose "attempt to insert the migrant self into the English landscape . . . paradoxically confirm[s] the inhospitability of England to this project" (Head 2003, 110), or Salman Rushdie, whose ability to depict the "unfettered migrant sensibility" is dependent upon his "turning away from the particular difficulties inherent in the actual geographical experience of the migrant self in post-war Britain" (Head 2003, 110), Smith's post-postcoloniality has been read as contributing to the project of imagining England as a "multicultural utopia" (Head 2003, 117). That is, if postcolonial writers such as Naipaul and Rushdie marked the inhospitability of a racist England to account for postcolonial, racialized, migrant subjectivities, does *White Teeth* recuperate England by celebrating its ability to incorporate the diverse formerly colonized populations that return to the metropole? Contemporary regimes of racial knowledge have unevenly repudiated white supremacy, delegitimated in no small part by its association with Nazi eugenics. Instead, contemporary neoliberal racism trumpets the panacea of a multicultural appreciation of difference, which erases the continuing existence of racialized exploitation. Such a multiculturalist move is part and parcel of a shift that marks the ascendancy of a contemporary neocolonial capitalism that operates by exploiting difference. I would argue that reading *White Teeth* as a multicultural celebration of difference is exactly to make it operate as a text of contemporary global capital. I read *White Teeth* against this tendency, asking if this text, which on the surface does seem to claim to be able to represent difference, gestures toward anything that is *unknowable* and *unrepresentable*.

I thus situate the novel's focus on racial mixing, multiculturalism, and hybridity as only one part of a larger engagement with the genealogy of race, which I posit as fundamentally a question of knowledge, an epistemological question. The histories of colonial and contemporary racism are not only revealed in the literal representations of racial purity or racial mixing in this novel, but also thoroughly infuse their engagement with Western epistemology and ontology. These representations of racial mixing are therefore intimately tied to this novel's other preoccupations regarding the possibility, or lack thereof, of knowing the "other" which are thematized as eugenicist science, genetic manipulation, and the eruption of colonial history in the present.

Thus, while *White Teeth* has been read as a utopian vision of a multicultural England that is capable of incorporating racialized difference, I want to read against the grain of such an interpretation by examining its engagement with the production of knowledge. Instead of congratulating ourselves for now being able to see that which was erased or subjugated at an earlier moment, *White Teeth* reminds us that we might do well to understand that there are things *we* must forget, epistemic erasures that our contemporary governmentality must erase, that we cannot see because we are of our moment. Chakrabarty suggests a methodology for such a project, a methodology that he calls "provincializing 'Europe,' the 'Europe' that Western imperialism and (third world) nationalism have by their collaborative venture and violence, made universal" (2000, 42). Yet if "Europe" is no longer the subject of all histories, but has rather been replaced by the "United States," *White*

Teeth takes this project one step further, and enacts the project of provincializing the United States. Put more accurately, White Teeth provincializes the dominant structure of feeling of the current geopolitical order. I end by suggesting the ways in which *White Teeth* gestures toward those erasures. Ultimately, *White Teeth* does not claim that we now know all; rather, it denies that we have reached the end of history.

***

Rather than merely exposing or revealing all the irrationality of the colonial endeavor—the affective, improper, desiring dimensions of this system once forcibly imagined as orderly and rational—*White Teeth* revels in it. The very title of the novel references a seemingly incidental episode in the novel that centers on a figure of colonial conquest. Archie's daughter Irie and Samad's identical twin sons Magid and Millat are sent by their school on a well-intentioned if somewhat condescending mission to deliver canned goods to the homes of the elderly. The beneficiary of their munificence is Mr. J. P. Hamilton, an aged, doddering relic of the colonial era. Mr. Hamilton, following the rules of propriety and good breeding as a colonial should, invites them to stay for tea, but his ability to be a good host is somewhat compromised by the fact that his attempts at polite conversation veer off into a disturbing reminiscence of his days as a soldier for the British army. After admonishing them about the importance of dental hygiene, Mr. Hamilton muses,

> "Clean white teeth are not always wise, now are they? Par exemplum: when I was in the Congo, the only way I could identify the nigger was by the whiteness of his teeth, if you see what I mean. Horrid business. Dark as buggery, it was. And they died because of it, you see? Poor bastards. Or rather, I survived, to look at it another way, do you see?"
>
> The children sat silently. And then Irie began to cry, ever so quietly.
>
> Mr. Hamilton continued, "Those are the split decisions you make in war. See a flash of white and bang! as it were. . . . Dark as buggery. Terrible times. All these beautiful boys lying dead there, right in front of me, right at my feet. Stomach open, you know, with their guts on my shoes. Like the end of the bloody world. Beautiful men, enlisted by the Krauts, black as the ace of spades; poor fools didn't even know why they were there, what people they were fighting for, who they were shooting at. The decision of the gun. So quick, children. So brutal. Biscuit?" (*WT*, 114)

In just a few sentences, this passage stages a revelation of the tangled ideologies of colonial racism, but not in order to represent such a revelation as profound. Rather, such a revelation is mundane, obvious.

As scholars like Ann Stoler have observed, colonial subjectivity and colonial violence always operated through desire—homosocial and homosexual—and not only through repulsion and abjection. Or, to put it another way, the repulsion and abjection of colonial racism produced desire as a corollary of hatred. Colonial subjects become the repository of darkness that not only signifies skin color ("black as the ace of spades") but also improper and perverse sexualities. The system of meaning is not only limited to skin color but is also one that encompasses all that is "other" to English colonial modernity. Yet darkness is not only repulsive, but also produces a fetishistic and sadistic fascination. The appeal of the "beautiful boys" is not contradicted but is rather enhanced, sadistically, by their death, their dismemberment, and their disembowlment.

These perverse desires are not contradicted by the drive toward propriety and the extension of domestic reproductive sexuality to the colonial territory, as marked by Mr. Hamilton's placid, polite conclusion to his story: "Biscuit?" Colonial subjectivity is here perfectly allegorized by the ritual of tea, which is the iconic representation of English domesticity and propriety but is also the trace of colonial violence and exploitation, dependent upon the commodities produced by colonial slavery and indentured servitude—tea and sugar. These two aspects—English propriety and colonial violence—do not contradict each other, as in the example of Mr. Hamilton, but rather coexist in an uncomplicated fashion. If at one point, as Ann Stoler notes, "who could be classified as 'European' was based on not skin color but on tenuously balanced assessments of who was judged to act with reason, affective appropriateness, and a sense of morality" (2002, 6), such proscriptions no longer seem to be very binding. The sadistic, the violent, the homosexual, the desiring, and the affective: if these were hidden in the colonial unconscious, *White Teeth* seems to say, they were not ever hidden particularly well. Hamilton's irrationality is represented less as a profoundly affecting revelation as much as it is a funny moment.

And there is, of course, the startling ridiculousness of this entire "white teeth" narrative altogether. *This* was the basis for colonial conquest? At one point in the novel, the erudite, cosmopolitan Samad says with disgust to the naïve and simple Archie, "How your lot ever conquered my lot is a bloody mystery" (*WT*, 101), and with Mr. Hamilton, this dubious example of colonial "rationality," one can see Samad's point. For *White Teeth*, colonial histories, and the epistemological contestations resulting from them, are exasperating, not painful; they are laughable, not tragic.

Even the most threatening of colonial irrationalities—Islam—becomes familiar and funny. Samad becomes the mouthpiece for a central fascination of *White Teeth* when he says, ranting and raving about his son Magid's idol, Sir S. V. Saraswati ("colonial throw-back, English licker-of-behinds," 239),

> He learns nothing from a man who knows nothing! Where is his beard? Where is his khamise? Where is his humility? If Allah says there will be storm, there will be storm. If he says earthquake, it will be earthquake. Of course it has to be! This is the very reason I sent the child there—to understand that essentially we are weak, that we are not in control. What does Islam mean? What does the word, the very word, mean? *I surrender*. I surrender to God. I surrender to him. This is not my life, this is his life. The life I call mine is his to do with what he will. Indeed, I shall be tossed and turned on the wave, and there shall be nothing to be done. Nothing! (*WT*, 240)

For if Magid did not learn this, certainly, *White Teeth* seems to say that our contemporary epistemology has learned to embrace "Islam," in a manner of speaking, if "Islam" is defined as invested with particular historical meanings for Western epistemologies.

White Teeth muses on the contemporary incorporation of previously unincorporable subjects through the story of Magid and Millat. Faced with what he sees as the utter corruption of the West (though it is more precisely the utter corruption of the suburb of London, Willesden Green, where they reside), Samad decides to send both boys back to Bangladesh, at the age of ten, to be raised as proper Muslims, inculcated with the traditional ways. This is what he decides, but, constrained by the meagerness of his income as a waiter in an Indian restaurant, he ends up only able to send Magid. Irony being what it is, which is to say, inescapable, Magid is educated in Bangladesh and ends up a fervid believer of rationality, Western state forms, science, and technology. He speaks the King's English, wants to study law, and wears a tweed suit and cravat. As his own mother notes upon his return seven years later, "His teeth, he brushes them six times a day. His underwear, he irons them. It is like sitting down to breakfast with David Niven" (*WT*, 351).

The joke is not that Samad's plan failed, but rather that it worked, albeit in an unanticipated way. He sends Magid to learn the traditional Bangladeshi ways, and so Magid does. He becomes colonized. Again, irony being inescapable and ubiquitous, Magid's twin brother Millat, prey to the presumable corruption of Western civilization, becomes a Muslim fundamentalist. Millat's fundamentalist "rebellion" against the West is represented as ultimately not very different from Magid's capitulation. Magid and Millat are, as Archie might say, two sides of the same coin.

In this way, *White Teeth* plays with the notion of Islamic fundamentalism as irrational, violent, and repressive, which is, as Talal Asad notes, a colonial construction. Fundamentalism is produced by rationality as its necessary correlative. Asad notes the secularization of "religion" as a category in Europe in the eighteenth and nineteenth centuries. Religion was understood as belonging to the newly emerging "private" sphere: "anchored in personal experience, expressible as belief statements, dependent on private institutions, and practiced in one's spare time. This construction of religion ensures that it is part of what is inessential to our common politics, economy, science, and morality. More strongly put: religion is what actually or potentially divides us, and if followed with passionate conviction, may set us intolerantly against one another" (1993, 207). Such a definition of religion as antithetical to the public sphere of political expression and dissent renders any form of political discourse that might happen to express itself through religion impossible to understand. It pathologizes what Asad calls "political religions"—Islam chief among them—as a danger to liberty and reason.

Yet if Islam once operated as an instance of all that was anti-Western, dangerous, and unimaginable, *White Teeth* represents it as no longer so. Millat's rebellion against Western values is simultaneously an embrace of them: Millat's desire to be a part of the Muslim fundamentalist organization Keepers of the Eternal and Victorious Islam Nation (KEVIN) has less to do with actual Islamic principles and more to do with wanting to be a gangster, or, more precisely, wanting to be Robert DeNiro. While many have read this moment in *White Teeth* as a sign of Millat's hypocrisy, there is actually a kind of sense to it. To Millat's mind, Islamic and American cultures are both modes of rebellion against British propriety and order. For the characters of *White Teeth*, Islam is a lifestyle, and the persecution of Islam is represented as absurd. The utter mundanity of the name KEVIN says it all: Islam is all too familiar, even as it tries to be militant and threatening.

In this way, *White Teeth* makes equivalent a variety of narratives that, in an earlier moment, may have been oppositional. There is no better example of this than the novel's evenhanded ridiculing of a variety of belief systems: apocalyptic Christianity, romantic sentimentality, and self-righteous rationality. The novel spins a narrative of Irie Jones's maternal line, the Bowdens, who are represented as carrying with them a long legacy of English irrationality. Irie's English colonial great-grandfather, Captain Charlie "Whitey" Dunham, for example, goes down in the Bowden family annals as that "no-good djam fool bwoy" (*WT*, 294) for his willingness to sacrifice thousands of Jamaicans for his own selfish ends. Having doomed the entire island of Jamaica to the ravages of illness and starvation after the great Kingston earthquake of 1907 will tarnish your reputation somewhat. Dunham, in love with Irie's great-grandmother Ambrosia, a young maid whom he impregnated, demands to have her with him on the ship back to England. His superior officer refuses, which leads Dunham to challenge his superior officer's authority to decide any such thing, using as proof the American war ships coming down to Jamaica full of provisions, coming to save Jamaica when England could not. His superior officer, of course, feels this affront to his authority keenly, and orders the American ships back, with no thought to the many "injured and weak, on their last legs and waiting for the boats" (*WT*, 310). Now is that the decision-making impulse of a rational man, or of a rational people? Of course not; these are the actions of a "no-good djam fool bwoy" and a deeply irrational colonial system. When an apocalyptic event happens, as it did in Jamaica in 1907, Captain Dunham's response is to save the one and let the thousands die.

Given how deeply irrational *White Teeth* represents English colonialism as being, it is no wonder that Ambrosia's daughter Hortense, Irie's grandmother, born during the great 1907 earthquake, lives within the apocalyptic temporality of the Jehovah's Witnesses. Convinced of imminent fiery holy wrath, Hortense runs her household as "a place of endgames and aftertimes, full-stops and finales; where to count on tomorrow was an indulgence, and every service in the house, from the milkman to the electricity, was paid for on a strictly daily basis so as not to spend money on utilities or goods that would be wasted should God turn up in all his holy vengeance the very next day" (*WT*, 327). This religious fervor, though based in the Jehovah's Witness creed, far exceeds it, and must be given another name: "Bowdenism, which was the Witnesses plus Revelation *and then some*" (*WT*, 327; italics in original). Certainly, if "Revelations is where all crazy people end up" (*WT*, 327), Hortense is as crazy as they come. But as Hortense waits daily for the imminent occurrence of the cataclysmic wrath of God, from which only the one hundred forty-four thousand Anointed (in whose ranks she hopes to be) will be saved, is she not just convinced of the same thing that Charlie Dunham believed? In other words, she is merely living a more grandiose and hyperbolic version of Dunham's decision to save the few (or the one) over the many. Hortense, in her irrational—no, out-and-out *anti*rational—faith in fiery vengeance is "more English than the English" (*WT*, 255). In this way, examples of everyday and ordinary otherness abound. Irrationality has a genealogy in this book, and one that seems not particularly lost to history.

We might see Hortense and Dunham as taking the opposite route from that chosen by Chalfen, who opts to sacrifice a few (mice, not people) to ostensibly serve the many (people, not mice). But Hortense, Dunham, and Chalfen are more alike, by *White Teeth*'s reckoning, than they are different. They are all under the sway of metanarratives: a sense that there is a larger purpose or guiding principle (God, love, and reason, respectively) that guides their decisions and makes sense of the consequences. They, like Magid, want "no second-guessing, no what-ifs, no might-have-beens. Just certainty. Just certainty in its purest form" (*WT*, 405). The only truly different subject is—unexpectedly—plain, sad sack Archie, who, as I observed at the beginning of this chapter, does not trouble himself much with grand ideas, but rather, in entrusting all his decisions to the flip of a coin, makes his peace with the randomness of the world. Archie, the representative of English decline, also personifies postmodernity as he blithely embraces the uselessness, the irrelevance of metanarratives of certainty. *White Teeth* thus establishes Archie as the figure for the rise of the new geopolitical order, and in so doing, allegorizes the way in which the decline of the previous order is the rise of the next.

This is what *White Teeth* does so well. That is, it makes ordinary and plain what previously had seemed very difficult to apprehend. Being able to see English irrationality makes it absolutely possible to understand "otherness," not as ungraspable, not as the subaltern who cannot speak, not as Foucauldian "subjugated knowledge," or as "what the modern represses in order to be," but rather as everyday and ordinary. *White Teeth* stages—literally—the crisis of Western rationality and the disruption of the metanarratives of Western scientificism that is, according to Jean-Francoise Lyotard, the hallmark of the postmodern condition. Rationality and scientificism is embodied, literalized, by Marcus Chalfen, for whom rational thinking is an aesthetic and a way of life. As the teenage Joshua Chalfen (rebelling against his father through a short-lived dalliance with radical animal-rights organizing) says bitterly, though accurately, of his father, "there's no point being reasonable with him because he thinks he *owns* reasonableness" (*WT*, 334–35). Having created Marcus Chalfen as the symbol of Western rationality, Smith puts such a rationality under siege in this novel's so-called "bad ending,"[9] in which a New Year's Eve press conference promoting Marcus Chalfen's genetically programmed mouse is the occasion for a variety of protests, by Joshua and his animal rights comrades (angered by the treatment of the mouse), Irie's grandmother Hortense's Jehovah's Witnesses (using the occasion to spread the gospel), and Millat's Islamic fundamentalist group KEVIN (outraged that Chalfen is implying imperfection in Allah's creations). Given that the metanarratives of Western rationality are themselves crumbling, the irrationality and nonsecularity that such metanarratives had previously relegated to the status of the unknowable are no longer the stuff of mystery.

Rather, the unknowable is the stuff of comedy in this novel. The very icon of unknowability for postcolonial studies—peasant insurrection—is downgraded to the status of a pub wager in *White Teeth*. The subaltern studies school of postcolonial studies takes up the complex and difficult task of excavating and narrating the history of peasant insurrection. Gayatri Spivak's oft-quoted essay "Can the Subaltern Speak?" examines the efforts of subaltern studies scholars, particularly Ranajit Guha, to narrate a history of the non-West, and observes that such histories cannot be empiricist histories of "'the way things really were'" (1988, 281), but rather, "the notion of what the work *cannot* say becomes important. . . . Elaborations of insurgency stand in the place of 'the utterance.' The sender—'the peasant'—is marked only as a pointer to an irretrievable consciousness" (1988, 287). Peasant insurrections, in other words, cannot be narrated through Western historiographical modes, which can only attribute agency to the West, or to those Indian elites whose subjectivities approximate the West. The subaltern cannot speak, therefore.

In *White Teeth*, subaltern insurrection is literally the insurrection of the "subaltern," not the subaltern as the metaphor for an unknowable peasant consciousness, but rather the subaltern in its literal meaning as a subordinate soldier. Samad's great-grandfather, Mangal Pande, a conscript into the British Army who fired the first shot of the first Indian mutiny, the Sepoy Rebellion of 1857, becomes the subject of a fervid and rancorous debate. To Samad, Pande is an unrecognized national hero who valiantly defended his religious obligations from the affront posed by the British. To Archie (and to most others, including, according to the novel, "British scholarship from 1957 to the present day," *WT*, 208), Pande is an incompetent and mutinous religious fanatic. Can the subaltern speak? Pande certainly cannot, but Samad and Archie can, and they debate the matter furiously in the dank, Arab-run Irish pub O'Connell's on New Year's Eve of 1989. This argument is never settled either way—it is impossible to know why Pande did what he did. The notion that the subaltern consciousness is unknowable not tragic but comic in *White Teeth*.

The problem of knowledge in *White Teeth* is not so much that of the difficulty of recovering subjugated knowledges, but instead that some knowledges are not quite subjugated enough. This is a text that quotes the following particular phrase from the Bible: "He that increaseth knowledge increaseth sorrow" (*WT*, 420). In the same vein, Samad's wife Alsana contends, "*Silence*, what is *not* said, is the very *best* recipe for family life" (*WT*, 65). When asked how she could have married someone whom she barely knew, she contends, "Yes, I was married to Samad Iqbal the same evening of the very day I met him. Yes, I didn't know him from Adam. But I liked him well enough. . . . Now, every time I learn something more about him, *I like him less*. So you see, we were better off the way we were" (*WT*, 66; italics in original). Likewise, Mr. Hamilton notes, "At my age it's not *more* information one requires but *less*" (*WT*, 142; italics in original). The repressed has returned, and Alsana, for one, and Mr. Hamilton, for another, are not entirely sure that this is a positive development. If the subaltern consciousness is ultimately never knowable, Alsana might maintain that that is quite all right.

When *White Teeth* represents irrationality, and in so doing, demonstrates the transparency and ease of doing so, it is symptomatic of this new geopolitical order. It stages—quite literally, in its "bad ending"—the meeting of rationality and religion, between Fascism and fundamentalism, between science, the secular, and the sacred—and in this way, nothing seems outside its purview. Yet it is not so very hard to poke fun at the old empire in 2000, remembering such moments of English ineffectuality and irrationality, and embodying late twentieth-century Britain as sad sack, ineffectual, paper-folding, middle-aged Archie, waffling and wavering and entrusting all his decisions, momentous or not, to a toss of a coin. Having a critique of English colonialism is what the new regime does best. But in its cheeky disrespect for the English empire, *White Teeth* does manage to comment on the new regime. As Smith has noted about her own book, to read it as claiming to know all is to misread it: "If you're talking about the big epic—encyclopedic is a better word, for these novels, I think those are not going to be around for long. . . . I don't think that is what [*White Teeth*] is at all. It's not the big book or the book which includes all of the information in the world" (O'Grady 2002, 108).

Instead, *White Teeth* ironically points to what cannot be known by imagining that it can know it all: by remembering the future, or, in other words, to write a "future history (for there is such a thing)" (*WT*, 383). When *White Teeth* laughs at the antirationality of English colonialism, it also asks us to imagine a moment when we might likewise be able to laugh at the antirationality of neocolonial capital—in other words, to remember the future. The writing of history is a difficult process with very high stakes, as the past is not transparent and can only be apprehended as it affects the present, or the future. Walter Benjamin writes, "Historicism contents itself with establishing a causal connection between various moments in history. But no fact that is a cause is for that very reason historical. It became historical posthumously, as it were, through events that may be separated from it by thousands of years. A historian who takes this as his point of departure stops telling the sequence of events like the beads of a rosary. Instead, he grasps the constellation which his own era has formed with a definite earlier one" (1969, 263). Benjamin's theorization of history rethinks "past" and "present" by lifting these terms out of chronological time.

If events are lifted out of the linear or "weak Messianic" time in which events happen discretely, strung along on a linear axis of time, there is no reason why an event in the past cannot be constellated with an event in the present, nor is there any reason why causality must operate in one direction. Benjamin calls linear temporality "*weak* Messianic" time because the end of history—as allegorized by the reappearance of the messiah—never actually comes, but instead exists as the only possible eventual future that organizes all prior events in a causal relationship to it (1969, 254). As Hortense would surely attest, *strong* Messianic time would be a completely different thing indeed. *White Teeth* lends itself to another implication from Benjamin's mediation on the past, present, and future: the implication that a variety of futures might exist, and that the ultimate triumph of U.S. global hegemony is not inevitable.

As such, *White Teeth* not only instructs us to remember the future but also actually stages such a seemingly impossible remembrance as its very conclusion. The novel ends on the following note:

> *But first the endgames.* Because it seems no matter what you think of them, they must be played, even if, like the independence of India or Jamaica, like the signing of peace treaties or the docking of passenger boats, the end is simply the beginning of an even longer story. The same focus group who picked out the color of this room, the carpet, the font for the posters, the height of the table, would no doubt check the box that asks all these things played to their finish. . . .
>
> And is it young professional women aged eighteen to thirty-two who would like a snapshot seven years hence of Irie, Joshua, and Hortense sitting by a Caribbean sea (for Irie and Joshua have become lovers in the end; you can only avoid your fate for so long), while Irie's fatherless little girl writes affectionate postcards to *Bad Uncle Millat* and *Good Uncle Magid* and feels free as Pinocchio, a puppet clipped of paternal strings? And could it be that it is largely the criminal class and the elderly who find themselves wanting to make bets on the winner of a blackjack game, the one played by Alsana and Samad, Archie and Clara, in O'Connells, December 31, 1999, that historic night when Abdul-Mickey finally opened his doors to women?
>
> But surely to tell these tall tales and others like them would be to speed the myth, the wicked lie, that the past is always tense and the future, perfect. And as Archie knows, it's never like that, it's never been like that. (*WT*, 447–48)

In other words, the point of writing a "future history" is not to actually see the future, but instead to remind ourselves that there is no such thing as the "end of history." This passage first offers an image of a lovely future in which all is resolved, wherein Irie returns to her island homeland and wherein O'Connell's is no longer Archie and Samad's homosocial refuge from their marriages, but rather becomes a site of marital harmony.

But by immediately undermining such an image as "the myth, the wicked lie, that the past is always tense, and the future, perfect," *White Teeth* casts doubt on a developmental temporality that posits a perfect future in which human progress and civilization are progressive and ultimately perfectible.

Although such developmentalism is no longer narrated as the triumph of British civilization, it does not mean that such a narrative no longer exists. It exists in a different guise, as the promise of focus groups that claim to be able to attend to all needs and wants, from those of "young professional women aged eighteen to thirty-two" to those of "the criminal class and the elderly." Contemporary capital's version of developmental perfectibility is represented by the endlessly proliferating tastes, consumerist choices, and commodification ostensibly promising evermore perfect forms of human satisfaction. It is not national identities, but rather demographics that inspire contemporary identification and describe traits and characteristics.

In encouraging us to write a "future history," *White Teeth* reminds us that although there may seem to be only one inevitable future in which global capital dominates all, there will come a moment when it seems as silly, ineffectual, and rife with contradictions as the earlier geopolitical organization of the world under British colonialism does to us now. Indeed, *White Teeth* seems to say that that future is *now* because we do not have to take recourse to a developmental historiography that lays events out in a linear temporality. In this way, perhaps *White Teeth* is the opening salvo, the first shot fired in a mutiny, the "tickle in the sneeze" (*WT*, 216), as Samad might say. Perhaps we may later remember Zadie Smith as the Mangal Pande of the new millennium.

Notes

1. Hereafter referred to as *WT*.
2. For a thorough discussion of the political and economic reorganization of the world economy through the Marshall Plan and the Bretton Woods System, see Wood 1986.
3. For a discussion of the epistemological implications of the demise of development, see Escobar 1992.
4. See Hardt and Negri 2000.
5. See Baker 2003.
6. My deployment of "structure of feeling" does not scrupulously adhere to William's definition, however. Williams uses this term to describe what he calls the "emergent." He notes, "There are the experiences to which the fixed forms do not speak at all, which indeed they do not recognize," and yet "although they are emergent or pre-emergent, they do not have to await definition, classification, or rationalization before they exert palpable pressures and effective limits on experience and on action" (1985, 130, 131–32). For Williams, structures of feeling are emergent precisely because they cannot be characterized by the dominant. My use of the term implies that the dominant can be a structure of feeling as well, and that the dominant structure of feeling is inarticulable not because it does not reproduce power (as in the emergent formation), but rather because power sometimes works invisibly, through affect, interpellation, and subject-formation.

7. Alejandro Portes and Manuel Castells (1989) define "informal economy" as "a process of income-generation characterized by one central feature: *it is unregulated by the institutions of society, in a legal and social environment in which similar actions are regulated*" (*WT*, 12; italics in original). Yet as many have noted, since the 1970s, the ability of nation-states to limit or regulate transnational corporations and finance capital has been severely undermined by accumulation and production processes that prioritize commodity chains across various nations. Thus, we can say that contemporary capital is *fundamentally* informal; in other words, informality is not a secondary characteristic of contemporary capitalism, but rather structures the very way it operates.
8. Laura Ho, Catherine Powell, and Leti Volpp argue that seemingly "non-modern" and "un-American" forms of exploitative labor practices are indeed exactly what sustain "modern American" corporations, attesting that "sweatshops . . . are a home-grown problem with peculiarly American roots" (1996, 385). See Edna Bonacich and Richard Appelbaum (2000) for a discussion of the re-emergence of the sweatshop in the late twentieth century, and for the ways in which the largest apparel manufacturing firms are dependent on quasi-legal forms of labor. Angela Davis notes that the California Department of Corrections invites corporations to establish shops on prison grounds, advertising prison labor as cheap and unable to unionize or demand minimum wage standards or health benefits (1997, 321). According to McMichael, about forty-six million children work for U.S. firms in nineteen different countries (2004, 100). Yet as Cathryne L. Schmitz et al. (2004) note, what constitutes "exploitative child labor" is exceedingly complex, and gives rise to the question: why is it worse to exploit children than it is to exploit adults? At what age does someone's right to be protected from exploitation expire? In other words, capitalism fundamentally depends on exploitative processes that we cannot arbitrarily delineate as acceptable or not based on characteristics such as age.
9. People seem to unanimously agree that the ending to *White Teeth* is "bad," including the author herself, who has said in an interview: "YES, 'WHITE TEETH IS TOO LONG.' It's like everyone thinks I haven't noticed. People say it took so long to read and the ending was a letdown. And I'm like, 'Dude, try writing it.' You sit for two years and write 500 pages and screw up the ending. You think that's fun? At least it only takes three weeks to read" (Zadie Smith quoted in Eberhart 2001, 7E).

References

Arrighi, Giovani. 1994. *The long twentieth century*. London: Verso.

Asad, Talal. 1993. *Genealogies of religion*. Baltimore: Johns Hopkins University Press.

Barnet, Richard. 1983. *The alliance: America, Europe, Japan, makers of the postwar world*. New York: Simon and Schuster.

Baker, Kevin. 2003. We're in the Army now: The GOP's plan to militarize our culture. *Harper's Magazine* (October): 35–46.

Benjamin, Walter. 1969. *Illuminations*. New York: Schocken Books.

Bonacich, Edna, and Richard P. Appelbaum. 2000. *Behind the label: Inequality in the Los Angeles apparel industry*. Berkeley: University of California Press.

Chakrabarty, Dipesh. 2000. *Provincializing Europe: Postcolonial thought and historical difference*. Princeton, NJ: Princeton University Press.

Davis, Angela. 1997. Interview. In *Politics of culture in the shadow of capital*, ed. Lisa Lowe and David Lloyd. Durham, NC: Duke University Press.

Davis, Mike. 2004. Planet of slums. *New Left Review* 26 (March–April): 5–34.

Eberhart, John Mark. 2001. *White teeth* author has a brush with fame in America. *Milwaukee Journal Sentinel*, July 8, sec. Cue, p. 7E.

Gibson-Graham, J. K. 1993. Waiting for the revolution, or How to smash capitalism while working at home in your spare time. *Rethinking Marxism* 6, no. 2 (Summer): 10–24.

Escobar, Arturo. 1992. Imagining a post-development era? Critical thought, development, and social movements. *Social Text* 31–32:20–56.

Hardt, Michael, and Antonio Negri. 2000. *Empire*. Cambridge, MA: Harvard University Press.

Head, Dominick. 2003. "Zadie Smith's *White teeth*." In *Contemporary British fiction*, ed. Richard J. Lane, Rod Mengham, and Philip Tew. Cambridge: Polity.

Ho, Laura, Catherine Powell, and Leti Volpp. 1996. (Dis)assembling women workers' rights along the global assemblyline: Human rights and the garment industry. *Harvard Civil Rights Civil Liberties Review* 31, no. 2 (Summer): 383–414.

Jameson, Fredric. 1992. *Postmodernism, or, the cultural logic of late capital*. Durham, NC: Duke University Press.

McMichael, Philip. 2004. *Development and social change: A global perspective*. Thousand Oaks, CA: Pine Forge Press.

Moss, Laura. 2003. The politics of everyday hybridity: Zadie Smith's *White teeth*. *Wasafiri 39*:11–17.

O'Grady, Kathleen. 2002. *White teeth*: A conversation with Zadie Smith. *Atlantis* 27, no. 1 (Fall/Winter): 105–11.

Portes, Alejandro, and Manuel Castells. 1989. World underneath: The origins, dynamics, and effects of the informal economy. In *The informal economy: Studies in advanced and less developed countries*, ed. Alejandro Portes, Manuel Castells, and Lauren A. Benton. Baltimore: Johns Hopkins University Press.

Robinson, Cedric. 1997. *Black movements in America*. New York: Routledge.

Said, Edward. 1979. *Orientalism*. New York: Vintage.

Schmitz, Cathryne L., Elizabeth Kim, Jin Traver, Desi Larson, and Pamela Pieris, eds. 2004. *Child labor: A global view*. Westport, CT: Greenwood.

Smith, Zadie. 2000. *White teeth*. New York: Random House.

Spivak, Gayatri. 1988. Can the subaltern speak? In *Marxism and the interpretation of culture*, ed. Cary Nelson and Lawrence Grossbert. London: Macmillan.

Stoler, Ann. 2002. *Carnal knowledge and imperial power: Race and the intimate in colonial rule*. Berkeley: University of California Press.

Williams, Raymond. 1985. *Marxism and literature*. Cambridge: Oxford University Press.

Wood, Robert. 1986. *From Marshall Plan to debt crisis: Foreign aid and development choices in the world economy*. Berkeley: University of California Press.

CHAPTER 2

Gender, Nation, and Globalization in *Monsoon Wedding* and *Dilwale Dulhania Le Jayenge*

Jenny Sharpe

The crossover success of Mira Nair's *Monsoon Wedding* (2001), whose characters speak English, Hindi, and Punjabi, lies in the skill with which the film acquaints a Western audience with the sights and sounds of the new global India. Set in a burgeoning New Delhi suburb, the film uses a lavish Punjabi wedding as an occasion for staging the reunion of family members who are scattered across the globe. But the idea of a global India does not simply refer to the large numbers of Indians (known as Non-Resident Indians or NRIs) living in the diaspora.[1] The term also signifies the social and cultural transformation India has undergone since 1991, when a new economic policy eliminated the bureaucratic red tape restricting imports and foreign investment. For the first time, the marketplace became flooded with consumer goods that had previously been available only on the black market, and designer labels became commonplace. Indian television went from the two channels of state TV to the more than sixty channels available on cable and satellite in some urban areas. Whereas the state-controlled television programming promoted agricultural shows aimed at farmers, the new satellite TV channels broadcast sexually explicit music videos and Hollywood soap operas such as *Santa Barbara* and *Baywatch* that engendered Indian imitations. Sexual topics that were previously unmentionable were now being openly discussed, and television brought these discussions into the inner sanctum of the home.

Monsoon Wedding presents the contradictions of everyday life that an opening of India to globalization has introduced. The film destroys any lingering image of a nation mired in some premodern space as a traditional land with ancient customs and beliefs. It reveals a postmodern world in which cell phones and e-mail coexist with age-old rituals and occupations.[2] The audience witnesses Delhi street scenes of pushcarts and bicycle rickshaws weaving in and out of cars driving by a monolithic statue of Shiva.[3] Golfers ride in golf carts across an immaculately landscaped golf course, while a row of women carrying sand in baskets on their heads (presumably for the sand pits) passes behind them. The camera often zooms in on television screens and monitors to emphasize the power of the new media, and it presents a TV talk show on film censorship where guests debate the erosion of Indian morality and Hindu tradition. The heroine, Aditi (Vasundhara Das), represents a new generation of Indian women who live double lives in order to reconcile their desires with the wishes of their parents. Aditi secretly meets the man she loves the night before she is to marry the Houston NRI her parents have arranged for her to marry.

In foregrounding the clash of modernity and tradition, Nair makes explicit the anxieties about a national identity underlying the commercially successful films of Indian cinema, commonly known as Bollywood in reference to Bombay as the Hollywood of the Indian film industry.[4] A hybrid form from its inception, Bombay cinema reworked the melodrama, musical, slapstick comedy, and gangster genres of the classic Hollywood era by infusing them with Hindu epic plots, Orientalist exoticism, and the visual and aural overload of Indian culture to create a new aesthetic style. Once derided for its melodrama and derivative plots, Bollywood has more recently begun to infiltrate a Euro-American consciousness through what can be identified as a new transnational cultural literacy. Indian films have always enjoyed an international audience, being popular among Arabs, Africans, Mexicans, and Southeast Asians. Indian film stars such as Raj Kapoor had an enormous following in third-world countries as well as the former Soviet Union, where loyal fans equally consumed the visual spectacle of his movies as his depiction of the angst of the common man. What is different today is that the Bollywood audience has expanded to include Western populations, while its cinematic style has been mainstreamed into British and American theater, film, and television.[5] Bollywood's crossover success can be attributed to the increased availability of Indian films on DVD, cable TV, and in theaters catering to South Asians living in the diaspora. But it is also an indication of how Indian films are becoming more global in appearance.

Glossy, high budget films shot on location in Europe and the United States and influenced by the slick cinematography of commercials are far removed from the feudal village drama of the 1950s and 1960s belonging to the golden age of Indian cinema. The story of the strength and courage of a peasant woman to overcome debt bondage in a classic postindependence film such as Mehboob's *Mother India* (1957) served as an allegory for the heroic effort of the Indian nation to achieve self-sufficiency through modernization. The 1970s and 1980s witnessed a shift to action films featuring the "angry young man" who embodied the triumph of India's underclasses over social injustice and political corruption.[6] The commercially successful films made since the mid-1990s, in contrast, emphasize wealth, fast cars, youth culture, and cosmopolitan lifestyles. Moreover, the folk-inspired song-and-dance sequences that were standard Bollywood fare have been replaced with a hip-hop style, Michael Jackson–inspired choreography, accompanied by the rapid editing and unconventional camera angles of MTV music videos—all appropriately "Indianized." The rural exists in the post-1990s films not as a geographical location so much as a signifier for a simpler way of life prior to globalization. As Govind Nihalani, a member of the new generation of directors, declares, "The village has been pushed to the farthest periphery of our imagination. Any reference to a rural background today is only a synthetic nod to the roots. The insistence is on gloss" (cited in Chopra 1997 69). Instead of the folkloric scenes belonging to earlier generations of films, the "rural" is emptied of the culture of everyday life.

The most successful genre to deploy the new cinematic style is the family melodrama, which was the most popular genre of the 1990s.[7] Instead of featuring India's underclasses as did earlier generations of films, the 1990s melodrama centers on wealthy Indian families with traditional values. These big-budget films, often shot on location in Europe and the United States, present "endless rounds of parties, beach dances, wedding celebrations, festive occasions, and an all-round feeling of well-being" (Kripalani 2001, 45). Films such as *Hum Aapke Hain Koun. . . !* (What Am I to You. . . ! 1994); *Dilwale Dulhania Le Jayenge* (The Brave-Hearted Will Take the Bride, 1995); *Pardes* (Foreign Land, 1997); and *Kuch Kuch Hota Hai* (Something Is Happening, 1998) allow their audiences to share in the extravagant lifestyles of the elite classes and cross the threshold of their luxurious homes, whether Western-style mansions or traditional Indian homes. Instead of the class conflict that dominated the "angry young man" films of the prior two decades, the conflict staged in these films is between modernity and tradition.[8] The 1990s family melodrama endorses traditional values through its staging of elaborate northern Indian marriage ceremonies and by making the joint family into the locus of the nation at a moment in time when the nuclear family was replacing the extended family among India's middle class (Uberoi 2001). The indebtedness of *Monsoon Wedding* to this genre of Bollywood film is unmistakable in its integration of song-and-dance sequences into the storyline, its indulgence in the rich culture of Punjabi weddings, and its tribute to the extended family.[9] In addition, through the shared knowledge its characters have of songs from popular Hindi films, Nair's film dramatizes how a commercialized, hybridized, and low cultural form such as Bombay cinema operates as the site of a collective Indian identity throughout the diaspora.[10]

But even as Nair integrates a Bollywood aesthetic into her film, she is critical of the rosy picture presented in its family dramas. Made under the aegis of her New York–based company, Mirabai Films, *Monsoon Wedding* moves fluidly from happy family reunion scenes to sexually intimate ones, and it weaves into its wedding motif the disturbing topic of sexual molestation—a subject too controversial for popular Indian cinema. Inasmuch as Nair eschews the glossy patina of blockbuster Bollywood films in favor of a documentary cinematic style by shooting with a handheld Super 16 camera, she merges the realism of American independent filmmaking with Bollywood's narrative style. Still, *Monsoon Wedding* was not only successful in Britain and the United States but in India as well, at least among its urban middle class. Its celebration of the Indian family aligns it more closely with the 1990s Bollywood blockbusters than its maverick approach to questions of female sexuality might lead one to suspect.

Nair reinvents even as she reproduces the lavish Punjabi wedding film that Yash Chopra popularized and that experienced a comeback with the success of *Hum Aapke Hain Koun. . . !* and Yash Chopra and Aditya Chopra's *Dilwale Dulhania Le Jayenge* (commonly referred to as *DDLJ*). Although *Monsoon Wedding* is generally located within a Hollywood tradition of wedding films ranging from Robert Altman's *A Wedding* (1978) to Ang Lee's *The Wedding Banquet* (1993), I want to consider it alongside a Bollywood wedding film such *DDLJ*, which also uses the marriage between an Indian and an NRI as an occasion for exploring the contradictions of the new global India. The first Bollywood film to fuse elements of Eastern and Western cultures into what one director calls "believable fantasies" (cited in Anupama Chopra's seminal study of the film 2002, 54–58), *DDLJ* perfected the cinematic style of "western gloss-*desi* soul" that became endlessly repeated in subsequent films hoping to reproduce its success.[11]

Although the hybridities of global cultures are generally explained as postnational phenomena, I want to examine how they constitute a new nationalism in India.[12] The vanishing rural in Bombay cinema undoubtedly reflects a turn in Indian films toward catering to urban and overseas markets, where the profit margin is greater than that of rural areas.[13] But it is also a sign of what Leela Fernandes (2001) identifies as a shift in the Indian national imaginary from an elimination of rural poverty through development to social mobility through consumerism. She argues that, rather than denoting a deterritorialization of the nation, "the global" is produced through nationalist narratives that shuttle between cultural hybridities and purities. "The lure of hybridity in this context," she explains, "holds within it the dangers of impurity. The potential disruption is managed through a remapping of the nation's boundaries through a politics of gender which centers around conflicts over the preservation of the purity of women's sexuality, a process which once again conflates the preservation of nationness with the protection of women" (2001, 157). Fernandes is alluding to how the purity of the Indian nation has historically been identified with the purity of the Hindu woman through the value attributed to Sita, the pure and devoted wife of Rama.[14]

Bollywood heroines commonly serve an iconic function in representing family values that Western decadence and materialism have undermined. In *Pardes* (which invites comparison with *DDLJ* because it not only has the same leading male actors—Shah Rukh Kahn and Amrish Puri—but also tells the story of an arranged marriage between an Indian and an NRI), the heroine is explicitly identified with traditional Indian values. A deeply religious woman who responds to the world with childlike innocence, she is appropriately named Ganga, meaning "pure," since the Hindu goddess Ganga is synonymous with the pure and chaste woman. The association between Ganga and the nation is reinforced throughout the film through patently allegorical statements expressing disapproval of an NRI father's attempt to reconnect with India through the marriage of his American-born son to Ganga. *Pardes* explicitly rejects the hybrid Indian identity of *DDLJ* in favor of cultural purity. The NRI father is informed that he is "trying to bring India's pure Ganges to these concrete jungles of America" and is accused of "wish[ing] to nestle an Indian girl, India itself, in America."

The potential violation of Indian values is presented through a trip Ganga takes to the entertainment capital of the world, Los Angeles, and the "sin city" of Las Vegas. Her introduction to amusement parks, nightclubs, and casinos in the two cities creates desire in the audience for "fascinating America" (Uberoi 1998, 330–31). But, even as the film offers the viewing pleasure of urban cool, foreign locales, and extravagant lifestyles, it also exhibits an anxiety about the loss of traditional Indian values. Although Ganga is seduced by the glamour and glitter of an American lifestyle, she refuses to engage in premarital sex with her fiancé. The positing of tradition as a pure origin at the moment of its perceived loss is enacted through her sexual purity and incorruptible nature.

As scholars of colonial and postcolonial cultures argue, modernity is less the negation of tradition than the grounds for its formation (Makdisi 1995, 111; Sharpe 1997; Mani 1998; Grewal and Kaplan 2001, 669–70). With this in mind, I want to consider the commodity culture of the new global India as a driving force behind the desire to see traditional family values in Bollywood cinema. The ascendance of the Bharatiya Janata Party (BJP), with its strong Hindu nationalist or Hindutva identity, has paralleled India's economic liberalization policy.[15] Its constituency includes an urban Hindu middle class and wealthy NRIs desiring to reconnect with their birthplace through the idea of a glorious Hindu past (Mishra 2004, 30–31). The strong assertion of a Hindustani identity in the 1990s family melodrama can be considered a response to the crisis in national identity produced by an embracing of values that were previously rejected for being synonymous with a Western lifestyle. With the introduction of the new commodity culture, individual desires began to be placed before social ones, and credit card purchases gained credence over the idea of financial conservatism.[16]

Historically the moral universe of commercial Indian cinema is a world in which social duties, love of nation, and kinship bonds outweigh individualism and personal desires (Thomas 1995, 164–66). The 1990s family melodrama broke with this convention by giving value to the acquisition of new wealth and the pursuit of personal desires. Its moral universe is maintained, however, through the symbolic functioning of the heroine as that which defines the boundaries of "Indianness." This functioning is evident in a film such as *Pardes*, whose heroine is a traditional Indian woman. What interests me about *DDLJ* is how the materialism of consumer culture is reconciled with traditional Indian values through its presentation of an Indian woman who is sexually chaste but who also has desires of her own. If, as Stuart Hall suggests, cinema is not "a second-order mirror held up to reflect what already exists, but . . . that form of representation which is able to constitute us as new kinds of subjects" (1996, 221), what kinds of female subjectivity does this film attempt to constitute? I want to argue that the cinematic staging of Indian tradition through transnational cultural hybridities relies on a female subject who is simultaneously modern and traditional, Westernized and Indian. I am interested in seeing how, on the one hand, a Bollywood film such as *DDLJ* appropriates feminist values in the service of tradition, and, on the other, a diasporic film such as *Monsoon Wedding* expands the heteronormative female sexual desire introduced into the family melodrama formula in order to explode it.[17] At the same time, Nair's splitting of Indian femininity along class lines leads one to question the gender politics of her feminist intervention.

The plot of *DDLJ* is simple enough to be captured by its promotional invitation to "come . . . fall in love." The heroine, Simran (Kajol), is the British-born daughter of a modest, middle-class Punjabi shopkeeper, Chaudhury Baldev Singh (Amrish Puri), while the hero, Raj (Shah Rukh Kahn), is also

British-born, except that he is an idle millionaire's son who wears a Harley-Davidson jacket, drives a Lamborghini, and jetsets across the globe. While Simran's family represents a prior era of migration when Indians had to struggle in small businesses to succeed, Raj's family history belongs to a more recent past in which enterprising NRIs have made their fortunes in computer and Internet-related businesses. The film presents the problem of the NRI's national identity through Baldev's desire to reconnect with his homeland by arranging a marriage between his daughter and the son of his best friend in Punjab. Although *DDLJ* ends in the idyllic Punjabi countryside, it does not tell the story of rural poverty. Rather, the rural exists as the nostalgic image of an uncontaminated homeland that resides in the expatriate's imagination. While feeding pigeons at London's Trafalgar Square, Baldev is magically transported to the golden mustard fields of Punjab, where women in colorful *salwar kameez*, the traditional Punjabi garb, are dancing.[18] The truth-value of this image is reconfirmed when he moves his family back home after twenty years of living abroad and sees from the train the same scene that he imagined.

DDLJ is considered a watershed film in Bombay cinema's depiction of NRIs inasmuch as its leading characters are British-born Indians. The NRI had always been a marginal character in Bollywood films, being stereotyped as a decadent debauchee and confused individual who smoked, drank, and gambled. *DDLJ* plays with and overturns this image, or, to quote Anupama Chopra, it "turned Bollywood's NRI stereotype on its head" (2002, 11–12). The film begins by leading the audience to believe that Raj is yet another decadent NRI who has been corrupted by living in the West. As a youth who relies on family fortune rather than his own intelligence for making his way in life, he is the first student in the history of a prestigious English university to have failed his exams. An early scene shows him tricking Baldev into selling him beer after he has closed his Southall shop for the night. The director wanted the disputed item to be a condom but decided that it would have been too transgressive for the audience to accept (Chopra 2002, 63). As a result, Raj's sexual dalliances are alluded to but not confirmed. By the end of the film, however, the audience realizes that the lazy, inept, beer-drinking, motorcycle-riding playboy does, after all, have traditional Indian values. The message of *DDLJ* is that, although the hero and heroine wear Western clothing and embrace youth culture, they have maintained their Indian values, particularly around questions of sexual morality. Raj will not challenge the authority of Simran's father by eloping with her, while Simran is hot spirited and independent, but also chaste and morally upright.

Even though Simran is not a traditional Indian woman, she is not exactly the second generation NRI that she is supposed to be. The intergenerational strife that is the subject of British-made Indian films such as *My Beautiful*

Laundrette (1985), *Bhaji on the Beach* (1993), and *Bend It Like Bekham* (2002) is muted in *DDLJ*. Whereas the British Indian films show immigrant parents who do not recognize their British-born daughters because their tastes, language, and customs are Westernized, the closest Simran comes to displaying such second-generation traits is to dance surreptitiously to pop music and to wear Western-style clothing. As Vijay Mishra observes in *Bollywood Cinema*, both Baldev's daughters "speak Hindi without an accent and, more important, have a body language that is totally Indian" (2002, 251). Despite its overturning of the NRI stereotype, then, the film is not about the overseas Indians coming home as much as it is about the India that resides within them. *DDLJ* does not attempt to reproduce the reality of the British Indian experience as much as it transplants a typically Indian family to a foreign locale.

The transformation of the NRI stereotype in Bollywood cinema is less an indication of the increased respectability of the NRI than it is a sign of the emergence of a new urban class in India. *DDLJ* lends credibility to the cosmopolitan lifestyles of India's urban middle class, which overlaps with but is not the same as Indians living in the diaspora. The "Indianness" of an Indian national identity can be established through the hybridized NRI precisely because the new consumer culture threw into crisis the home/world opposition underpinning the nationalist claim to an authentic, spiritual self that the British were unable to colonize.[19] *DDLJ* invokes the perceived independence of NRI daughters to establish Simran's desire for a love match that conflicts with her father's wishes. At the same time, even though she is not happy at the idea of an arranged marriage, she accepts his decision by tearing up the love poems she has written to the unknown man of her dreams.

Once she is in India, Simran abandons her Western clothing in favor of the Punjabi *salwar kameez*, which follows the Bollywood formula of the heroines (more so than heroes) wearing Indian clothes as a sign of their national identity. And, in preparation for her marriage, she decides to keep *Karva chauth*, which is a northern Indian ritual in which women engage in a daylong fast for the prosperity of their husbands. The feminist twist on this gender-biased tradition is that Simran is secretly fasting for Raj as the man she wants to marry rather than her husband-to-be, and Raj, out of love and sympathy for her, also refrains from eating or drinking. Yet he does not take the ritual as seriously as she does, as he attempts to sneak her some sweets when she complains of hunger. Since it is women who define the boundaries of "Indianness," Raj can be depicted as playing with traditional practices while Simran has to observe them. The film nonetheless establishes her as a strong, independent woman, and a sexual being with desires of her own.

The song-and-dance sequence, which generally serves as a fantasy space in Bollywood films, provides an occasion for staging female desire, even if this desire is contained in the last instance. The audience is first introduced to Simran as she stands at the window with a dreamy look on her face, the wind blowing in her hair. Her mother, Lajjo (Farida Jalal), has found her daughter's diary and enters reading aloud the love poem she has committed to its pages. After Simran recites the poem to her mother, the film cuts to a song, "Mere Khwabon Mein" (The one who comes in my dreams), which is about the man she hopes to meet. There is considerable ambivalence to the film's staging of Simran's desires. Although the lyrics position the unknown man as the object of her desire, the sequence of images that presents Raj as the embodiment of this man establishes him as an agent. He is shown scoring in soccer and bowling, picking up an attractive female hitchhiker on his motorcycle, driving a racing car, and even attempting to outrun an airplane.

Unlike Raj, who is out in the rough and competitive world of sports, Simran is in the inner sanctuary of her bedroom—one that, with its stuffed animals and lace decor, belongs to a girl who is not quite a woman. Yet, at the same time, her dreams are constitutive of him as an ideal type, since the real Raj is much more bumbling and ineffectual than the almost superhuman man of her dreams. In this regard, the film gives value to Simran's dreams as the expression of female desire. When she moves outside the home to help her mother bring in clothes from the rain, her dance and clothing become more sensual. The domestic chore of removing clothes from the clothesline is an occasion for offering voyeuristic pleasure to the audience. Since the rain song has conventionally been used as a metaphor for sex in order to circumvent the restrictions of the Indian censor board, the song plays with this convention in order to hint at Simran as a sexual—but not necessarily a sexually active—being (Chopra 2002, 60). The film entertains (even if it does not go so far as to declare) the possibility for female sexual agency.

In a subsequent song, "Zara Sa Jhoom Loon Main" (What madness love is), Simran does act on her desires, even if, because she is drunk on cognac, she is not quite herself. She steals a red mini-skirted dress (surely the sign of a sexually promiscuous woman) from a store window and wears it while chasing Raj through the Swiss Alps out of a desire to embrace him. The song ends when she wakes up in his bed wearing his shirt and has no memory of how she got there. Raj leads her to believe that they have spent a passionate night together, but on seeing how much his words upset her, exclaims, "I know what you think of me. You think I'm a wastrel. I'm not scum, Simran. I'm Hindustani. And I know what honor means for a Hindustani woman." This moment constitutes a turning point in the film, one in which both Raj's and

Simran's true Indian identities are established. Both of them observe traditional Indian rules of moral conduct prior to marriage, and it is only after exercising restraint that they realize they have fallen in love. The assertion of a hybrid (rather than a pure) Indian identity is thus contingent on the containment (rather than the negation) of female sexuality.

There exists a gender difference in each leading character's fulfilment of his or her desire inasmuch as Simran, aided and abetted by her mother, is willing to elope, while Raj is not. Although rebellion is built into the Bollywood formula for romance, it is generally the hero, rather than the heroine, who goes against the parents' wishes (Chopra 2002, 75). This is not the case in *DDLJ*, which endorses a woman's right to choose. As a film genre, Indian women's melodrama has characteristically raised the issue of women's choice and desires within an overarching frame of patriarchal discourse (Prasad 1998, 86). Although *DDLJ* establishes Simran's right to choose her marriage partner, it displaces agency away from the youthful female protagonist by having patriarchal authority questioned by a prior generation of women who had greater restrictions placed on them.

The most moving scene in the film occurs when Lajjo confesses to Simran that, although she vowed her daughter would not have to make the same sacrifices she did, she wants her to give up Raj in order to make her father happy. As Patricia Uberoi remarks about this scene, "the condemnation of the injustice of 'tradition' (*parampara*) is paradoxically the *very* ground on which the mother asks Simran to *give up* her own aspirations and 'sacrifice' her personal happiness" (1998, 324; emphasis original). Yet the film does not leave this paradox unresolved. Lajjo later reverses her position, saying, "I was wrong, Simran! My daughter won't sacrifice her happiness. She isn't going to sacrifice her love," and she encourages her to elope with Raj.[20] Lajjo's words reconfirm her earlier belief that daughters should not be expected to sacrifice their personal happiness. Simran's mother exhibits an independence and bravery in her willingness to side with her daughter against her husband. Baldev, however, does not possess the patriarchal virtues of wisdom and self-sacrifice that the fathers in Bollywood films have conventionally held.[21] The value he ascribes to his personal desires over the welfare of his family compromises his role as patriarch. The arranged marriage is revealed to be not in his daughter's best interest, as the man he has chosen for her is an uncouth lout who plans to commit adultery after marriage. Since *DDLJ* shows that Baldev has made the wrong choice for his daughter by placing his desires for reconnecting with his homeland above the well-being of his family, it questions a patriarchal authority based on personal desires. At the same time, the male authority that Lajjo challenges in her husband is reconstituted in the man that Simran wishes to marry.

Although Simran rejects the husband her father has chosen for her in favor of eloping with Raj, Raj refuses to marry her unless he has her father's approval. He follows her to India, thereby undermining Baldev's efforts to separate the lovers. But he also dashes Simran's hopes that he has come to take her away. "No Simran," he informs her, "I haven't come here to steal you. I might have been born in England, but I am Hindustani. I've come here to take you as my bride. I'll take you only when your Babaji gives me your hand." Raj's refusal to undermine Baldev's parental authority is identified with the Indian values he possesses despite being British-born. Hence, when Lajjo brings the couple her jewellery so that they might elope, she is forced to concur with Raj when he says, "I want to be given Simran. I don't want to steal her." His repeated phrasing of elopement as "theft" reaffirms Baldev's propriety over his daughter.

In the film's final scene, when Simran begs her father to let her go to Raj, the camera focuses on the two men looking at each other followed by a literal handing over of daughter from father to future son-in-law. The audience is presented with a close-up shot of Baldev releasing Simran's hand as she struggles to run after Raj, who is leaving on a train. There is a second close-up of Raj grasping her hand to pull her on board the train and, as he clasps her, he exchanges a thumbs-up with Baldev. This closing scene reassures the audience that any choice Simran might have exercised conforms to the rules of patriarchal authority. The traditional values of arranged marriages are affirmed in the love match through the handing over of the daughter from father to husband. The triumph of romantic love over an arranged marriage thus occurs through what Uberoi identifies as an "arranged love marriage" (1998, 306), which is a love match that receives parental approval and consequently is treated as if it were an arranged marriage.[22] The assertion of tradition is contingent on demonstrating that women can exercise their choice, but it is a choice that should not undermine patriarchal authority, even if the father's decision is proven to be wrong.

I have been establishing the cinematic conventions of the family melodrama as well as the uniqueness of *DDLJ* in order to situate *Monsoon Wedding* as a metanarrative commentary on the 1990s genre. Calling her film "a Bollywood movie, made on my own terms" (cited in Hoffman 2002, 28), Nair exposes the myth of a nation at work in Bollywood films about the NRI. Rather than transporting the Indian experience of globalization to Britain or the United States, Nair stages the identity crisis it is creating within India. The wealthy father is not the high school dropout-turned-London-millionaire or immigrant shopkeeper of *DDLJ*. He is the homespun Punjabi Lalit Verma (Naseeruddin Shah), who has made his fortune as a garment exporter for American clothing stores.[23] The setting is not the golden mustard fields of rural Punjab, with its pastoral harmony of joint family life, but rather the suburban sprawl of New Delhi, with its high-rises and carefully manicured golf course. Sexual frankness is not simply a Western import, for a Hindi film dubbist is shown simulating the sounds of sexual pleasure on a talk show called Delhi.com. The question that one of show's panelists raises makes explicit the anxieties underpinning Bollywood's endorsement of traditional values: "Just because India has gone global," he queries, "should we embrace everything? What about our ancient culture, our traditions, our values?"

Countering the tendency in Bollywood cinema to make the Indian woman into a receptacle of traditional Indian values, Nair centers her film on an upper-middle-class Hindu woman's desires and subjectivity. Unlike the heroine of *Pardes*, Aditi is not an innocent Punjabi girl whose honor is potentially under attack; rather, she is a savvy Delhi woman who reads *Cosmopolitan* magazine and is having an affair with a married man. She is the ideal type of a Punjabi beauty—fair-skinned with big doe eyes (although the actress who plays her is from Bangalore)—but she is also a modern Indian woman with cropped, hennaed hair. The audience is first introduced to Aditi when she visits a TV station to meet her lover, Vikram Mehta, the host of Delhi.com. We are immediately confronted with an extreme close-up, over-the-shoulder shot of her face as her lover kisses her in a scene that self-consciously thumbs its nose at the Indian prohibition of on-screen kissing.[24]

Nair melds the sexual frankness of Hollywood with the visual and affective extravagance of Bollywood in order to establish her heroine as a desiring subject. Much of the film's dramatic action focuses on Aditi attempting to arrange a liaison with Vikram and agonizing over the difficult choices she has to make. She has agreed to an arranged marriage with a Houston computer engineer, Hemant (Parvin Dabas), but only because she is tired of waiting for Vikram to divorce his wife. Aditi nonetheless is still in love with Vikram and sneaks out to meet him on the night before her wedding. The police humiliate the lovers, however, when they are caught half-naked in Vikram's car, which is parked in a remote spot in the middle of a torrential rainstorm. Aditi decides to reveal the affair to her future husband so that she can enter the marriage with a clean slate. Hemant is initially upset but then admits to having been in love himself and decides to make a go of it anyway, saying, "What marriage isn't a risk? Whether our parents introduce us or we meet in a club, what difference does it make?" These words are directed at a Western audience that regards arranged marriages to be a holdover from India's feudal past. For an Indian audience, though, they endorse the idea of an arranged love marriage that has been incorporated into the Bollywood family film formula.

Monsoon Wedding reveals that it is not the question of a woman's sexual abstinence prior to marriage that lies at the heart of the battle between tradition and modernity, but rather that it is her right to choose that is withheld through the double standards upheld for men and women. The monsoon that is regarded in India as a cathartic release from the oppressive summer heat serves as a metaphor for Indian women's liberation from the patriarchal strictures imposed on them. One such instance occurs when Uncle Tej (Rajat Kapoor), the man who serves as the family benefactor after Lalit's older brother dies, is exposed as having sexually abused his niece, Ria (Shefali Shetty), when she was a child. Noticing the attention that Tej is giving her younger cousin, Aliya, Ria publicly denounces him. Lalit is able to prevent his family from unravelling, not by deferring to Tej's authority as an elder male relative and family benefactor, but instead by respecting his niece's right not to have to face her molester anymore.

Tej's ejection from the wedding involves a symbolic removal of the traditional Punjabi turban he is wearing for the wedding. While posing for the formal wedding photo, Ria is made to sit at the feet of her Uncle Tej, who is seated in a chair next to the bride in reference to his status as the extended family's patriarch. In the scene in which Lalit asks Tej to leave the wedding, the camera pans across the female family members to emphasize that the father is making his choice out of respect for them over his obligations to an elder male relative. The film's dramatization of Tej removing his turban before leaving the Verma home makes explicit the superficiality of locating traditional values in appearances. Lalit's decision demonstrates that the strength of the Indian family lies in a male head of household who respects all of its members' needs over his own desire to save face in public. The torrential rain represents not only the freeing of women's sexual desire through a disengagement of male honor from women's virginity, but also a refusal to sacrifice women in the name of family honor. Rather than reaffirming traditional patriarchal values through the ruse of modernity as does *DDLJ*, *Monsoon Wedding* reworks those values for the modern Indian family.

But even as Nair infuses the Punjabi wedding film with the grittiness of art-house cinema and a feminist sensibility, she adheres to the conventions of Bollywood filmmaking in the parallel love story between the wedding planner, P. K. Dubey (Vijay Raaz), and the Verma family servant, Alice (Tilotama Shome). Dubey's upward mobility is evident through his frequent conversations with his mother over stock options and his claim to be running a business he calls a " Y2K dot.com event management," which is essentially the age-old task of wedding decorating gone high-tech. He is shown continuously talking on his cell phone or using consumer gadgets such as a wristwatch calculator or pager. Dubey represents the much larger group of India's lower middle class that aspires to participate in the new wealth being generated by economic liberalization. When he gives Alice his business card, he tries to explain to her the electronic transmission of letters, to which she responds with a single, knowing word: "e-mail." The exchange suggests that the new information technology extends far beyond the upwardly mobile classes to the servant classes. At the same time, the lowly servant girl serves as a visual image of a nation that has been untouched by the commodity culture of globalization.

Although *Monsoon Wedding* abandons the traditional Bollywood heroine in Aditi, she is reconstituted in Alice, who appears as a pure and virginal object of desire. While decorating the outside of the house, Dubey spies Alice through the window and watches as she surreptitiously tries on Aditi's jewellery. The image of Alice posing in the mirror all adorned in jewels is shot from the voyeuristic angle of a camera that embodies the male gaze. The audience views her reflection in the mirror from Dubey's perspective outside the room looking through the window. Alice is unaware that she is being watched because she is too engrossed in admiring herself in the mirror. As a feminist filmmaker, Nair is careful to show that the pleasure a member of the servant class derives from adorning herself in fineries she can never hope to own.

Yet the woman as surveyor is displaced in favor of what John Berger in *Ways of Seeing* calls "the surveyed female," which is a woman who does not act but rather appears as an "object of vision" (1972, 47). The camera lingers on Alice putting on Aditi's necklace, earrings, *bindi*, and ankle bracelets. As she lets down her hair and strikes the pose of a Bollywood heroine's seductive coyness by wrapping the end of her sari around her head and face, she is transformed into the virginal woman of Bombay cinema. Alice, however, does not embody the perfect vision of upper-caste Hindu femininity that Bollywood has created, as Nair avoids using the soft lens designed to make the heroine emit an aura of beauty. Rather, she operates as a figure of working-class authenticity. When Dubey leaves the soap opera drama of Lalit's unravelling family to return to his home in the ancient city of Old Delhi, he recalls the vision of Alice's adorned reflection. The juxtaposition of her image with Delhi street scenes shot in the cinema vérité style of documentary filmmaking identifies her with the less materialistic and hence "more authentic" world of India's working classes.

Alice's singularity makes her iconic status in the film all the more apparent. She is the only servant present in the Verma home, which would be unusual for a country in which even a modestly middle-class family can afford several servants. She is also the only Christian—identified by the cross around her neck and a larger one hanging on the kitchen wall—among Hindus, and the only villager in an urban setting, since she claims to be from the largely rural state of Bihar. Having a Christian occupy the position of the pure Indian woman undermines the Hindutva identification of the nation with the chaste, upper-caste Hindu woman and a Bollywood stereotyping of Indian Christians as mini-skirted, sexually loose women. Yet a reliance on Indian cinematic conventions for filming the parallel love story begs the question as to the narrative function of Alice's character.

I would go so far as to argue that Nair's feminist endorsement of arranged marriages—which are as much determined by class, money, and family alliances as they are by a couple's compatibility—is structurally contingent on the relationship between Dubey and Alice. The latter relationship is not for material gain (that is, a dowry) since Dubey is marrying beneath his class and outside his caste. Dubey and Alice share a propensity for eating marigolds, which are used to decorate the Verma home for the wedding. Dubey declares his love by presenting Alice with a heart of marigolds, which she accepts with a nod of assent. The chasteness to their mutual declaration of affection places the exchange firmly within a trope of romantic love. Dubey says he is looking for a "decent, simple girl," and there is no indication that Alice is looking for the sexual passion that Aditi desires in a man. The camera cuts from Hemant and Aditi passionately kissing to Alice accepting Dubey's chaste declaration of love, thereby reinforcing the audience's belief that Aditi will find love in her arranged marriage. If the marriage between a woman from Delhi's wealthy cosmopolitan class and the son of a Houston NRI is complicated by prior relationships and family obligations, the relationship between Dubey and Alice is extraordinarily uncomplicated.[25] The latter belongs to the film's utopian desires for an egalitarian nation.

Through its parallel story of a pure and innocent love, *Monsoon Wedding* expresses an anxiety about a widening of the gap between rich and poor in the new global India. In the director's commentary on the DVD release of *Monsoon Wedding*, Nair remarks that she did not know how to end her film, and then knew that it had to be with a shot of Lalit happy with where his family had taken him. The film's final shot, however, shows Lalit reaching out for Alice's hand as he invites her to join the wedding guests dancing exuberantly to a Bally Sagoo fusion of *bhangra* and disco music. Are the viewers to understand this closing scene as a gesture toward a classless society? If so, the utopian vision needs to be located with the frame of the new global nation for which the film creates desire in the audience.

The film's locating of the love between Dubey and Alice outside the global network that structures the post-1990s family melodramas is evident in Nair's citation of films from the golden age of Bombay cinema for staging their romance. In contrast to the extravagant wedding taking place on the same premises, Dubey and Alice exchange simple vows under a marigold umbrella that alludes to a scene between Raj Kapoor and Nargis in *Awaara* (The vagabond, 1951). The scene in which Dubey declares his love for Alice by presenting her with a heart made of marigolds invokes the ending of Guru Dutt's *Pyaasa* (Thirst, 1957), when Gulabo, who is a prostitute, decides to leave with the idealistic poet Vijay, played by Dutt. It is not inconsequential to Nair's film that Dutt's film denounces the corrupt and materialistic world in which the hero finds himself. However, despite her efforts to remain faithful to his shooting of the scene from the perspective of a mobile camera that heightens Gulabo's (and by extension, Alice's) agency, she cannot escape the Bollywood cliché that Dutt's signature shot has become for representing Indian women as objects of desire. In other words, there is no possibility for a simple return to an earlier (and perhaps purer) moment of Bombay cinema.

Just as *DDLJ* gives value to the hybridized Indian through the traditional values of the NRI, *Monsoon Wedding* requires the innocence of the parallel love story for its endorsement of the materialism of India's wealthy cosmopolitan class. The film suggests that the marginal groups to which Alice belongs—a Christian minority in the face of an increasingly Hindu-identified nation, a servant class that journeys from impoverished rural areas to urban centers seeking employment—can participate in the social mobility that economic liberalization has introduced. Since Bihar is India's most underdeveloped state, with the lowest per capita income in the nation, what does it mean for Alice to share in a knowledge of e-mail? *Monsoon Wedding* does not allow the audience to entertain this question. Its vision of a dot-com nation follows a cartography in which the "global" consists of a series of urban centers connecting India's cosmopolitan classes to Indians in the diaspora. It is not inconsequential to its storyline that guests travel from the four corners of the South Asian diaspora—the United States, Britain, the Gulf States, and Australia—for the wedding.

The idea of a global India is endorsed through the visibility of those classes that have the financial ability to participate in the transnational cultures of globalization. However, despite the media's fascination with the success stories of India's growing middle class, its economic liberalization policy has been much more uneven in its effects. The government's incentives for foreign investments were accompanied by cuts in agricultural spending and subsidies during the 1990s. Moreover, agribusiness and biotechnology have not brought wealth to small farmers as have the new technologies in urban areas. Rather, transnational agricultural giants such as DuPont and Cargill engage in practices that activists call biopiracy—namely, the patenting of seeds and indigenous knowledge that prevents farmers from saving seeds to replant the following year (Mehta 1994; Shiva 2000). As a result, farmers are forced to plant patented hybrid seeds, which requires more water and fertilizers. An increased reliance on purchased seeds, fertilizers, and irrigation systems has placed small farmers even deeper in debt. In Bihar, Monsanto's introduction of hybrid corn resulted in a four billion rupee loss for small farmers. The late 1990s witnessed the emergence of farmer suicides, which has reached the proportion of a national crisis. Approximately twenty-five thousand farmers have committed suicide during the past five years over their increased indebtedness to lenders charging exorbitant rates (Shiva 2004; Huggler 2004).

The diminished iconic value of the village in Bombay cinema does not mean that the problems of rural development have been resolved. Among rural Indians, 97 percent still do not have basic facilities, and debt bondage remains as much a problem as ever. The rural vote that helped Sonia Gandhi and the Congress Party defeat the BJP in the 2004 Indian elections has forced the media to address the disastrous cost of economic liberalization on the rural poor. The BJP had hoped to win a second term in office by running a glossy "India Shining" advertising campaign that capitalized on its economic achievements. However, the 1990s enthusiasm for economic liberalization has been replaced with a more sober attitude. "'Shining' India Fails To Lighten Gloom in Villages," declared a *London Times* headline just prior to the April elections (Philp 2004). The difficulty I have with *Monsoon Wedding* is not that it centers on a wealthy Delhi family, so much as it suggests, through its "upstairs, downstairs" narrative, that this family's world is the entire story. Although Nair makes visible the anxieties about globalization that Bollywood family melodramas gloss over, her film renders invisible the widening gap between rich and poor, and urban and rural areas under India's economic liberalization policy. The vanishing rural in Bollywood cinema is mirrored in an independent film such as *Monsoon Wedding* through a universalizing of the class experience that lends credibility to the image of a shining India.

Notes

1. The term "Non-Resident Indian" generally refers to the post-1960s migrants from India to Australia, Britain, Canada, and the United States. The profile of the NRI has changed since the 1990s, when a U.S. immigration reform act tripled the quotas for skilled immigrants, thereby producing a surge in migration from India to the United States. Unlike previous generations of Indians, particularly those who went to Britain in the 1960s and 1970s, this new group constitutes a transnational class that has the financial ability to live between their country of origin and place of residence. It is not unusual for this new class of NRIs to maintain strong ties with India not only through their participation in cultural clubs and religious centers but also by sending their children to India so that they might maintain the cultural identity they would otherwise risk losing.
2. It is estimated that there are now approximately ten million cell phone users in India.
3. The Shiva statue, a modern replica, is on the Delhi-Jaipur road.

4. Approximately two hundred of the eight hundred films made in India each year are made in Bombay, which was renamed Mumbai in 1995.
5. The 2001 nomination of *Lagaan* for an Academy Award in the best foreign film category is one of the many indications of the increased respectability of commercial Indian cinema in the United States. Other indications are the numerous British and American productions of films, television shows, and musicals that Bollywood has influenced. Baz Luhrmann's film *Moulin Rouge* (2001) and Andrew Lloyd Webber's West End and Broadway theatrical productions of *Bombay Dreams* (2002) pay homage to Bollywood's "filmi" style, while Daisy von Scherler Mayer's parody of Bollywood's musical interludes in *The Guru* (2002), presumes the audience's prior knowledge of Hindi film conventions. Nair is currently working on a television series for ABC about a diasporic Indian family in New Jersey, while Gurinder Chadha, whose British-made film *Bend It Like Beckham* (2002) did surprisingly well with an American audience, has also made *Bride and Prejudice* (2004), a Bollywood rendition of Jane Austen's novel.
6. The film most representative of this genre is *Sholay* (Embers 1975), which was released the same year that Indira Gandhi declared a state of emergency in India. *Sholay*, which reworked the spaghetti western for an Indian audience, starred Amitabh Bachchan, India's greatest actor of all time, in his characteristic angry young rebel role.
7. Although Bollywood directors have more recently experimented with less traditional genres such as the thriller, science fiction, and gangster films, these are considered niche films and do not have the popular appeal of the family melodrama.
8. *Sholay* was the longest running film in Indian cinema until *Dilwale Dulhania Le Jayenge* broke its record in 2001 (Chopra 2002, 8–9).
9. Interestingly enough, the Indian press treats *Monsoon Wedding* as a Bollywood film, even though it was not made in Mumbai. Bollywood has more recently witnessed the phenomenon of the "Hinglish" film, which are made in both Hindi and English. Both of these events are an indication of the increasingly symbiotic relationship between the Bollywood film industry and the NRIs, who have also emerged as financial backers for Indian films.
10. For discussions of Bollywood as one of the primary cultural sites for constructing an imaginary of the modern Indian nation, see Chakravarty 1993; Prasad 1998; Mishra 2002, 235–69; and Rajadhyaksha 2003.
11. Aditya Chopra, who was only twenty-three years old when he made *DDLJ*, belongs to a group identified as Bollywood's Generation Next: "Raised on Hollywood but firmly grounded in Bollywood, the new kids on the block—directors, writers, musicians, choreographers, art directors, editors, stylists, distributors, publicists—are serving up a clever cocktail of *desi* values draped in Yankee slickness" (Chopra and Chowdhury 1999). *Desi*, meaning "local," is a term that has particularly been embraced by South Asians living overseas.
12. For explanations of globalization as a process of cultural hybridization rather than homogenization, see Appadurai 1990; and Pieterse 2003.
13. The ticket price in a multiplex theater in Indian cities is fifty rupees, compared to the five rupees charged in rural areas. The profit margin for tickets sold in

Western nations is even larger, if one considers the exchange rate of forty-five rupees per U.S. dollar.

14. For a reading of the gender politics of national articulations of the *Ramayana* between 1920 and 1990, see Zacharias 2001.
15. The BJP's efforts to remove the mosque built on top of Rama's birthplace in the northern city of Ayodhya culminated in the December 1992 communal violence during which thousands of Muslims were killed.
16. During the mid-1990s, middle-class savings gave way to debt accumulation as the use of credit cards grew by 100 percent (Varma 1998, 177).
17. For discussions of how *Monsoon Wedding* asserts the heteronomativity of female sexual desire through a containment of queerness in the effeminate male character of Aditi's brother, Varun, see Desai 2004, 223–28; and Gopinath 2005, chap. 4.
18. Vijay Mishra attributes the replacement of a northern Indian ethos in Hindi films with a Punjabi one to the predominance of Punjabis in the diaspora and an identification of the Punjab with a pastoral way of life (2002, 260).
19. For a discussion of the home/world opposition in Indian nationalist discourse, see Chatterjee 1993, 119–21.
20. A similar moment occurs in *Pardes* when Ganga's grandmother helps her escape from the barn in which her father has locked her for refusing to go through with the arranged marriage. The family matriarch informs the two fathers who have arranged the marriage that "for centuries we women have been taking poison only" and instructs Ganga not to swallow the poison anymore.
21. I am grateful to Parama Roy for pointing this out to me.
22. The term "arranged love marriage" was first used by the hero of *Hum Aapke Hain Koun . . . !* in response to the question of whether he preferred an arranged or love marriage.
23. *Monsoon Wedding* alludes to the stereotyping of the NRI as one who returns after having made his fortune abroad, when Lalit exclaims, "I'm not a Non-Resident Indian" to a price quote of two *lakhs* for a waterproof wedding canopy.
24. The censorship of kissing is a holdover from strict British censorship codes that were established when India was still a colony. Although the prohibition of kissing has been lifted, filmmakers are reluctant to depict it since public displays of intimacy are considered to be un-Indian. The increasing availability of cell phone cameras has begun to undermine this particular form of Bollywood myth making. The video clip of an actor and his costar passionately kissing in a Mumbai restaurant, which was surreptitiously filmed with the assistance of a cell phone camera, caused an uproar when shown on national TV.
25. One wonders what Dubey's stock-obsessed mother would think of his marriage to a servant girl.

References

Appadurai, Arjun. 1990. *Modernity at large: Cultural dimensions of globalization.* Minneapolis: University of Minnesota Press.

Berger, John. 1972. *Ways of seeing*. London: Penguin.
Chakravarty, Sumita S. 1993. *National identity in Indian popular cinema, 1947–1987*. Austin: University of Texas Press.
Chatterjee, Partha. 1993. *The nation and its fragments*. Princeton, NJ: Princeton University Press.
Chopra, Anupama. 1997. Bollywood: Bye-bye Bharat." *India Today* (December 1): 69.
———. 2002. *Dilwale dulhania le jayenge* [The brave-hearted will take the bride]. London: British Film Institute.
Chopra, Anupama, and Nanda Chowdhury. 1999. New blood: The new Bollywood brigade." *India Today* (June 28): 66.
Desai, Jignai. 2004. *Beyond Bollywood: The cultural politics of South Asian diasporic film*. New York: Routledge.
Dilwale Dulhania Le Jayenge. 1995. Directed by Aditja Chopra. Mumbai, India: Yash Raj Studios.
Fernandes, Leela. 2001. Rethinking globalization: Gender and the nation in India. In *Feminist locations: Global and local, theory and practice*, ed. Marianne DeKoven, 147–67. Piscataway, NJ: Rutgers University Press.
Gopinath, Gayatri. 2005. *Impossible desires: Queer diasporas and South Asian public cultures*. Durham, NC: Duke University Press.
Grewal, Inderpal, and Caren Kaplan. 2001. Global identities: Theorizing transnational studies of sexuality. *GLQ* 7 (4): 663–79.
Hall, Stuart. 1996. Cultural identity and cinematic representation. In *Black British Cultural Studies*, ed. Houston A. Baker Jr., Manthia Diawara, and Ruth H. Lindeborg, 210–22. Chicago: University of Chicago Press.
Hoffman, Adina. 2002. The big bash theory: Mira Nair's latest movie revels and reels. *American Prospect* (March 25): 28–29.
Huggler, Justin. 2004. India acts over suicide crisis on farms. *The Independent* (London) (July 2): 31.
Kripalani, Coonoor. 2001. Coming of age: Bollywood productions of the nineties. *Asian Cinema* 12 (Spring/Summer): 29–48.
Makdisi, Saree. 1995. "Postcolonial" literature in a neocolonial world: Modern Arabic culture and the end of modernity." *boundary 2* 22, no. 1 (Spring): 85–115.
Mani, Lata. 1998. *Contentious traditions: The debate on Sati in colonial India*. Berkeley: University of California Press.
Mehta, Chirag. 1994. The seed *Satyagraha*: Indian farmers and global capital face off. *Dollars & Sense* 125 (September/October): 25–27.
Mishra, Pankaj. 2004. India: The neglected majority wins! *New York Review of Books*, August 12, pp. 30–32, 37.
Mishra, Vijay. 2002. *Bollywood cinema: Temples of desire*. London: Routledge.
Monsoon Wedding. 2001. Directed by Mira Nair. New York: Mirabai Films, 2001.
Pardes. 1997. Directed and produced by Subhash Ghai. Mumbai: Mukta Arts.
Philp, Catherine. 2004. "Shining" India fails to lighten gloom in villages. *London Times*, April 6, p. 16.
Pieterse, Jan Nederveen. 2003. *Globalization and culture*. Lanham, MD: Rowman and Littlefield.

Prasad, M. Madhava. 1998. *Ideology of the Hindi film: A historical construction.* New Delhi: Oxford University Press.

Rajadhyaksha, Ashish. 2003. The "Bollywoodization" of the Indian cinema: Cultural nationalism in a global arena. *Inter-Asia Cultural Studies* 4 (1): 25–39.

Sharpe, Jenny. 1997. "The Limits of What Is Possible": Reimagining *sharam* in Salman Rushdie's *Shame*." *jouvert* 1 (Fall): 18 paragraphs.

Shiva, Vandana. 2000. War against nature and the people of the south. In *Views from the south: The effects of globalization and the WTO on third world countries*, ed. Sarah Anderson, 91–125. Oakland, CA: Food First Books and International Forum on Globalization.

———. 2004. The suicide economy of corporate globalisation. *Znet.* http://www.countercurrents.org/glo-shiva050404.htm (accessed April 5, 2004).

Thomas, Rosie. 1995. Melodrama and the negotiation of morality in mainstream Hindi film. In *Consuming modernity: Public culture in a South Asian world*, ed. Carol A. Breckenridge, 157–82. Minneapolis: University of Minnesota Press.

Uberoi, Patricia. 1998. The diaspora comes home: Disciplining desire in *DDLJ*. *Contributions to Indian sociology* 32 (2): 305–36.

———. 2001. Imagining the family: An ethnography of viewing *Hum Aapke Hain Koun. . . !* In *Pleasure and the nation: The history, politics and consumption of public culture in India*, ed. Rachel Dwyer and Christopher Pinney, 309–51. Oxford: Oxford University Press.

Varma, Pavan K. 1998. *The great Indian middle class.* New Delhi: Viking.

Zacharias, Usha. 2001. Trial by fire: Gender, power, and citizenship in narratives of the nation. *Social Text* 19 (Winter): 29–51.

CHAPTER 3

Comparing Emirati and Egyptian Narratives On Marriage, Sexuality, and the Body[1]

Frances S. Hasso

On March 3, 2004, I turned on my television to the al-Jazeera Arabic satellite station, based in Doha, Qatar. The weekly program, "For Women Only" (*lil nisaa' faqad*) was on, and the topic was a comparison of "love" versus "traditional" (arranged) marriages. Most of those e-mailing and calling, and they were predominantly men, argued that "traditional" marriages had a higher rate of success. In addition to the host, and in typical fashion for this program, there were three female guests. In this case, one was a PhD and well-known Algerian poet and author who was hooked into the studio by satellite from Paris. The other two women, a Lebanese sociologist and professor, and an Egyptian physician of Islamist orientation whose clinical practice focused on sexual problems among married couples, were in-studio. It appeared that all the women were Muslim.

The program revolved around a few questions that continuously engaged everyone: First, what is marital love? Is it more than what the Islamist physician continuously insisted it was, the Qur'anic dictum of "affection [*mawwada*] and compassion [*rahma*]"? Or was this a necessary but not sufficient aspect of it, as the Algerian poet argued, insisting that the Qur'an was equally clear on the importance of men's and women's sexual pleasure and the importance of emotional and intellectual partnership in marriage at various points? This debate was framed in "Eastern" versus "Western" ways by the Islamist doctor, who argued that one did not have to rely on Greek sources, Western sexual norms, or commodified images to have a happy, sexually fulfilled marriage. At the same time, she and the Algerian disagreed on the extent to which women should rely on previous generations of related women for information. The Islamist physician was consistently modernist in her argument that "wrong" information frequently came from such women, whereas the Algerian poet argued that aunts, grandmothers, and other female relatives with successful marital relationships were excellent sources of information for younger women.

Other questions included to what extent poverty was important in determining the success or failure of marriage in the region, as the Lebanese sociologist argued. Program participants also discussed the role of sexual or bodily culture in marital relations, referred to by the women as *thiqafa jinsiyya* or *thiqafa jasadiyya*. Here, the reference was not only to sexual chemistry, which most agreed was important but all agreed was unlikely to last given the daily requirements of family life, but also to the "arts" of spouses sexually pleasuring each other in *halal* (religiously correct) ways in order to maintain marital happiness. The women agreed that commodified images and sexualities, sold through satellite television, serial television programs, and the Internet, made the situation worse for married women in relation to their husbands. They also agreed chat groups, relationship blogs, Islamic and Arab Web sites, and cell phones and other technologies increased the possibilities for "hooking up" for men as well as women and girls.

As the this example indicates, marriage and sexuality are very much part of public-sphere discussions in the Arab world. This paper is based on my own research on the rise of *`urfi* (customary), *misyaar* (ambulant), and other nontraditional sexual and marital contracts among Sunni Muslims from various walks of life in the United Arab Emirates (UAE) and Egypt. I argue that, in fact, satellite technologies and other aspects of globalization have had an important impact on relationships and sexualities in the region, although these less-bounded processes coexist (and even articulate in novel ways) with patriarchies, including legalized gender inequality as encapsulated in state family laws and competing Islamic legal precepts.

Marriage, Sexuality, and the State

Heterosexual marriage and procreation within such marriage has been and remains fundamental to the organization of Arab societies across ethnic, religious, and class boundaries (Hoodfar 1997, 51, 241; Sherif 1999, 619; Singerman 1995, 74). Islam in particular "extols the virtues of marriage, regarding it as *Sunna*, or the way of the prophet Muhammad, and as the 'completion of half of the religion' (with worship and service to God completing the remaining half). . . . In addition, among Egyptians of all denominations, marriage is regarded as a protection for both a woman and a man, especially against the desire for illicit sexuality and procreation, both of which must occur with the confines of marriage" (Inhorn 2003, 226–27). This is so much so that the extended or nuclear family, rather than the individual, is often viewed as the basic unit in Arab societies (Altorki 2000; Joseph 2000). How does one explain, then, the apparent rise of nontraditional, often transient marital and relationship forms, such as customary marriage, ambulant or traveler marriage, and a range of other relationships and sexual contracts in parts of the Middle East and North Africa (MENA) beginning in the 1990s?

Based on Egyptian press accounts of *`urfi* marriages that I have perused, the "woman as victim" narrative is prevalent, underestimating how regular marital contracts and personal status laws (across religious denominations) in most Middle East and North Africa (MENA) states fundamentally privilege men over women. In the twentieth century, most postcolonial MENA states rationalized and formalized *shari`a*-based (Islamic juridical tenets, broadly defined) marital contracts (Sonbol 1996; Charrad 2001; Amawi 2000; Ismael and Ismael 2000; Mir-Hosseini 1993), in many cases decreasing previous flexibility and negotiability that had allowed women and men to choose among different juridical schools in making and breaking contracts (Sonbol 1996; Mir-Hosseini 1993). Overall, however, all five major juridical guilds (*Shi`i*, *Hanbali*, *Hanafi*, *Shafi`i*, and *Maliki*) privilege men in terms of divorce, child custody, and postmarriage alimony support. The rationalization through codification of family law has increased the power of often authoritarian states and their religious appointees, as well as male-biased lawmakers (religious and secular), over marital contracts and personal status or family laws. At the same time, historical and contemporary-focused research on different parts of MENA demonstrate frequent disjuncture between lived experiences and legal, religious, and cultural precepts with respect to marriage and sexuality, indicating significant maneuvering and violation (Haeri 1989; Singerman 1995; Hoodfar 1997, 78–79; Longinotto and Mir-Hosseini 1998; Moors 1995; Moors 1999).

Recent Challenges to "Traditional" Marriage

According to a recent large-scale survey in Egypt, the three leading problems of adolescents listed by their parents were associated with marriage. In order of significance, these were finding an apartment or house for marriage, lack of money, and furnishing the marital home (Singerman and Ibrahim 2001, 96). While these economic problems are particularly relevant in Egypt, the explanations for rising marital ages and new relationship forms may be overly economistic, underestimating other factors. As more than one informant in Egypt indicated, despite economic problems, the very poor majority of Egyptians (particularly those living in rural areas) have lower expectations in terms of marital support and resources, and upper–middle-class families have the resources to provide for the marriage of children. Among the upper middle classes, some parents are sharing the costs of marriage, and among the working poor, many are foregoing the *mahr*, or dowry. So the economic obstacles to marriage in Egypt seem to be most important to the middle class and are particularly related to the limited supply and cost of housing, a responsibility of the groom.

As marriage has become increasingly expensive for young men and their families—who are required, largely by custom, to provide a range of material resources to wives before consummation, and are religiously required to provide for household maintenance—states have attempted to lower its cost for men. State officials in the United Arab Emirates are so concerned with out-group marriage among Emirati men, marriage delays, and high rates of singlehood among Emirati educated women that they established the "Marriage Fund" (*sandouq al-zawaj*) in the early 1990s to coordinate state-sponsored group wedding ceremonies and parties, and to provide large grants and free or inexpensive wedding halls for Emirati-Emirati weddings. State leaders also made an ineffective decree limiting the amount of dowry a bride's family can demand from a groom's family. There are similar programs, on a much lower scale, in Egypt. From the perspectives of women and their parents in both countries, however, increasing the cost of marriage for men makes the cost of divorce and remarriage higher, since men have much more institutional, cultural, and legal leverage in both cases.

While the term *`urfi* implies that this is a traditional practice, the emerging contracts associated with *`urfi* relationships are very much contemporary innovations. What seems to make them "customary" is that they evade registration with formal religious and state authorities. Until a controversial legal revision of personal status law narrowly passed by the parliament in late January 2000, such contracts in Egypt violated a 1931 Egyptian statute "mandating registration of all marriages with a *ma'zoun* (civil marriage registrar) (Zerrini 2000). In order to be "legitimate," according to some Islamic legal scholars, *`urfi* marriages must follow the same basic requirements as regular marital contracts (*nikah*): both partners consent, two men (or one man and two women) act as witnesses to the contract in addition to an overseer with knowledge of Islamic law, a wedding gift is given to the bride, and a public announcement of the marriage, "at least to family and neighbors," is made (Zerrini 2000; Shahine 1999; Ahmed 1999). In such relationships, the publicity requirement has been transformed from the very public wedding to—as one Emirati man told me—"having the girl tell seven to eight of her trusted friends and having the guy tell seven to eight of his trusted friends"

(Abdel Rahim 2003). Three of the four Sunni schools of jurisprudence also stipulate that a woman who has not been married before must be accompanied by her legitimate guardian (usually her father, brother, or uncle, a *wali* while signing the contract (Shahine 1999).

Misyaar marriage "is an official relationship between man and woman, but does not involve that the two live together, nor that the man is economically responsible [for the wife or household]." This type of relationship "allows the man to have a normal wife in addition to his *misyar* wife(s). The *misyaar* wife is expected to live with her parents, and her husband can visit her according to a predetermined schedule" (Kjeilen 2002). *Misyaar* relationships have been practiced in Egypt and Saudi Arabia "for years" (they appear to have begun in significant numbers in the early 1990s), often involve a middleman or broker, and were legitimized by Egyptian Sheikh Mohammad Sayyed Tantawi and Saudi Arabian Sheikh Abdel Aziz bin Baz in 1999 by *fatawa* (plural), or nonbinding religious edicts (Kjeilen 2002; Comparative Index to Islam 2002; Reuters 1997; Arabi 2001). They are also recognized as legitimate by religious courts in the Emirates, although the completed marital contracts do not significantly differ from regular contracts (indeed, the same form is utilized by the courts), since the more innovative aspects are agreed upon in advance by the couple. According to Oussama Arabi, a philosopher and scholar of Islamic law in Lebanon who has studied *misyaar* in Saudi Arabia, the practice is "an original *bricolage*, a patchwork production of law using the flexible resources of the [Sunni] Islamic marriage contract to cater to the needs of certain Saudi middle-class segments" (2001, 155), that, post facto, has been recognized by the judicial establishment as abiding by *shari`a* criteria (Arabi 2001).

Customary marriages in Egypt, while often contracted in writing, usually only come to public or state attention when legal problems arise, most often when a woman files for divorce or maintenance for herself or a child (Abaza 2002). This is also the case in the Emirates. The secrecy is one reason that *`urfi* marriages are considered illegitimate by some religious scholars, who view them as violating rules against fornication and adultery (Shahine 1999; Arabi 2001, 164–65). In the Emirates, however, *misyaar* marriages are registered with the state, although whether a first wife is aware of such a marriage depends on whether she researches court records.

Islam, Sexuality, and the Fragmentation of Authority

`Urfi and *misyaar* relationships occur in cultural environments that treat sexual desire and pleasure as natural and necessary, even sacred, but seek to regulate and channel them into licit (usually contractual) relationships that

explicate mutual obligations (Hoodfar 1997, 251, 253; Bouhdiba 1998, 14–15, 187; Sherif 1999, 626–27). Oussama Arabi argues, on the contrary, that two attitudes on sexuality coexist in Islam: one is pietistic and ascetic, depending on controlling desire and channeling energy into prayer, and the other is about lawful sexual indulgence (Arabi 2001, 152). Which one becomes dominant depends on the person articulating the correct life and the context and purpose for this.

These relationships allow men to gain access to ostensibly *halal* (licit) sex with significantly fewer economic obligations. Women gain sexual relationships without the social constraints required of traditional marital relationships (Shahine 1999; Ahmed 1999; Reuters 1997; Arabi 2001), or because they would like to have sexual relations or have a child but remain unmarried in the traditional sense. Other women engage in such relationships because they strongly desire a man who does not want to or cannot marry them in the traditional sense for a variety of reasons.

These relationships may be one ironic consequence of the resurgence of different forms of Islam as a basis for personal life and imagined community (Anderson 1991). While she is not addressing these emergent relationships or gender and sexuality, Andrea Rugh argues that the pursuit of an "Islamic society" for activists in late 1980s and early 1990s Egypt was "drawing upon a tendency already present in contemporary Egypt in which individuals operate more independently of their families than has been the custom in the past" (Rugh 1993, 151). In a period of widespread economic, social, and political discontent, many Egyptians were looking for personal meaning, authenticity, and "cultural self-assertion," as well as political participation, within a more broadly defined community (of Muslims) that often undermined the idea of families or nations as the fundamental framework in which an individual situates him- or herself (Rugh 1993, 155, 157). Carrie Wickham argues that the middle-class male Islamists she studied promoted an "ethic of civic obligation demanding that every Muslim participate in the Islamic reform of society and state" in Egypt, regardless of costs (Wickham 2002, 15). The consequences of people acting on such mobilization discourses, I believe, are neither predictable nor fully under the control of the mobilizing movements.[2] Dale Eickelmann and James Piscatori have found, for example, increasing "fragmentation of sacred authority" in Muslim societies (in Wickham 2002, 126), with younger Islamic activists competing with traditional and state-affiliated Muslim jurists and scholars. Such fragmentation, by definition, increasingly devolves into more fragmentation, with counterelites challenged by grassroots tendencies (some virtual). This gives rise to often conflicting definitions of what is correct human living in Islamic terms, in this case, in relation to marriage and sexuality.[3] The fragmentation of authority has led to interpretive proliferations at lay levels with respect to what is sexually right or wrong in Islamic terms. Such processes create a feedback loop in which officials affiliated with states and formal religious institutions in turn produce religious edicts and legislation in response to popular pressures that are at times multidirectional in that they reflect competing ideologies and beliefs.

Indeed, *`urfi* and *misyaar* relationships are often rationalized by lay articulations and interpretations of cultural and Muslim religious precepts and sacred texts in relation to personal life. In some respects, this is similar to the ways in which new social movements or identity movements in the United States and Europe have worked to seek personal answers to larger problems. One difference is the methodological principle of *ijtihad* in Islam, which allows, and many have argued requires, continual assessment of sacred sources to seek religiously correct answers, although the term and practice of *ijtihad* have historically been deployed differently depending on context and political ideologies and motivations. Suffice to say here that while plural sources of legislation and competing sources of authority have always existed in Islam, these have proliferated, intensified, and occurred much more quickly with the explosion of the World Wide Web and satellite television.

Sexual Desire and Globalization

When explaining the phenomena of *`urfi*, *misyaar*, and other nontraditional sexual and marital contracts among Sunni Muslims, men and women from various walks of life in the UAE and Egypt often evoked "Islamic" conceptualizations of sexual desire and satisfaction as natural and good, combined with discourses of "instinctive" physical needs whose fulfillment was imperative. In defense of *misyaar* marriages, an Emirati young man argued that it was more in the interest of women "because they get the status of being married and satisfy their sexual instincts."Women further benefited, he argued, in that they could work but had "total freedom in terms of marriage. The child is registered by the state under the man, but she has childrearing power" (Abdel Rahim 2003). A young Emirati woman professor of political science also deployed bodily and biological explanations, but in a different way as follows:

> If we are talking about why . . . women they accept this kind of marriage, *al-misyaar* is not hidden, but there are no rights for women—*nafaqa* and—in Arabic, I analogize it to a man whose role is like [*fahl al-thor*] a male bull [or stud], that's it—he goes to fertilize the female. . . . The problem, of course, [is that] the Arab societies are not like the Western societies. The woman does not

> have the unrestraint and openness in terms of bodily issues as men do. And in the end, she suffers more—I mean, there have to be limits on her—it is codified (*muqanan*) for her how she can enter into a bodily relationship—it has to be according to certain codes. So she is forced—there is also a view toward women that if she is not married, she has no value. There is an Egyptian saying that "the shadow of a man, and not the shadow of a wall" [*thellah ragil wa la thellah hayta*]. This shows how there is a view about women that she is inferior [*dooniya*].

Biological metaphors were also used by a modernist religious male scholar I interviewed in the UAE:

> If marriage does not come to a woman, what does she do? How can you demand of a woman in this society, sexual films, phenomena, newspapers, magazines, and it is a human necessity—sex is like food and drink—is it possible for one to live without food and drink? It is not possible. He must eat. It is the same thing here—this kind of desire [*shahwat al-fal*] and the stomach's appetite—the erotic appetite and the appetite [*shahwatun wa shahiyya*]. So in Islam, before the laws, marriage was very easy—with anything the marriage could be *shar`I* . . . in the past it was very inexpensive . . . Now, it is in the millions! . . . So they say, this [*`urfi and misyaar*] resolves a problem. The important thing is that it is *halal* and not *haram*. . . . So it is a solution to the problem of fornication.

I began to consider that the prevalence of biologist ideas of desire might be recent and rearticulated, rather than "traditional," during an interview with an Egyptian physician of middle-class background. She mentioned that young people, even in middle and high schools, were having sexual relations using *`urfi* contracts. Contrasting the contemporary situation with her less sexualized 1960s teen and young adult years—during which political desires and work, studies, and a range of extra-curricular "fun" activities with friends occupied much of her cohorts' time—and reflecting on some of her hospital experiences with patients, she believed that bodily and sexual self-awareness had become more prevalent and articulated by young people (El Afify 2003). My findings were consistent in that embodied narratives of sexual desire and satisfaction, not dissimilar to those structuring discussions of the consumption and need for products, often permeated discussions explaining such relationship forms, whether the speaker approved or disapproved of them.

Egyptians and Emiratis argued that economic barriers delaying heterosexual marriage, the only culturally and religiously licit channel for assuaging heterosexual desire, have increased the necessity for innovations in fulfilling sexual "instincts," although the scale and nature of these barriers dramatically differed since Egypt is one of the poorest countries in the region and the UAE one of the wealthiest. Indeed, more than one person mentioned that Emirati men of less means will frequently marry Egyptian women (using regular and *`urfi* contracts) since the marriage costs and expectations of their families are lower. Moreover, people in both countries also mentioned the phenomenon of poor Egyptian men essentially selling their young daughters to wealthy Gulf men for what the latter, according to a young Emirati man, consider to be "pocket money" in what usually turn out to be a form of temporary marriage.

In Egypt, the increasing gap between rich and poor as a result of neoliberalization policies, high underemployment and unemployment, and increasing consumption aspirations has delayed the age of marriage, particularly of young men in the urban lower middle and middle classes. In some cases, wealthy men, particularly from Gulf countries, use the secret contracts to legitimize brief sexual relationships with prostitutes in Egypt while on summer holiday (al-Gawhary 1995). Among the native (and minority) Emirati population, a number of factors have delayed or reduced marriage rates and encouraged new sexual forms. These include high levels of consumption of expensive goods, the costly wedding "traditions," and demands made by the parents of Emirati brides. In addition, regional male migration, as well as the state's active importation of men and women laborers in an adamantly tariff- and tax-free, investment and tourist-friendly economy, facilitates the out-marriage of Emirati men, as well as their taking of non-Emirati sexual partners using various modalities (concubinage, *misyaar*, or *`urfi*). In both places, then, "globalization" was seen as important in its impact on these forms and options, although in different ways.

As Frederic Jameson has argued and Kamran Asdar Ali has found in the context of Egypt, the "labor practices globalization" also require people to endorse the "ideology of consumption" (Jameson, cited in Ali 2002, 5). The goal, in Ali's words, "is to create wants, desires, and demands that are linked to new notions of individuality and selves, in order to increase consumption among the diverse populations of the world" (Ali 2002, 4–5). In Egypt, Ali argues, this is a project cooperatively endorsed by the state and international agencies with the goal to lower fertility rates. While luxury consumption and free markets are dominant and encouraged in the UAE, the state depends on its minority Emirati population to procreate with each other given that most of the country's population is comprised of permanent or migrant noncitizen workers. That is, state rulers are actively threatened by the sexual implications of free consumption and assuaging of desires, at the same time that state wealth, economic structure, and policies require and encourage this. While the Egyptian state is also conservative in this regard, its existence is unlikely to be threatened by out-marriage, new forms of marriage, or polymorphous sexualities. Despite the biopolitics of both states, Egyptians and Emiratis are receiving positive messages about consumption and encouragement for sexual expression from, in Arjun Appadurai's terms, the less bounded mediascapes, ethnoscapes (of tourists and immigrants), and ideoscapes (ideologies of states and counterideologies of movements) that are part of global and transnational flows (Appadurai 2001, 52–53).

Especially in the UAE, some viewed these desires and ideas as stoked by widely available media and communication technology such as satellite television, which broadcasts the popular Mexican, Egyptian, and U.S. soap operas and movies. On the World Wide Web, a number of cross-national and national Muslim chat rooms are popular in both Egypt and the UAE, enhancing the feasibility and spread of these relationships. In the UAE, a gender segregated society for Emirati women, the possibilities for engaging in illicit or at least nonnormative relations are also facilitated by text messaging and the prevalence of mobile phones, which allowed unmarried girls and women to avoid family surveillance and control, as well as to negotiate trysts. Parents are well aware of these possibilities and have successfully pressured the gender-segregated national universities and colleges to ban the use of cell phones on women's campuses, a requirement that faculty members (who reported this phenomenon to me) ambivalently police. This brings to mind Timothy Mitchell's important point in *Rule of Experts* that "nonhuman elements," in this case the technologies of communication and entertainment and the flows they facilitate, are not passive in their "partnership" with human agents. The outcomes of such interactions are dynamic, multiple, and never fully predictable or controllable, even when they are deployed with particular intentions by capitalists, bureaucrats, policy makers, or educators (Mitchell 2002, 199).

Gender Inequality, Sex, and Marriage in the Accounts of Egyptians and Emiratis

Among the middle-class Egyptian female students at Cairo University I interviewed in late December 2003, while concern about their economic futures and careers was predominant, there was also a strong fear about the sort of person the man they married might turn out to be. At the same time, they assumed that getting to know such a man in advance through dating and sexual relations would tarnish their reputations and reduce their value, especially in his eyes. As two female students argued,

Student 1: If he goes out with a girl, it's impossible that he will marry her . . .

Student 2: Meaning, he encourages her freedom in this respect, it is normal for us to sit together and talk to each other [he says], and the problem—it's normal—it's not shameful, become liberated [he says]. [liberated, says another student.] And then when she says, well, let us get married. . . . He says, "No, you should remain liberated." [laughter] Once I was arguing with my brother, and my brother is in the first year of university, okay? He does not yet have relations with girls at all, but his thoughts . . . I wanted to tell him that there is not a problem with this if there are good feelings between you and a girl. So he said to me, "Look, guys like us"—he is young in years, so for him to say "one of us," and "men like us" [laughter]—He says, " . . . Men like us know many girls but when he wants to get married"—and he had an expression that I will never forget—"when he wants to get married, he takes a girl who remains in her wrapping." As if she is a piece of chocolate, as if she is a piece of chocolate or a bonbon! In its wrapping?! My God, they all think like this example.

With the exception of the first speaker in the following interchange that occurred during the same group interview with eight female students at Cairo University, the remaining women believed that women involved in *`urfi* relationships suffered from "naïveté" (*sazga* in Egyptian colloquial, or *sazaajatun*):

Student 1: I think that in the future it will be considered a natural occurrence given the economic changes that have occurred, and the ideas of parents about marriage—the idea that marriage needs *shabka* [jewelry, especially gold, for the bride] and *mahr* [dowry] and an apartment and the apartment has to have specific things. They do it to be liberated from the traditional ideas of the family. So the response—I don't agree with it—but I think that is a response to these pressures.

Student 2: I also think that in *`urfi* marriages—the young men think that they have love—meaning, they will have love without paying anything.

Student 3: It's completely free. [laughter]

Student 2: Exactly, but here—usually he has to pay money to take love, but here [with *`urfi*] it is not a problem . . . she agrees, a paper is written between the two and that's it . . .

Student 3: The real intention of the boy is that this is a sexual need that will build.

Student 2: I [meaning the boy] will fulfill it! [laughter]

Student 3: I will fulfill it to its farthest extent. It's amazing. In terms of the girl, she does this because she feels he is her true love and she—If she gives him . . .

Student 2: She thinks he will be her husband— . . . in my opinion, there is absolutely no justification for *`urfi* marriage because it is very reasonable and

> clear that almost everything about it works to the benefit of the boy. And it totally works against the girl. Sana [pseudonym] says that the girl is sometimes scared that he is her true love and he will leave—this is naïveté also.

This was similar to the analysis of most Emirati women I interviewed. According to the fiancé of a young Emirati man (they met on the internet), "I am against [*`urfi* and *misyaar* type relationships] because [they do] not protect women's rights. Husbands in these situations are not committed to *mahr* or living costs. And people will always think it was done for pleasure and not take such a marriage seriously." She believed that in the Emirates, "women may accept such a marriage because her parents may have refused a guy, so she accepts because a *wali* [male guardian] is not required." Emirati women, particularly the high proportion that is college-educated, are increasingly less inclined to marry young Emirati men schooled in relatively patriarchal conceptualizations of family and marriage. Their potential Emirati male partners were also likely to have attended post-secondary military or police academies, since they are guaranteed employment in these sectors. An Emirati man believed that the rural, less educated men who join the police and army are more likely to hit women and "more likely to marry village [poor] girls from Syria and Egypt." Indeed, some of the Emirati women intellectuals interviewed believed that the cultural gap produced by the two forms of post-secondary education, liberal arts and military or police academies, one dominated by women and the other by men, partly explained what are perceived to be high divorce rates among nationals.

The Emirati female college students interviewed at Sharjah Arab University in 2003, aged between twenty and twenty-two, were most dramatically concerned with remaining unmarried and being defined as spinsters, which they argued occurred by the early twenties at the latest. They believed that Emirati women who were educated and worked were most likely to be chosen as second wives of men in their late thirties and early forties. Mostly, however, they thought that such men, as one student put it, were likely to choose a "migrant [*wafida*], she has a passport [*mutajanisa*], she would be, meaning, sometimes it is normal, she would be any religion, but the important thing is that she differs from the first wife. Meaning, she could be employed. Meaning, he tries sometimes to leave his family, to travel, et cetera, a totally different life. . . . This woman would be open in terms of dress, in terms of food." When I asked the students whether this was common or the rare case throughout the Emirates, there was a chorus of yeses for its ubiquity.

For the most part, single Emirati male university students interviewed at UAE University, Al-`Ain, in 2003, on the other hand, argued that it was in-laws and parents, as well as women insisting on working after marriage and not fulfilling their duties to husbands in particular, that likely led to the high rate of marriage dissolution in the Emirates. One male student believed that it was possible that young men were not ready for the responsibilities of marriage and that their "inattentiveness to religion and some distraction with other things" has created some of these problems. (This position is in fact the dominant one among Emirati state and religious authorities; male irresponsibility and immaturity are the main problems and thus men are the main targets of large-scale state education campaigns with respect to marriage.) The young married man in the classroom, on the other hand, believed that part of the problem was that Emirati women were getting unreasonable ideas in their heads as follows:

Student: Some of the women's media write, whether external or internal [media], for example, they give women more than is their right. They make women feel that she should reach the summit of the pyramid, and with this knowledge she makes herself superior to men. . . . A small example, Toujan Faisal [Jordanian political activist and feminist]—

Interviewer: I know her, I mean I know of her—

Student: At the end she said, as a man marries more than one wife, why shouldn't a woman—

Interviewer: But she is against a man marrying more than one wife. She does not want women to marry four men, but she is against men marrying more than one wife.

Male Professor: She wants equality. Why should men have this right and not women.

Interviewer: But really she is against it.

Male Professor: But really if she goes to Tibet, she can do that. [Students laugh]

In a society in which marriages arranged by parents remain the norm, younger, less educated girls and women are often viewed as preferable wives since they are assumed to be less sexually knowledgeable and more malleable. Consistent with this, it does appear that while both Emirati men and women's expectations of marriage increase with a college education, women's expectations for marital happiness and partnership increase significantly more. As indicated earlier, some Emirati men argued that the two-directional migrations of Emirati men and the immigration and importation of non-Emirati men and women for work, as well as television programming from places such as Egypt and Lebanon, have produced local male appetites for more expressive feminine sexualities than has been considered appropriate locally. Other men, particularly some of the university students interviewed, seemed to see Emirati gender segregation and control of Emirati women's mobility as reducing the potential for intellectual partnership in marriage—since men gain more cosmopolitan orientations given their higher levels of freedom in mobility and mixing with men and non-Emirati women. On the other hand, the male students I interviewed argued not for increased mobility and gender-mixing for women, but rather for more "courses" for them.

Emirati women, in turn, stressed the double standard of local men and cultural norms, which deem sexually expressive sartorial or bodily practices unacceptable if coming from national women, and would lead to their social exclusion (as "sluts") in a society whose state and family forms are premised on a benign patriarchy. Moreover, national women who traveled for business or education, or who worked in professional mixed-gender settings, were stigmatized as marriage prospects and often did not marry. Many of these women are nevertheless using new forms of communication to explore and negotiate sexual and relationship possibilities.

To conclude, in both Egypt and the Emirates, new bodies and desires are being articulated as people selectively draw on a range of "traditional" and contemporary discourses and practices—facilitated by cultural flows, human migration, and communication technologies and products—even as the contexts in which this occurs are very much structured by socioeconomic, political, and cultural limits and opportunities. This indicates the extent to which local, religious, "cultural," purely economic, or regionally bounded explanations are limited in the tools they provide to understand such phenomena. This awareness forces scholars, in keeping with Sami Zubaida's important interventions (Zubaida 1993), to avoid reducing explanations for these phenomena to "Islam" or "Muslim culture," in the process, treating both as transhistorical essences. The definitions of the good Muslim life are plural and contested, and religious sentiment is always situated in time and imbricated with other locations and identities.

Notes

1. This paper is a slightly revised version of a Rockefeller fellow lecture presented on May 11, 2004, at the University of California, Riverside. I am grateful to Dr. Emory Elliot and the Rockefeller cofellows and staff at the Center for Ideas and Society, as well as Dr. Rima Sabban.
2. The popular literature produced by the counterelites studied by Wickham argue against the spread of perversions, deviations, vice, and depravity "perpetrated in the unbridled pursuit of material and sensual pleasures" (Wickham 2002, 141), instead encouraging fasting and prayer to reduce sexual longing (170).
3. One of the ironic consequences of modern fundamentalists' selective rearticulations of sacred textual sources, posited as rightful and necessary aspects of being members of the Muslim community, is that Muslim feminists have done the

same, challenging dominant interpretations through popular and scholarly engagement with scriptures.

References

Abaza, Mona. 2002. Circuiting or transgression? Perceptions of *`urfi* marriage and changing sexual norms in Egyptian press. Paper presented at the World Congress of Middle Eastern Studies, University of Mainz, Germany, September 2002.

Abdel Rahim, Muhammad. 2003. Interview by the author in Dubai, United Arab Emirates, December 1.

El Afify, Nadia Abdel Wahab. 2003. Interview by the author in Cairo, Palestine Hospital, December 28.

Ahmed, Sarwat. 1999. Closet consummations. *Cairo Times Online* 2, no. 19 (November 12–25). http://www.cairotimes.com/content/issues/Women/marriage.html (accessed December 16, 2001).

Ali, Kamran Asdar. 2002. *Planning the family in Egypt: New bodies, new selves*. Austin: University of Texas Press.

Altorki, Soraya. 2000. The concept and practice of citizenship in Saudi Arabia. In *Gender and citizenship in the Middle East*, ed. Suad Joseph, 215–36. Syracuse, NY: Syracuse University Press.

Amawi, Abla. 2000. Gender and citizenship in Jordan. In *Gender and citizenship in the Middle East*, ed. Suad Joseph, 158–84. Syracuse, NY: Syracuse University Press.

Anderson, Benedict R. 1991. *Imagined communities: Reflections on the origin and spread of nationalism*. 2nd ed. London: Verso.

Appadurai, Arjun. 2001. Disjuncture and difference in the global cultural economy. In *The anthropology of globalization: A reader*, ed. Jonathan Xavier Inda and Renato Rosaldo, 46–64. London: Blackwell.

Arabi, Oussama. 2001. *Studies in modern Islamic law and jurisprudence*. The Hague: Kluwer Law International.

Bouhdiba, Abdelwahab. 1998. *Sexuality in Islam*. Trans. Alan Sheridan. London: Saqi Books. Originally published, 1975.

Charrad, Mounira M. 2001. *States and women's rights: The making of postcolonial Tunisia, Algeria, and Morocco*. Berkeley: University of California Press.

Comparative Index to Islam. 2002. Misyar marriage. http://www.answering-islam.org/Index/M/misyar.html (accessed December 16, 2002).

Al-Gawhary, Karim. 1995. Sex tourism in Cairo. *Middle East Report* 25, no. 5 (September–October): 26–27.

Haeri, Shahla Haeri. 1989. *Law of desire: Temporary marriage in Shi`i Iran*. Syracuse, NY: Syracuse University Press.

Hoodfar, Homa. 1997. *Between marriage and the market: Intimate politics and survival in Cairo*. Berkeley: University of California Press.

Inhorn, Marcia C. 2003. *Local babies, global science: Gender, religion, and in vitro fertilization in Egypt*. New York: Routledge.

Ismael, Jacqueline S., and Shereen T. Ismael. 2000. Gender and state in Iraq. In *Gender and citizenship in the Middle East*, ed. Suad Joseph, 185–211. Syracuse, NY: Syracuse University Press.

Joseph, Suad. 2000. Introd. to *Gender and citizenship in the Middle East*, ed. Suad Joseph, 3–30. Syracuse, NY: Syracuse University Press.

Kjeilen, Tore. 2002. Misyar marriage. In *Encyclopaedia of the Orient*. http://lexicorient.com/cgi-bin/eo-direct.pl?misyar.htm (accessed December 16, 2002).

Longinotto, Kim, and Ziba Mir-Hosseini. 1998. *Divorce Iranian style*. Women Make Movies. Videorecording. 76 minutes.

Mir-Hosseini, Ziba. 1993. *Marriage on trial: A study of Islamic family law, Iran and Morocco compared*. London: I. B. Tauris.

Mitchell, Timothy. 2002. *Rule of experts: Egypt, techno-politics, modernity*. Berkeley: University of California Press.

Moors, Annelies. 1995. *Women, property, and Islam: Palestinian experiences, 1920–1990*. New York: Cambridge University Press.

———. 1999. Debating Islamic family law: Legal texts and social practices. In *A social history of women and gender in the modern Middle East*, ed. Margaret L. Meriwether and Judith E. Tucker, 141–75. Boulder, CO: Westview.

Reuters. 1997. Marriages with few strings stir Saudi passions. http://www.payk.net/mailingLists/iran-news/html/1997/msg02563.html (accessed December 16, 2002).

Rugh, Andrea B. 1993. Reshaping personal relations in Egypt. In *Fundamentalisms and society: Reclaiming the sciences, the family, and education*, ed. Martin E. Marty and R. Scott Appleby, 151–80. Chicago: University of Chicago Press.

Shahine, Gihan. 1998. The double bind. *Al-Ahram Weekly online*. October 1–7. http://www.ahram.org.eg/weekly/1998/397/fe1.htm (accessed December 16, 2001).

———. 1999. Illegitimate, illegal or just ill-advised? *Al-Ahram Weekly online*. February 18–24. http://www.ahram.org.eg/weekly/1999/417/li1.htm (accessed December 16, 2002).

Sherif, Bahira. 1999. The prayer of a married man is equal to seventy prayers of a single man: The central role of marriage among upper-middle-class Muslim Egyptians. *Journal of Family Issues* 20, no. 5 (September): 617–32.

Singerman, Diane. 1995. *Avenues of participation: Family, politics, and networks in urban quarters of Cairo*. Princeton, NJ: Princeton University Press.

Singerman, Diane, and Barbara Ibrahim. 2001. The cost of marriage in Egypt: A hidden variable in the new Arab demography. In "The New Arab Family," ed. Nicholas S. Hopkins. Special issue, *Cairo Papers in Social Science* 24, nos. 1–2 (Spring/Summer). Cairo: American University in Cairo Press: 80–116.

Sonbol, Amira El Azhary, ed. 1996. *Women, the family, and divorce laws in Islamic history*. Syracuse, NY: Syracuse University Press.

Wickham, Carrie Rosefsky. 2002. *Mobilizing Islam: Religion, activism, and political change in Egypt*. New York: Columbia University Press.

Zerrini, Caroline. 2000. Triumphant milestone for *`urfi* marriages. *Arabia.com*, January 14. http://www.arabia.com/life/article/print/english/0,4973,37528,00.html (accessed December 16, 2001).

Zubaida, Sami. 1993. *Islam, the people and the state: Political ideas and movements in the Middle East*. London: I. B. Tauris.

PART 2

U.S. Immigration and Culture

CHAPTER 4

Third World Newsreel

Third Cinema Practice in the United States[1]

Cynthia Young

On September 9, 1971, 1,300 inmates, almost half the prison population, captured more than three dozen guards and employees at Attica Correctional Facility in upstate New York. The mostly Black and Latino inmates did so to protest the intolerable living conditions and vicious brutality of the prison guards. Inside Attica, they were subjected to severe overcrowding, up to 16 hours per day in solitary confinement, severely restricted medical aid, and rectal searches before and after they received visitors despite the fact that they were separated from their visitors by a wire mesh barrier. In addition, the authorities arbitrarily withheld inmates' correspondence, denied them access to newspapers and magazines, curtailed the religious freedom of Muslim inmates, and separated politicized inmates from the rest of the prison population (Bell 1985).[2]

That same month, two inexperienced filmmakers, Susan Robeson, the granddaughter of singer, actor, and international activist Paul Robeson, and Christine Choy, a Chinese-Korean immigrant, found themselves in the midst of their own battle: one to transform Newsreel, the unofficial filmmaking arm of the New Left, into a collective that would center the concerns of what I have elsewhere called U.S. Third World Leftists.[3] When the rebellion erupted, the two novice filmmakers began shooting the unfolding events, eventually producing *Teach Our Children*, the first film on Attica. For Choy and Robeson, the reorientation of a film collective and the making of a film on the Attica rebellion bled into one another, transforming the resulting film into a visual manifesto for the group that would soon change its name to Third World Newsreel (TWN).

The fact that the Attica rebellion and the founding of Third World Newsreel are linked is anything but coincidental. In fact, the relationship between the two speaks to the importance of film to radical politics during the 1960s and 1970s, and the centrality of state violence to the U.S. Third World Left's understanding of itself and the United States from which it emerged. At this historical conjuncture, film and prison rebellion, Third World Newsreel and the Attica inmates, First World minorities and Third World majorities found themselves "articulated" to one another in intriguing and sometimes paradoxical ways. Stuart Hall has defined articulation this way: "An articulation is thus the form of the connection that *can* make a unity of two different elements, under certain conditions. It is a linkage which is not necessary, determined, absolute and essential for all time. . . . The 'unity' which matters is a linkage between that articulated discourse and the social forces with which it can, under certain historical conditions, but need not necessarily, be connected" (Hall 1996, 141–42). Hall continues, "The theory of articulation asks how an ideology discovers its subjects," and I understand him to mean that it helps us understand how a particular ideology disrupts "common sense," speaking to a subject in a new, historically specific way (Hall 1996, 141–42).

Similar to Louis Althusser's theory of interpellation, Hall's articulation theory allows for infinitely more dialecticism, acknowledging that groups and individuals speak back to ideologies, transform them, and even discard them altogether (Althusser 2001, 85–133). Articulation is useful in thinking about Third World Newsreel and U.S. Third World Leftists generally because it requires that one account for the historical factors that lead to an ideological shift, but it also provides a way of exploring why and how a given political project, site of contestation, or discourse becomes prominent and assumes a palpable urgency.

Informed by Hall's concept, I wish to make three interrelated claims about Third World Newsreel in the 1970s. The group's adaptation of Third Cinema themes and practices developed by Cuban documentary and *Brazilian Cinema Novo*, particularly in *Teach Our Children*, enacts and reflects upon modes of transnational cultural exchange. That film's focus on state violence as it manifests itself in police brutality, prison practices, and welfare bureaucracies offers a window into U.S. state structures that articulates people of color in the United States to their Third World counterparts. And finally, Third World Newsreel's praxis contests conventional paradigms of struggle—be they Marxist, cultural nationalist, or feminist—creating instead a community of struggle based upon the juggling of multiple identity categories. Rather than privileging a working class, racial, ethnic, or national identity, Third World Newsreel and other U.S. Third World Leftists tried to visualize a radical Third World subject and a radical Third World public capable of transcending such categories in the name of a concrete, if diffuse political project.

That Third World subject and its larger public take as their object of focus, and are constituted by, their resistance to state violence as it is manifested in prisons, policing practices, and the parallel structure of poverty maintenance—welfare, substandard housing, low wages, et cetera—the "modes of oppression"[4] that articulate U.S. people of color to Third World colonized subjects. Central to this ideological and political work, of course, is the question of whether this enterprise fixes the Third World as simply "a screen for [U.S. Third World Leftist] desire," one that is held together by multiple suturings of place, position, and power (Renov 1988, 10–12). In order to consider these multiple displacements and complex unities, one needs to go back to 1970, to the period of internal struggle that preceded Attica and led to Third World Newsreel's founding. Consequently, the first section of this essay considers the institutional history that precipitated the group's founding, while the second section focuses on *Teach Our Children's* thematics and aesthetics.

Third World Newsreel Builds a Cultural and Political Community

In early 1970, a debate erupted within Newsreel, Third World Newsreel's predecessor, over whether or not White members were qualified to make films about peoples of color. This ushered in an extended period of bitter factionalism during which Newsreel was battered by conflicts over enduring race, class, and gender inequality. Accounts of this internal struggle vary. Film scholar Michael Renov writes, "New York Newsreel members split themselves into 'haves' and 'have-nots,' with the distinctions among ethnicity, class background, and functional class position somewhat blurred" (Renov 1987b, 26). TWN cofounder Susan Robeson's recollections are more pointed. She argues that the organization was explicitly divided along racial and ethnic lines into a White caucus and a Third World caucus.[5] It was the White caucus, according to cofounder Christine Choy, that divided along class lines into the "haves" and the "have-nots," and eventually the "haves" decided to leave Newsreel.

During this period, Newsreel essentially consisted of two parallel organizations; the White and the Third World caucuses were each responsible for their own distribution, production, and finance. While the White caucus engaged in self-criticism and debate, the Third World caucus initiated a major reorientation of the group, calling for the production of films by and about Third World peoples in the United States. In an attempt to rid New York

Newsreel of what were felt to be its voyeuristic tendencies, control of production on films about Third World peoples was to be put in the hands of Third World peoples. White members of Newsreel could no longer use footage of New York's communities of color to politicize White, middle-class students. Instead, the goal was to foster media activism within those communities by "help[ing] the people involved in [local] struggles create their own propaganda" (Nichols 1980, 31). Not content to solely transform New York Newsreel, the caucus even issued an edict to all of the other extant Newsreels demanding that they recruit and train U.S. Third World peoples.[6]

The Third World caucus had set itself a clear political agenda. However, this agenda left the White caucus rudderless and unable to define its purpose. According to Choy, the "have-nots" began to debate "working class issues, working class filmmaking, definitions of and strategies for cultural work, filmmaking, and organizing work" (Milner 1985, 21). For the first time, White Newsreel members explicitly and extensively addressed the issue of a White, working-class film praxis. Previously, they had been content to represent the White student movement and radical groups of color such as the Black Panthers and the Young Lords with little attention to their own class and race composition. A caucus in crisis, the White members agreed that they could not continue to make films of Black, Latino, and Latina communities, but they had no idea who the new subjects of their films would be. Nor did they know how the caucus could best show its support for Third World struggles and at the same time address the issue of racism within the White community. In short, the White caucus could not agree upon or articulate a politics that would determine their reconstituted role within Newsreel. After repeated failures to produce a coherent statement of their political and filmmaking objectives, the White caucus disbanded in late 1971, leaving the organization to the Third World members.[7]

After the white members' departure, the Third World caucus changed the group's name to Third World Newsreel in April 1972 (Nichols 1980, 30). A series of events precipitated the change in nomenclature. Soon after the White members departed, all of Newsreel's filmmaking equipment was mysteriously stolen. This loss of equipment coupled with the loss of individuals who were financially able to sustain the organization's work seriously impaired the group. Desperate, the Third World members turned to the former Newsreelers for equipment and skills training, but most of them refused. In a 1982 interview, Choy recalled that "only one or two [former members] were sincere enough to teach us how to use the camera. The rest wouldn't have anything to do with us. So it was out of anger that we called ourselves 'Third World Newsreel'" (Milner 1985, 21). The new name was meant to underscore the pseudocolonial relation that had previously existed between the White and non-White members of Newsreel; it was an angry commentary on the racist paternalism that had marred Newsreel's radical face. In that same interview, Choy defined the group's use of the term "Third World" as follows: "[It is] more applicable to an underdeveloped country, and domestically speaking, it applies to a national minority struggling for equality. When we use the term Third World, we use it superficially, since we distribute films from Latin America, Africa and Asia. But the production we do does not relate to Third World issues but to conditions in the United States, especially among minorities and working-class people as a whole" (Milner 1985, 21). The historical record troubles Choy's observation that the group used the term "Third World" "superficially." If one only considers the literal meaning of the term "Third World," then of course Choy is correct; the group's members were not living in the Third World nor were their films (exclusively) about the Third World. But if one probes deeper, thinks of the term as a metaphoric shorthand for complex material structures, then TWN's adoption of the term recontextualizes it, stretching it to include U.S. national minorities who were facing conditions akin to those in Third World colonies, such as segregation, cultural denigration, racial discrimination, and exploitation.

The term "Third World" helped provide a language for national minorities who were not juridically colonized but nonetheless faced many of the selfsame structures underpinning colonialism. It lent them access to a theoretical rubric that would be extremely helpful in challenging their own particular forms of oppression. Affiliating with anticolonial struggles and connecting economic exploitation and cultural supremacy in the First and Third worlds was an important political move precisely because it depended upon and helped solidify a global analysis, one that forged transnational forms of solidarity and support. Choy's reduction of TWN's complicated history may in part reflect her position as an Asian immigrant mindful of the tremendous differences between the United States and the Third World. Her focus in those years was clearly on the social and political inequities in the United States, but that focus was always related to global power dynamics. For example, her 1976 film *From Spikes to Spindles* takes pains to connect happenings in New York City's Chinatown to the trade inequities between Hong Kong and the United States.

Choy's comments may also be explained by the interview's conditions of production. The published interview was the result of two different interview sessions with Choy in December 1978 and two years later in January 1980. Another two years after that, the interview was spliced together from those earlier sessions and published in *Jump Cut*. Consequently, it is difficult to determine whether Choy's comments were refashioned and taken out of their original context. By 1982, if Choy had any input into the interview's final form, she must have been mindful of repositioning TWN for a Reagan-era audience hostile to Leftist rhetoric of the 1960s variety.

Whether her distancing of the organization from its name was intentional or unwitting, Choy's comments uneasily coexist with the collective's cultural reorientation, a process in which she herself participated. By the time the White caucus left, the Third World caucus had declined from twelve to only three members, Robert Zelner, Christine Choy, and Susan Robeson, the latter two of whom were the most active. Choy had been recruited by Newsreel cofounder Norm Fruchter in 1970 and was the first non-White woman in the group. A Chinese-Korean immigrant, Choy was born in Shanghai where she grew up on a steady diet of Chinese, Russian, Polish, and Czechoslovakian films. She spent her teen years in Korea before emigrating alone to New York. Once there, she attended Manhattanville College for one semester before transferring to Columbia University to study architecture. Her mentor in the field, Buckminster Fuller, left Columbia for Washington University in St. Louis, and Choy enrolled there for two years between 1969 and 1971. Choy eventually earned a scholarship to Princeton University, where she, in her words, "met a bunch of radical philosophers, activists, Marxists" (MacDonald 1998, 200). When the bombing of Cambodia came to public light, she joined those radicals in staging protests demanding the establishment of a Third World Center. Fed up with Princeton, Choy began working for the Urban Institute in Newark, where she met Tom Hayden, Steve Friedman, and Norm Fruchter. While completing her architecture degree at Columbia University, she became increasingly interested in Newsreel, attending a screening at the suggestion of Norm Fruchter. While Choy was immediately excited by Newsreel's political commitment, she was struck by its lack of non-White members. Despite her misgivings, however, she soon became a dedicated member, serving as the head of distribution and film maintenance and eventually founding the Third World caucus (MacDonald 1998, 200–202).

When Susan Robeson joined Newsreel in the summer of 1971, she was an eighteen-year-old student fresh from a summer filmmaking course at New York University. Robeson, who is the granddaughter of acclaimed actor, singer, and political activist Paul Robeson, was born in West Harlem in 1953. The child of a White mother and Black father, she spent much of her early childhood in the Manhattanville Projects until her family moved with her grandfather to the Upper West Side of Manhattan in 1965. Because of the Robesons' involvement in the Left circle—her parents were both members of the Harlem youth branch of the Communist Party until 1960—Robeson grew up in what she describes as a "politically charged atmosphere."[8] By the time she joined Newsreel, Robeson was a fledgling photographer and had completed her first year at Antioch College in Ohio. Although she had little filmmaking experience, she seems to have possessed a precocious political vision and tireless energy. The self-described "scribe" for early TWN, Robeson's desire to forge links to Third World communities at the local, national, and international levels critically informed the group's early direction.[9] TWN's predominantly female leadership also ensured that the contribution of women of color to the struggles within Black, Asian, and Latino communities was highlighted, a focus that explicitly countered the conventional phallocentric perspective on 1960s and 1970s activism. In fact, to this day, TWN continues to be run by women of color. Choy and Robeson's early work challenged the exclusive focus on male-gendered modes of resistance—armed revolt and public demonstrations—that came to eclipse other effective forms of protest.

In October of 1972, TWN released a statement entitled "Act First, Then Speak" that presented its perspective on the mass exodus from Newsreel (Third World Newsreel 1972).[10] The group emphasized the inability of members of the White caucus to define a film praxis based on their political beliefs, and then outlined its own vision for the organization. Stressing the fact that TWN did not solely want to make films about Third World people, it insisted that it wanted to "build a working relationship with Third World organizations and community people"(Third World Newsreel 1972).[11] This approach would enable TWN to produce public artifacts that would have both an integral relationship to disenfranchised communities and intrinsic use and value. As the group members described it, they wanted to "pass on [their] knowledge and produce what [their] people need[ed]" (TWN 1972). But who their people were and exactly what they needed was far from self-evident. Shortly after the "Act First, Then Speak" statement, TWN drafted and released a manifesto entitled "Organizational Principles of TWN." Here, the members more clearly defined their mission and their audience, producing the philosophy that would guide the organization for much of the decade.

In that document, the collective defined itself as a "propaganda organ for the progressive forces in general and the proletarian forces in particular" (TWN 1973).[12] As Newsreel had, TWN willingly embraced its propaganda role, positioning itself as a conscious alternative to the mass media, which it deemed an "instrument of social control" (TWN 1973).[13] However, the collective did not define its constituency, the "proletarian forces," in specifically race- or ethnicity-based terms. Instead, TWN emphasized their structural position in the U.S. economy. The "proletarian forces" were the "working people," and "the most exploited sectors of this country." Claiming Marxism-Leninism as its guiding political theory, TWN declared itself willing to work with "all progressive, Communist, and labor groups which have the interests of the masses at heart" (TWN 1973). In doing so, TWN forthrightly rejected the sectarianism that has often been attributed to the advocates of so-called "identity politics" and blamed for the New Left's demise. Instead, the collective stressed solidarity along economic rather than race, ethnicity, or gender lines. This entailed, however, an attention to how race, ethnicity, and gender structure economic relations. Eschewing a rigidly defined identity politics, TWN never defined its mission in narrowly nationalist terms. Instead, they understood that, to paraphrase Stuart Hall, race (and other identity categories) are all modalities through which class is lived (Hall 1980).

As Hall reminds us in the seminal essay "Race, Articulation and Societies Structured in Dominance," "Race is thus, also, the modality in which class is 'lived,' the medium through which class relations are experienced." He continues, "This has consequences for the whole class, not specifically for its 'racially defined' segment" (Hall 1980, 308). The group's nuanced understanding of race, one that privileged the structural position of groups rather than their biological essences, depended on a recognition that racism derived in large part from economic exploitation and from the very colonialism that the name Third World Newsreel was meant to underscore. Colonialism was first and foremost a system of economic exploitation that simultaneously spawned a set of racial hierarchies. By attacking racist commonsense, the group was also therefore attacking the racial hierarchy that maintained exploitative social relations. Commonality between members of the film collective and communities of color was forged on the basis of a counterhegemonic understanding of history, what Antonio Gramsci might have termed an "oppositional common sense" that TWN sought to (re)produce with its films. Its films produced a viable imagined community based on identification with those who lived under colonialism and those suffering its aftereffects. This meant an acknowledgement of colonialism's devastations and a recognition of the fact that the United States' rise to world dominance depended upon that devastation as well as the scope and success of its own imperial projects. Located as U.S. national minorities, then, TWN members were subject to the racist and exploitative common sense that animated Third World colonialism and imperialism even as they were also uneven beneficiaries of U.S. world supremacy. Theirs was always a tricky balancing act, one that animated their best work.

What is also apparent in TWN's early formulations is the belief that oppositional cultural production contributes to a group's sense of shared political purpose. The collective's first priority was to produce "revolutionary propaganda" defined as much by the conditions of its production as its content. Their manifesto declared, "Revolutionary propaganda involves the conscious class elements integrating themselves wholly with the masses in order to . . . serve the masses, and depict realistically the struggle of the masses in order to show the common links of the various levels of the mass struggle" (TWN 1973). TWN would not only portray instances of local political struggle, but it would also put those struggles in a context that would emphasize their structural affinities to national and international events. This was a radical departure from Newsreel's earlier film praxis in which analysis was secondary to reportage. Newsreel films were records of events not necessarily analytical pieces meant to draw connections between disparate phenomena. From its inception, TWN was also aware that its efforts were acts of solidarity rather than proof that members were either "authentic" members of the working class or its designated leaders. With this redefined role, the collective consciously rejected much of the vanguardism that animated Newsreel and other New Left organizations during the 1960s. The filmmakers eschewed membership in what philosopher Herbert Marcuse termed the "young middle-class intelligentsia" who were supposed to inspire the masses to revolt by their radical example (Marcuse 1969, 51). Nor did they see themselves as a "group of intellectuals or isolated individuals producing works . . . to distribute to the people" (TWN 1973).

Instead, they hoped that the subjects as much as the filmmakers themselves would guide film production. This perspective was yet another departure from Newsreel's earlier cultural and political practices. By insisting that the group's production be concretely tied to oppositional groups or movements, TWN sought to avoid the voyeurism and romanticism that had characterized its predecessor. Although the group's films were in part designed to educate communities of color, TWN openly acknowledged that it had as much to learn from U.S. Third World communities as those communities did from it. This perspective redefined the role and function of cultural producers, positioning them as "organic intellectuals" in the Gramscian sense, rather than cultural or political missionaries. TWN films were intended to be group articulations, a collective "call to arms." Accomplishing this lofty goal was not always easy since TWN filmmakers' educational and cultural capital distinguished them from the communities they represented. Nonetheless, their efforts were important steps in that direction, enacting an important collaboration between middle- and working-class people of color.

Teach Our Children and the Discourse of Internal Colonization

During the transition from Newsreel to TWN, Choy and Robeson were shooting *Teach Our Children*. In many ways, the film executes the cultural and ideological vision of TWN evident in its internal struggles and initial public pronouncements. Despite their lack of experience and being in the midst of Newsreel's dissolution, Choy and Robeson decided to complete the film. Many of the tendencies and tensions within TWN's early history are apparent in its first film, *Teach Our Children*. It is no accident that the film is a stinging indictment of the Attica prison rebellion's violent conclusion. Not only was this event involving hundreds of prisoners of color a seminal political event for U.S. Third World activists, but it also starkly demonstrated the similarities between Third World colonies and U.S. communities of color. In fact, *Teach Our Children* was only the first of a series of four films on prisons and their social control function.[14] These films made TWN an important source of prison films and thus a valuable resource for community groups agitating for prisoners' rights. They employed and expanded upon an extant internal colony discourse equating U.S. Black, Latino, and Asian communities with Third World colonies.

The use of prison as a metaphor for Third World oppression was a standard device in the decade between 1965 and 1975. In 1978, Newsreel historian Bill Nichols remarked that "the degree to which prison represents a vivid and often all-too-real symbol of Third World oppression by a capitalist system is beyond doubt" (Nichols 1980, 53). By emphasizing the social control function of U.S. prisons, TWN added material substance to the analogy of inner cities to internal colonies. The likening of Black communities to internal colonies has a long history in communist and Black Left politics. As early as 1916, Vladimir Ilyich Lenin suggested that Southern Blacks should be considered an "oppressed nation" because their freedoms had been increasingly curtailed in the aftermath of Reconstruction (Foner and Allen 1987, xiii). In 1928, the Sixth World Congress of the Communist International affirmed this position, declaring Black Southerners' right to control their political and economic destiny, and their right to complete self-determination and territorial secession (Kelley 1990, 13–14). This "Black Belt Nation Thesis" signified a break with both Karl Marx and Friedrich Engels who had distinguished between "nations" and "nationalities," the latter of which were incapable of economic independence. If Lenin was its original architect, Joseph Stalin refined the concept, arguing that the Black South was a nation because it was "a historically established, stable community of people, coming into existence on the basis of a community of language, territory, economic life, and psychological constitution, which manifest themselves in a community of culture" (Robinson 1983, 308–9).

As Robin D. G. Kelley demonstrated in *Hammer and Hoe*, the Black Belt Nation Thesis ignited an organizing drive during the 1930s among sharecroppers and tenant farmers in Alabama and fostered a generation of Black communists, including Harry Haywood, Hosea Hudson, and Angelo Herndon. The late 1960s witnessed a resurgence of the internal colony discourse with the appearance of Harold Cruse's *The Crisis of the Negro Intellectual* (1967),

Robert Allen's *Black Awakening in Capitalist America* (1969), Amiri Baraka's formulations in his journal *The Black Nation*, Mario Barerra, Carlos Munoz, and Charles Ornelas's essay "The Barrio as Internal Colony" (1972), and Nelson Peery's *The Negro National Colonial Question* (1972), among other texts. *Teach Our Children* relies upon the internal colony paradigm, comparing conditions in Attica with those in urban communities of color.

The film is a collage of news footage and personal interviews set to a soul- and gospel-inflected soundtrack that retells the tragic events of the Attica prison rebellion. Before the September takeover, Attica inmates had twice sought a peaceful resolution of their grievances. In May, a group of inmates mailed a manifesto of thirty demands to Police Commissioner Russell Oswald, an administrator known as a "liberal reformer." Receiving no response, a five-man negotiating committee mailed Oswald a similar list in July, asking most notably to be "granted the right to join or form labor unions."[15] During the Attica rebellion, Oswald agreed to thirteen of the prisoners' demands, but when he refused to concede to the lawful prosecution of prison guards for cruel and unusual punishment, negotiations broke down. Refusing to meet with the rebels, Governor Nelson Rockefeller ordered a police attack—what independent investigator Malcolm Bell described as a "turkey shoot"—during which ten hostages and twenty-nine inmates were killed and eighty-nine others were seriously wounded (Bell 1985, 1). In the aftermath of the massacre, state police engaged in rampant torture, indiscriminately beating inmates suspected of inciting the rebellion. In the fallout after Attica, conservative and liberal media alike criticized police authorities for attempting to cover up instances of abuse. Years later, vice-presidential nominee Nelson Rockefeller was even dropped from Gerald Ford's 1976 presidential ticket over the controversy.

As one might expect, *Teach Our Children* does not solely focus on the events of the rebellion. Instead, the film links the conditions at Attica—overcrowding, police brutality, and labor exploitation—with the conditions in poor Black and Latino communities. The result is an angry, humorous, and ultimately powerful indictment of both prison and urban community life. The film opens with a voice reading from a statement delivered by the rebels at a press conference during the siege: "To segregation of prisoners from the mainline population because of their political beliefs, we demand an immediate end."[16] While the viewers struggle to decipher the phrase's context and meaning, this brief sound bite is immediately juxtaposed with the voice of Malcolm X declaring, "Don't be shocked when I say I was in prison. You're still in prison. That's what America means, prison." The film then moves from Malcolm X to black-and-white footage of an inner city community in which kids play in abandoned lots, women idly stare through the bars of their tenement windows, and unemployed men congregate on the city streets. From *Teach Our Children's* initial seconds, the rebelling inmates are defined as freedom fighters whose existence can be explained by the state of their communities. They are not solitary heroes, but rather inextricably bound up in a larger Third World public. This near deification of the Attica rebels is certainly problematic. Choy and Robeson risk obscuring precisely what it is that makes these inmates such compelling and ultimately recognizable figures: namely, that their demands are reasonable and their methods ordinary. They have simply used the limited means available to them to wring concessions from the state. However prone to mythmaking such a comparison may be, it does invert the dehumanizing logic of the state apparatus, which treats the inmates as expendable, and it challenges the mainstream media's construction of the inmates as hapless victims of police brutality.

The film represents the inmates primarily through the use of excerpts from their own speeches. In one segment from the Attica press conference, a speaker shouts, "We are men! We are not beasts and we do not intend to be beaten or driven as such. The entire prison populace (and that means each and every one of us here) has set forth to change forever the ruthless brutalization and disregard of human lives of the prisoners here and throughout the United States. What has happened here is but the sound before the fury of those who are oppressed. . . . We call upon all the conscientious citizens of America to assist us in putting an end to this situation that threatens the lives of not only us but of each and every one of you as well."

Attica, the prisoners insist with a Shakespearean flourish, is but one scrimmage in a much larger battle. The upheaval in Attica and other U.S. prisons is only the latest symptom of an ailing body politic. The film reinforces this point by flashing the names of nine other correctional facilities that have been the site of recent protests. Clearly, these uprisings are a response to deteriorating conditions, but they are also a response to a widespread pattern of police corruption and state violence. For example, Attica inmates were angry over the 1969 murder of Fred Hampton, who was ambushed by an FBI orchestrated police raid while he lay sleeping in Chicago's Black Panther Party headquarters. And just one month before the Attica uprising, George Jackson, a radical writer and prison organizer, was shot to death by San Quentin guards during an escape attempt because they claimed to believe he was hiding a gun in his Afro. In his honor, Attica inmates held a one-day hunger strike and wore black armbands (Bell 1985, 18).

While Black radicals were a spectacularly visible target of state violence during the 1960s and 1970s, *Teach Our Children* demonstrates that unchecked police power affects far more than just individual Black rebels. In lengthy footage from the 1967 Newark Rebellion, during which National Guard troops wounded 1200 Newark residents, we see police roaming the streets, harassing pedestrians, conducting arbitrary searches, and violently subduing anyone deemed to be resisting their absolute authority. As we watch this graphic footage, we cannot help but compare urban communities of color with their Third World counterparts. Newark, and by inference, U.S. Third World communities generally, are quite literally occupied territories, figurative extensions of Attica prison.

This assertion is strengthened by interviews with inner-city residents. Their poignant testimony links squalid prison conditions and desolate inner-city life, illustrating that communities of color are economically and politically disenfranchised in much the same way that Third World countries have been under colonialism. We meet Carlos, a middle-aged, Puerto Rican man, who sits in a crumbling New York apartment surrounded by his wife and several children. An ex-convict, he contends that Third World peoples' civil rights are routinely violated once they are arrested. He states, "Over here, real justice for the Puerto Ricans and Blacks and other minorities that find themselves in prison does not exist. . . . For example, we are poor and we don't have the money to pay for a lawyer, a good lawyer. We have to take those lawyers that are paid for by the city. . . . We have to take this defense and this is no defense . . . because those people are paid for by the state. Those people are going to work for the state." Carlos not only questions the legitimacy of the legal system, but he also indirectly raises the question of whether Attica inmates are criminals or economic and political prisoners as he describes the structural conditions that plague the people in his neighborhood as follows:

> In Brooklyn, you have that part in the south where mostly all Blacks and Puerto Ricans live. They're condemned to live in those places which are slums. . . . At the jobs we have the worst jobs, the worst paying jobs, jobs that no White would want to do, salaries are the lowest and you either have to take it or leave it. . . . We don't have sufficient money to pay the rent which is high for decent apartments where only upper-middle-class people with good salaries are able to live in. But we can only afford to live in apartments that are infested with rats and roaches.

Carlos concludes his trenchant critique by saying, "There's really no difference in the places we live in and the way we live and the life in prison. There's no difference. The only difference may be that in our communities the walls are invisible and we don't see them and in the prisons we do." As he concludes, the camera pans from the faces of his children to a view of the gated fences that enclose his apartment complex.

By focusing on Carlos, a middle-aged family man, *Teach Our Children* complicates the film's thus far romantic view of Black and Latino men. Men are not only valiant war heroes; they are also dedicated family men frustrated by their circumstances. Unlike the Attica inmates, Carlos is neither slim, particularly attractive, nor garbed in the early 1970s style many have come to associate with militant youth—bell bottoms, army fatigue jackets, and perfectly manicured Afros. Nonetheless, his words illustrate that he is acutely aware of and dissatisfied with his circumscribed life and is anxious to change it. The leap from Carlos to the Attica inmates, the filmmakers assert, is a small but significant one.

If the depiction of Carlos counters the predominant view of 1960s radicals, so does the presence of angry, articulate women, many of them mothers who present the too-often invisible aspect of male incarceration. Although she is not nearly as prominent as Carlos is, his wife angrily describes the ways in which she was harassed after his arrest as follows: "The system tries to force a lot of things on me, but I cannot give in like they would like me to. . . . When Carlos was first arrested, they tried to throw me out of where I was living. They tried a lot of things. The police would be around where I lived." Although brief, her comments impart political significance to the domestic space and her critical role there. *Teach Our Children* implies that her fight to keep her family intact is every bit as "revolutionary" as the actions of the Attica rebels. The very fact that she and her several children have resisted bureaucratic attempts to evict them and break up their family attests to her persistence in the face of state interference. Her actions may not be as spectacularly visible as the Attica rebellion, but they contribute to the community's ultimate survival. The inclusion of her testimony undermines male-centered definitions of political action and revolt.

The centrality of women's roles in the domestic and public sphere is further emphasized by the film's inclusion of another vocal woman. This time, the speaker is a young Black mother. A moving counterpart to Carlos and his family, she speaks in detail about the perils of raising children alone in the ghetto. In the following excerpt, she describes the area in which her children play: "I have five children and I can speak about genocide in every aspect that you can look at it in. I live in a housing project. We have no facilities here for children to play. We have a lot out there, a concrete lot about twenty by forty feet. We have here in this one building about seventy children. Can you see little kids out there playing in a concrete lot with glass and everything?" Because the children are forbidden to play on the grass, they play in the project's busy parking lot. A car, the woman explains, recently hit a boy who was riding his bike on this makeshift playground. "Genocide," according to this woman, literally truncates the lives of poor Black people, but it also robs them of the ability to lead meaningful lives—in her words, "keep[ing] people from knowing who they are and what they are and what they should be about doing." A local community activist, this woman has organized protests against the callous and inhumane treatment that plagues her community. She, like Carlos and his wife, has maintained the ability to both critique the state apparatuses that restrict her existence *and* imagine an alternative existence outside of them. By demonstrating the persistence of this collective, oppositional imaginary, *Teach Our Children* situates U.S. Third World communities squarely at the center of their own destinies.

As a narrative bridge between this community testimony and eyewitness accounts of Attica survivors, the film includes a long cartoon interlude skewering U.S. imperialism. A grotesque Uncle Sam clutching a U.S. flag shaped like a hatchet morphs into the head of Richard Nixon and then the head of Russell Oswald. These images are then superimposed onto a sketch of Africa, Southeast Asia, and South America. The men's grimacing countenances completely obscure the landscape they have invaded. The sketch concludes with a series of scales being gleefully manipulated by Uncle Sam on which various people(s) are balanced. Three young children are outweighed by a menacing U.S. soldier, a Black factory worker by three White politicians, and a Vietnamese mother and son by an older White woman proudly waving a U.S. flag. Admittedly, the crude politics espoused in the sketch is not nearly complicated enough to hold together the various elements the film embraces—Attica, anticolonial struggles, and inner-city devastation. Russell Oswald is not Nixon, nor are African Americans the North Vietnamese. However, as the film amply demonstrates, certain power inequities and structural similarities hold true in the U.S. and in north Vietnam.

What is wonderful about this interlude is the fact that the film does not take itself too seriously here. The humorous spoofing of White hegemony allows the film a Utopian moment of inversion during which Black men, women, and children trapped behind prison bars are replaced by the "real" criminals, Nixon, Rockefeller, and Oswald. As the film is well aware, that inversion would involve a dramatic shift in U.S. ideology, economic policy, and political perspective, but such playful whimsy is a memorable part of the "oppositional imaginary" constructed and articulated by the film. The section focuses on the events of the revolt with one young inmate's voice as follows: "To all people of color worldwide, so many times and so often the Black man in the federal penal institution and concentration camps throughout America read about you on the other side of Babylon calling for what you label as 'nation time.' All I want to say is please, those people on the other side of Babylon, let our actions here in Attica concentration camp be a prime example to you." Speaking at a press conference, it is the Attica inmates who most directly link the perilous situation of people of color in the United States with those in the developing world. As this excerpt from the press conference illustrates, the prisoners were speaking to and acting in solidarity with a real and imagined international constituency, those people calling for "nation time." Just as the film depicts a community of politicized urban residents, it presents the Attica inmates as articulate, committed political prisoners who have been energized by a larger Third World community.

Choy and Robeson interview the surviving rebels, and in these segments they describe the variety of incidents that preceded the rebellion. We hear one inmate tell of a truncated visit with his two sisters, one of whom he had not seen for many years. When he challenged the guards' refusal to extend the visit or even allow him to say goodbye, they attacked him. He recalls, "They bit me, punched me, threw me on the ground, put the shackles on my legs, put chains around my waist with a padlock, put the handcuffs on, and you know commenced to beating me . . . they maced me, blinded me, kicked me in the cell." Once in solitary confinement, the guards sprayed him with "nausea gas" for seventeen hours. This gas, he notes, has been banned from use in Vietnam. This incident has its quite literal counterpart in U.S. imperial adventures in Vietnam.

Another prisoner describes the dangerous working conditions that inmates face in Attica's metal shop, where fingers, arms, and legs are frequent fodder for obsolete machinery. Such dangerous work is the only way to secure even small amenities such as soap and cigarettes, and retribution in the form of solitary confinement comes swiftly to those who refuse to work. Placed in this context, the inmates' demands for the right to organize into a union assume greater significance. Unionization, a seemingly mainstream demand, would at least allow the inmates to negotiate the conditions of and compensation for their labor. In this instance, the ability to form unions challenges the prison's dehumanizing logic that seems determined to banish inmates from the very realm of civil society with its attendant protections.[17] Here, *Teach Our Children* links the situation at Attica to other instances of economic exploitation. The film contrasts images of prisoners working in the metal shop with sketches of Black slaves toiling in the fields of colonial America. Admittedly, such juxtapositions flatten the very real and quite different structures of slave and prison labor economies. Nonetheless, as a cinematic strategy, the comparison serves to highlight the justice of the inmates' list of demands: working conditions that meet New York state standards, minimum wage pay, adequate visiting conditions, and the lawful prosecution of correctional officers. These reforms can only be viewed as radical if one believes Attica inmates to be less than fully entitled to the guarantees of a liberal democracy. Once the inmates refuse to compromise on these demands, though, they become revolutionary actors, refusing to accept Oswald's indecent proposal.

The violent response with which the inmates are met serves to strengthen the comparison between them and the Third World guerrilla forces they self-consciously emulate. Despite the fact that officials knew the men to be armed only with sticks and homemade knives, the state troopers armed themselves for combat. One inmate describes the attack as follows: "They came in there with bazookas, AK-47s. They came in there with machine guns, they came in there with flame-throwers . . . they came in and shot us down like animals. They seen [sic] one brother that was holding a Black liberation flag (red, black, and green flag). They shot him off the balcony, and they continued to shoot him while he was on the ground. The brother was still clenching onto the flagpole. They stomped him in his head, they stomped him and continued to shoot him." Even a wholly symbolic statement of political or cultural independence—such as the flag held by the slain inmate—must be swiftly and violently repudiated. The surviving inmates' accounts of troopers who murdered or brutally punished inmates as they surrendered is supported by mainstream media accounts of the incident, but the prisoner's testimony crackles with righteous indignation and anger. As one of the leaders recalls, he and fifty-nine other inmates were stripped, marked with an "X," and made to crawl around the muddy perimeter during a downpour. As he describes this episode, the film juxtaposes footage of the Attica aftermath with still photography of World War II concentration camp victims.

With this extreme juxtaposition, Attica is elevated to the level of a historic tragedy every bit as brutal as Hitler's crusade against the Jews and every bit as central to a community's collective memory. In light of contemporary opposition to reparations for the descendents of African slaves, this analogy is all the more striking. Claiming Attica's parity with the Holocaust is both politically loaded and audacious, considering White Americans have historically resisted any attempt to label enslavement as genocide or an African American holocaust. Though it is clearly inaccurate to compare Attica and the Jewish Holocaust—on the level of scale and sheer horror, the Jewish Holocaust far surpasses Attica—the comparison raises the issue of the relative value placed on Jewish and Black American life. The film asks the viewer to consider whether the murder of unarmed men is less morally reprehensible if the victim is a Black prisoner. The outrageous comparison forces the viewer to confront the everyday forms of racist state violence that go unmarked and unresisted, raising the possibility that future generations may view Attica in terms no less harsh than they will the Jewish Holocaust. This is, of course, wishful thinking, as race and class oppression militate against the memorializing of the Black and Latino victims of Attica.

However bloody the suppression of the Attica rebellion was, *Teach Our Children* refuses to dwell on the rebellion's defeat. Instead the film alludes to the militant action Attica may ultimately inspire in urban communities around the United States. To the upbeat, soul-inflected gospel anthem "Let

Us Sing This Simple Song for Freedom," *Teach Our Children* argues that the spirit of Attica thrives in individual and collective memory. We see inmates pumping iron in U.S. jails and then shots of massing guerrilla armies in Southeast Asia, Latin America, and Africa. The voices of women and children intone, "We the people here don't want no more," while Malcolm X's voice excoriates U.S. imperialism: "They are violent when their interests are at stake, all that violence that they display at the international level. When you and I want a little bit of freedom, we're supposed to be nonviolent. They're violent in Korea. They're violent in Germany, in the South Pacific. They're violent in Cuba. They're violent wherever they go." As his words and the images of Third World armies fade, we are left with a view of Black and Latino children playing amid the broken bottles and the hostile eyes of the police. Rather than passive victims or murdered inmates, the film asserts, these children will eventually mobilize to liberate their communities by "any means necessary."

Teach Our Children marked a clear departure from earlier Newsreel films. It was the first production made by filmmakers of color about communities of color. As directed by TWN cofounders Choy and Robeson, the film presents a sympathetic yet fairly complicated portrait of New York's marginalized communities. In telling the story of Attica, *Teach Our Children* does not focus solely on the sensational aspects of the rebellion, as early Newsreel would have done in order to jolt the viewer into unthinking sympathy. Instead, the film places Attica in a context that stresses its relation to a larger anticolonial struggle. The viewer is given an analytical framework in which to understand a controversial event. Rather than treating the inmates as if they had emerged fully formed from the proverbial revolutionary womb, *Teach Our Children* traces the roots of their dissatisfaction within the correctional system itself and in the communities in which they live. In doing so, *Teach Our Children* integrates women's perspectives, recontextualizing an event that on its surface appeared to be a collective male expression of outrage.

In many ways, *Teach Our Children*'s style is clearly influenced by the Third Cinema techniques perfected by renowned Cuban documentarian Santiago Alvarez, who cofounded Instituto Cubano del Arte e Industria Cinematográficos (ICAIC) and directed its Newsreel Division. A tireless supporter of Castro's revolution and a fierce opponent of Western imperialism, Alvarez traveled throughout Latin America, Africa, the Caribbean, and Asia, filming everything from north Vietnamese troops to Cuban athletes training in Puerto Rico. Alvarez's eclectic mix of original and found footage, cartoons and still images, strategic alternation of color and black-and-white, and judicious selection of music characterized a style shaped to meet the dictates of the event he was documenting. For Alvarez, newsreels did not simply provide information, but rather, he argued, could "join things up in such a way that they pass before the spectator as a complete entity, with a single line of argument" (Chanan 1985, 180). Alvarez's new conception of newsreel revolutionized the genre, transforming it into a documentary form that could at once provide information and analysis while capturing a particular mood, whether of exuberant excitement or devastating loss.

Teach Our Children relies upon Alvarez's towering example. The film mixes found footage of the 1967 Newark rebellion, Oswald's official statements, and the Attica inmates' press conference with original interview footage of the Attica survivors and community residents. Most of the film is shot in grainy black-and-white, and some segments feel as if they have been put together in haste as if to stress the urgency of this report. The cartoon interlude awash in color mimics those used by Alvarez in films such as *LBJ* (1968) and *Hanoi Martes 13* (1967) in which Alvarez lampoons a club-and-gun-wielding President Johnson, who is figured as a grotesque Texas cowboy riding a bronco (Chanan 1985). Choy and Robeson's use of the soul anthem "Let Us Sing this Simple Song for Freedom" echoes Alvarez's use of Lena Horne's riff on "Hava Nagila" to comment on U.S. racism in the 1965 film *Now*. Alvarez, in critic Michael Chanan's words, "uses the cultural associations of his chosen music (its iconography) to orient the viewer's frame of reference" (Chanan 1985, 181). Above all, *Teach Our Children* unabashedly bolsters its moral and political point of view through the juxtaposition of perspectives—those of the Attica inmates and the inner-city residents—the framing device of Malcolm X speeches and the footage of anticolonial fighters, and the use of realist techniques such as on-the-spot reportage and personal interviews. Connecting the fight against U.S. and Western imperialism in the Third World with the fight for justice in U.S. prisons provides the kind of uncompromising global framework to which Alvarez dedicated his career.

The borrowing of Third Cinema techniques gives Third World Newsreel a filmic vocabulary for making claims that are both local and global in scope. It helps it expand mainstream civil rights discourse beyond its domestic borders. Secondly, these Third Cinema techniques situate the filmmakers within an "organic community"; they locate Choy and Robeson in relation to the film's subjects by serving as the alibi or the structuring ground upon which differences in cultural and political power—Choy and Robeson possess a certain cultural and economic capital that their subjects do not—can be overcome, if not erased. This is not to question the filmmakers' sincerity, but rather to point out that this triangulation between filmmaker, technique, and filmic subjects brings Third World Newsreel even closer to Third Cinema filmmakers because such techniques performed the same function vis-à-vis Alvarez and other Latin American filmmakers who themselves possessed a great deal of cultural, economic, and political capital that they sought to deploy in the name of the masses. These questions of position, cultural capital, dislocation, and relocation (of aesthetic techniques, ideological formulations, political and military tactics, cultural privilege, and political dispossession) enact the structuring features of diasporas and transnational exchange within those diasporas. That is to say that diasporic exchange always necessarily involves a dizzying series of juxtapositions and tradeoffs that simultaneously expand and contract political and cultural space. What becomes possible is also, of course, the obverse of what becomes impossible.

In constructing an oppositional Third World community to which the film is addressed, *Teach Our Children* reveals certain parallels between U.S. peoples of color and Third World colonized and decolonizing peoples. If the film convincingly argues that non-White freedom is incompatible with the U.S. nation-state's current configuration, it simultaneously reaffirms that this is also true for Third World peoples: within current imperial and global configurations, freedom for colonized peoples cannot be fully achieved. It goes a step further, however, juggling multiple subject positions—ex-convict, inmate, male, female, middle class, and working class—in an attempt to transcend or evade the particular constrictions that accompany the feminist, Marxist, or nationalist prescription for liberation. It does this, however, by juxtaposing U.S. black and brown bodies that get to speak with anonymous Southeast Asian and African bodies. In other words, the transcendence of narrowly conceived identity politics requires the obliteration of the identities, the particular histories that structure each anticolonial struggle that is referenced. What becomes an escape route for Choy and Robeson becomes a straightjacket for Third World anticolonialists; their struggles are in some metaphorical sense recolonized in the name of U.S. Third World peoples' emancipation.

This problematic reveals the very real differences between the oppression of national minorities in the most powerful country in the West and that of national majorities in developing and hyper-exploited regions of the globe. This critique might also be leveled on the domestic front. Is there an "organic" relationship between the testimony of surviving Attica inmates and that of the inner-city residents, or, for that matter, between inner-city residents who are Latino and those who are Black? Can bridging the inside/outside divide, the divide materialized by the prison wall or the line of racial and ethnic segregation, be sutured by the film's series of juxtapositions? We do not, after all, ever see the film's subjects—be they Latino and Black, or those inside and outside the prison—joined within a single frame.

Even as *Teach Our Children* points our attention to a Utopian future certain fundamental questions of power and difference must be addressed so that one group's future freedom will not become the structuring ground for someone else's oppression. On one level, the film does address these fundamental questions by challenging the representations of the 1960s bequeathed to us. By presenting a multigenerational, multiethnic group of men and women, *Teach Our Children* challenges the very notion of radicalism that pervaded the decade of the 1960s. Radicalism was not only armed revolt, but also intellectual critique and communal survival. Rebels were not only bright-eyed, camera-ready soul brothers, but also world-weary, middle-aged women demanding that playgrounds be built and rogue police be prosecuted.

Third World Newsreel's first film successfully incorporated the domestic and international planks of earlier Newsreel filmmaking. The result was a scathing critique of the forces that placed Third World communities under siege in the United States and abroad. This emphasis, one that foregrounds ordinary people of color in extraordinary circumstances, may well help explain why Third World Newsreel's activities have so often been eclipsed by those of Newsreel. In many ways, Newsreel's films confirm the conventional narrative of 1960s activism, one that foregrounds White students and Black civil rights activists. Third World Newsreel's work during the period challenged that familiar story worked in the seams between various racial and ethnic groups, and between various local, national, and international spaces, documenting the daily struggles that at times united and at times divided different urban populations and members of the First and Third World. Recovering and acknowledging Third World Newsreel's important efforts is certainly about supplementing 1960s film historiography. But, more importantly, it is also about expanding our view of the 1960s and 1970s so that we can see the complexity of local and global influences that shaped the cultural production and political activism of the period.

Notes

1. This chapter is excerpted from Cynthia Young, "Third World Newsreel Visualizes the Internal Colony," *Soul Power: Culture, Radicalism and the Formation of a U.S. Third World Left (*Durham, NC: Duke University Press, 2006).
2. For more on how prisons work to define captured people as beyond the protection of civil society, see Dylan Rodriguez, *Forced Passages: Imprisoned Radical Intellectuals and the U.S. Prison Regime* (Minneapolis: University of Minnesota Press, 2006).
3. See Cynthia Young, *Soul Power: Culture, Radicalism and the Making of a U.S. Third World Left (*Durham, NC: Duke University Press, 2006).
4. The phrase "modes of oppression" in connection with this project emerged in a fruitful exchange I had with Professor Robert Hill at UCLA's Third World Lecture Series on May 17, 2002.
5. Susan Robeson, interview by the author, November 3, 1997, New York.

6. This mandate is mentioned in a position paper distributed by San Francisco Newsreel in the midst of their group's dissolution. It was obtained from Susan Robeson's personal files.
7. Susan Robeson, interview by the author, November 3,1997.
8. Ibid.
9. In 1971, before Robeson even joined Newsreel, she wrote a long position paper in which she outlined her intention to create a national Third World media center that would bring together Black and Third World political artists to make films and operate a mobile film and sound unit that would show films in the streets to local communities. This paper was obtained from the personal files of Susan Robeson.
10. This statement was originally obtained from Susan Robeson's personal files. There is some conflicting evidence concerning the document's moment of production. Susan Robeson wrote 1973 on the top of her copy, but when the author surveyed TWN's files, this document was attached to Newsreel's national newsletter, entitled "Focal Point," and dated October 1972.
11. Hereafter referred to as TWN.
12. This statement was obtained from Susan Robeson's personal files.
13. This was obtained from Susan Robeson's personal files.
14. In the next few years, Third World Newsreel released *We Demand Freedom* (1972), *In the Event Anyone Disappears* (1973), and *Inside Women Inside* (1975). Each film elucidated the structural similarities between Third World life inside and outside the U.S. penal system. In *We Demand Freedom*, contrasting footage of U.S. prisons, Japanese-American concentration camps, and Vietnam "trace[d] the development of prison philosophy," demonstrating how "prisons have been used historically" and examining "their function today," according to an undated TWN catalog most likely from 1973. *In the Event Anyone Disappears* and *Inside Women Inside* explored the nascent prisoners' rights movement largely through testimonials from male and female inmates in New Jersey prisons.
15. Joseph Martin, Nat Kantner, Donald Flynn, Alex Michelini, Jean Perry, and Donald Singleton, "Attica, Anatomy of a Tragedy," *New York Daily News*, special report, October 4–8, 1971.
16. All quotations are taken from the author's transcription.
17. For insight into the connection between the prison system and civic death, I am indebted to Dylan Rodriguez's paper delivered at the American Studies Association Annual Conference, October 18, 2003.

References

Althusser, Louis. 2001. Ideology and ideological state apparatuses: Notes towards an investigation. In *Lenin and philosophy and other essays*, trans. Ben Brewster, 85–133. New York: Monthly Review Press.

Bell, Malcolm. 1985. *The turkey shoot: Tracking the Attica cover-up*. New York: Grove Press.

Chanan, Michael. 1983. *Twenty-five years of the new Latin American cinema*. London: BFI Books.

———. 1985. *The Cuban image: Cinema and cultural politics in Cuba*. London: British Film Institute.

Foner, Philip, and James Allen. 1987. *American communism and Black Americans: A documentary history, 1919–1929*. Philadelphia: Temple University Press.

Hall, Stuart. 1996. On postmodernism and articulation: An interview with Stuart Hall. Ed. Lawrence Grossberg. In *Stuart Hall: Critical dialogues in cultural studies*, ed. David Morley and Kuan-Hsing hen, 131–50. London: Routledge.

Kelley, R. D. G. 1990. *Hammer and hoe: Alabama communists during the Great Depression*. Chapel Hill: University of North Carolina Press.

MacDonald, Scott. 1998. *A critical cinema 3: Interviews with independent filmmakers*. Berkeley: University of California Press.

Marcuse, Herbert. 1969. *An essay on liberation*. Boston: Beacon Press.

Milner, Sherry. 1985. TWN: Interview with Christine Choy. In *Jump cut: Hollywood, politics, and counter cinema*, ed. P. Steven. New York City: Praeger.

Nichols, William. 1980. *Newsreel: Documentary filmmaking on the American left (1971–1975)*. New York: Arno Press.

Renov, Michael. 1987a. Early Newsreel: The construction of a political imaginary for the new Left. *Afterimage* 14 (7): 10–12.

———. 1987b. Newsreel: Old and new—towards an historical profile. *Film Quarterly* 41 (1): 20–33.

———. 1988. Imaging the other: Representations of Vietnam in '60s political documentary. *Afterimage*, December 16: 10–12.

Robinson, Cedric. 1983. *Black Marxism: The making of the Black radical tradition*. London: Zed.

Third World Newsreel. 1972. *Act first, then speak*. New York: Author.

———. 1972. *Teach our children*.

———. 1973. *Organizational principles of Third World Newsreel*. New York: Author.

———. n.d. *The higher ground cinema statement of purpose*. New York: Author.

CHAPTER 5

Defying the Taboo on the Study of Internalized Racial Oppression[1]

Karen D. Pyke

Internalized racial oppression is a controversial and largely ignored topic in race scholarship, yet it is vital to informing critical race theory. In sociology, a discipline committed to cataloging the social mechanisms and consequences of racism, internalized racial oppression has received only scattered, often cursory, attention (Anzaldua 1993; Collins 1990; Osajima 1993). More recently, attention to the problem of colorism among African Americans includes reference to internalized racism as a largely peripheral concern (Hunter 2005; Thompson and Keith 2001; for an exception, see Russell, Wilson, and Hall 1992). Yet internalized racial oppression has been repeatedly acknowledged as a problem in the writings, films, and speeches of antiracist activists, public intellectuals, and artists, most prominently among African Americans (e.g., filmmaker Spike Lee; novelist Toni Morrison; Malcolm X; and see hooks 1995; Lipsky 1987; Sandler 1993; Woodson 1933/1990). Those who study the effects of colonialism on the oppressed have also engaged the topic, sometimes referring to internalized oppression as "mental colonization" (see Freire 1968; Fanon 1963; Memmi 1965). Psychologists have long studied internalized racism's deleterious effects on a variety of outcomes, including health, self-esteem, and marital satisfaction (see Butler, Tull, Chambers, and Taylor 2002; Taylor 1990; Taylor and Jackson 1991), while clinical psychologists have developed therapeutic responses to the psychological harm of internalized racial oppression (see Fortes De Leff 2002; Semmier and Williams 2000; Watts-Jones 2002). Nevertheless, in sociology, we have yet to create a subfield devoted to the study of internalized racial oppression. In fact, the concept of internalized racial oppression inspires such emotional aversion and shame in those areas of scholarship most directly linked to antiracist politics that its mention has been largely taboo.

In this chapter, I discuss some of the factors contributing to the taboo of the study of internalized racism and why race scholars we ought to defy it. I argue that the silence surrounding the topic contributes to an incomplete knowledge of the "hidden injuries" of racism, undermines the potential contribution of race scholarship to strategies of racial uplift, and bolsters white privilege. I regard this project as especially pressing given the current regime of "color-blind racism," so-named for the embeddedness of white privilege in societal structure, institutions, and culture that renders racism invisible (Barlow 2003; Bonilla-Silva 2001). My argument, which is partial and suggestive, is not intended to be uncompromising. It is, however, designed to encourage a serious, abiding theoretical and empirical engagement with internalized racial oppression as a means of understanding the subtle and not-so-subtle mechanisms that reproduce racial hierarchies and white privilege. As Ruth Frankenberg observes, "knowledge about a situation is a critical tool to dismantling it" (1993, 10).

Because internalized racial oppression is frequently misinterpreted, I first clarify my use of the term. I then describe the journey leading to my accidental engagement with this concept and the issues and concerns I have had to contemplate before continuing my work on this topic. In elaborating internalized racism, I briefly draw on examples from my research based on intensive interviews with over four hundred second-generation Vietnamese and Korean Americans. Although the dynamics these empirical cases provide are based on specific racial-ethnic groups, I suggest they capture more general features of internalized racial oppression. In the last section of the chapter, I consider why we have not devoted more scholarly attention to the internalization of racial oppression, and why doing so is crucial for advancing antiracist knowledge.

What Is Internalized Racial Oppression?

To understand internalized racial oppression, we need to consider the broader category of internalized oppression. All systems of inequality, including gender, race, class, sexuality, age, and their various intersections, have mechanisms that promote the internalization of oppression among the subjugated. Internalized oppression is a generic feature of inequality and a method by which inequality is reproduced (Schwalbe et al. 2000). It takes distinct forms in different situations and affects subordinated groups and individuals in diverse ways and to varying degrees. Yet certain fundamental dynamics mark the overall process as one of internalized oppression. I draw on these shared properties in framing my understanding of that particular form associated with racism.

Internalized oppression is rooted in a process of "othering," a constitutive component of inequality. "Othering" occurs when a dominant class defines into existence groups of individuals marked as different and inferior, that is, as "other." The dominant group's purpose in generating these social categories and attendant identities is the creation and justification of a class of exploited and subordinated individuals whose existence is fundamental to marking the dominant group as superior. It is not to signify some other meaningful social, cultural, or biological distinction, though subjugated identities are typically essentialized in ways that blur the social, arbitrary, and elective aspect of their construction. Indeed, the reification of these social categories as inevitable and natural, as if flowing out of "real" differences and samenesses, obscures how they are mechanisms for exerting power over those so contained. The process of generating categories that constitute subordinated individuals includes the discursive detailing of the alleged inferiority of the subordinated through stereotypes, myths, ideologies, images, and symbols disseminated throughout the society as "truths." Discourses asserting the dominant group's supremacy are also spun and promulgated. These so-called truths become commonsense knowledge that legitimates and naturalizes inequality, and explains the power and privilege of elites as inevitable (see Gramsci 1971). The dominant class secures compliance without coercive force by getting the subjugated to participate in cultural and structural practices and beliefs that justify as natural and inevitable the supremacy of the dominant class and inferiority of the oppressed.

I hasten to add, lest I insinuate a false dichotomy between culture and structure, that the construction of inequality as essential and legitimate also has a material basis. Systems of inequality depend upon, indeed they are defined by, institutional practices and structural arrangements granting greater resources to oppressors on the basis of their membership in the dominant group (Barlow 2003, 16). These structures are ideologically endorsed as rational, commonsensical, and the best or only way to organize social life. Privilege and subjugation are thus embedded in standard operating practices, deeming them "normal." This process obscures how inequality informs the arrangement of institutions, organizations, and everyday social life. This social machinery propagates inequality, according more and more resources and privileges to the oppressors, whose accumulated capital is regarded as further evidence of their supremacy, making it more difficult to dispute (see Brodkin 1998). While the subjugated can and do recognize some aspects of the oppressive machinery within which they negotiate sites of power, disrupt oppressive social relations, or strike bargains with the dominant regimes, the oppressive practices instilled in some social arrangements are so successfully concealed behind a veil of normalcy that they go unnoticed (Kandiyoti 1988; Sa'ar 2005). This draws members of the subordinated group into participation and endorsement of such arrangements and practices, thereby enlisting their unwitting collusion in the reproduction of inequality, ultimately resulting in a subtle and often invisible dynamic of internalized oppression. This co-optation happens at the individual level as described by social psychologists, and, equally important, shapes collective interaction between the oppressors and oppressed, and among members of subordinated.

The dominant group minimizes revolt and other forms of resistance by getting the oppressed to buy into the myths about themselves and view the system of inequality as justified and inevitable. Hence coercive force and overt repression are no longer needed to maintain domination. Such is the case with racial domination in the United States, which shifted in the mid-twentieth century from an overt state-sponsored system of Jim Crow marked by racial exclusion, segregation, and military and police repression, to a subtle system of color-blind racism characterized by structural and institutional arrangements that, on the surface, appear to be neutral and objective but are actually shaped by racial domination. With racism's entrenchment in the standard operating practices, procedures, and norms of day-to-day society, white privilege no longer depends on a discourse of racial superiority. This system allows a state-supported liberal discourse endorsing racial equality that, in turn, is used to suggest that racism is no longer a problem (Barlow 2003; Omi and Winant 1986). Indeed, the best defense of racism is for a society to deny its existence. Denial of racism permeates contemporary U.S. society in discourses that render racial inequality invisible and obscure white privilege. On-going problems endured by people of color, including internalized oppression, are presented as of their own making. In order for color-blind racism to function, subordinates must be made to embrace the precepts of institutional racism and white privilege. The internalization of racial oppression and white supremacy among the oppressed is thus central to the maintenance of this system.

My description of color-blind racism in the United States relies on the concept of hegemony. Hegemony is a practice of consent, not coercion. White privilege and domination are not enforced completely by repressive, coercive mechanisms, thus the concept of hegemony is appropriate for understanding racial hierarchies in contemporary United States society. Given that compliance is not overtly, physically coerced, but is rather lived at the level of "common sense," to understand dynamics of racial oppression, race scholars must speak about internalized racial oppression.

Because the ideas, beliefs, and ideologies legitimizing and normalizing racism are omnipresent, they infiltrate and give meaning to the subjective identities of everyone in society, including the subjugated, influencing their experiences, attitudes, and interactions. In one of the few sociological studies directly engaging the concept of internalized racism, Keith Osajima describes how racism encourages the internalization of negative self-identities among the subordinated as follows: "People come to accept and believe the myths and stereotypes about their group as part of their natural definitions of self. Moreover, in questioning their own position in society, members of oppressed groups often belie that the source of their problems lie not in the structural relations in society but in themselves, in their own inadequacies and inabilities to be anything other than what the dominant image describes" (1993, 83). Osajima examined racism's effect on how thirty Asian American students construct their everyday view of themselves—their "racial subjectivities"—at two predominately white private colleges in the Northeast (1993, 82). He finds that students responded to the negative stereotypes about their group either by accepting those images as true and trying to be more like whites, or by distancing themselves from the negative stereotypes, which was typically expressed as a general disgust toward others of Asian descent.

As these findings illustrate, the internalization of racial oppression revolves around an ideology of white superiority. Indeed, internalized racism and internalized white supremacy are flip sides of the same coin, and thus I use the terms synonymously. The new field of critical white studies provides tools for elaborating this synonymy. "White supremacy," "white privilege," "the wages of whiteness," and "the culturelessness of whiteness" are all ways of conceptualizing the benefits whites derive from racialized hierarchies (Frankenberg 1993; Rasmussen et al. 2001). George Lipsitz (2006, viii) argues that white people are invested in white identity, and thus identity politics, as it confers psychological, cultural, and material rewards. He refers to this dynamic as a "possessive investment of whiteness" (2006, viii). Although whites can divest themselves of interests in white supremacy through commitment to antiracism, few actually do so. Lipsitz notes that people of color can also invest in whiteness and serve as active agents of white supremacy. Generally, when referring to people of color who take stock in whiteness for personal gains, race scholars and activists point to the rare, notorious, and extreme examples of nonwhite individuals who actively endorse policies that promote white privilege like the antiaffirmative stance of Supreme Court Justice Clarence Thomas. Race scholars tend to treat the investment in whiteness among nonwhites as an outlying tendency, a special case. There has been far less attention to the subtle, less extreme, everyday ways that racialized structures encourage people of color to collude in sustaining whiteness and white privilege.

In fact, there is a stubborn tendency to blame and shame the individual who demonstrates internalized white supremacist thinking, like the black American who comments on the "good" hair of another or the Korean American who invokes anti-Asian stereotypes and glorified images of white masculinity in denigrating "typical Asian" males as unromantic and tyrannical in their relationships with women. When discussing internalized racial oppression in my classes, I have observed students slipping seamlessly between blaming white racism and faulting the victim. Denouncing people of color who display some aspect of internalized racism reflects our failure to theoretically grasp this extremely destructive aspect of white racism. Further, blaming the victim forestalls enlightened and compassionate responses to internalized oppression and the development of strategies for resisting the mental colonization of the subjugated. Instead, feelings of shame, embarrassment, and repulsion have relegated the discussion and study of internalized racism to the shadows.

Because of the tendency to blame the victim, I want to make clear what internalized racism is *not*. Internalized oppression is *not* the result of any specific feature attributed to the subjugated. It is *not* a result of their internal organization or culture, their psychological makeup, or some essentialized or idiosyncratic trait. Nor is it a result of any inherent deficiencies or shortcomings. It *is*, however, a condition of their oppression. *All* forms of oppression are to some degree inculcated into the consciousness of the subordinated through no fault of their own. I find this point to be the most difficult for scholars and students to incorporate into their understanding of internalized racism. Instead there is a tendency to view internalized racism as reflecting some failure or weakness of the oppressed, contributing to anger and resentment when the topic is discussed. Nonetheless, until we closely study internalized racial oppression, we will never fully understand white racism and privilege. And until we stop blaming the victims, internalized racism will be undertheorized in antiracist scholarship and critical race theory.

How I Came to the Study of Internalized Racism

I never intended to study internalized racial oppression when I began interviewing the sons and daughters of Korean and Vietnamese immigrants. My initial glimpse of internalized racism emerged in an analysis of the first seventy-three interviews. Many respondents juxtaposed negative accounts of their family life against notions of a "normal" American family life (meaning white and middle class; Pyke 2000). Respondents grounded notions of a "normal" American family with examples from television shows like *The*

Brady Bunch, the families of their white friends, and assumptions and prescriptions about family life that reflect the discourse circulated throughout the dominant culture by schools, social commentators, politicians, the clergy, mass media, and the political-legal system. For many respondents, the ethnic practices of their immigrant families marked them as inferior to the white, middle-class ideal of how a "normal" family should look or act. One respondent in my interview study, a twenty-four-year-old Korean American male who immigrated at age seven, had unusual insight into these dynamics. He said, "I still find myself envying white American families and wishing that my family was perfect like theirs. So basically I find myself suckered into this ideal image of the American family. And I realize, sadly, that my family is not the American family and never will be. God, you know, this really upsets me when I keep striving for this intangible thing because then I never really feel happiness or satisfaction" (for a description of the interview methods, see Pyke 2000).

Around the same time, I became interested in my respondents' routine use of the term "FOB," an acronym for "fresh off the boat," to identify and denigrate more recently arrived, less acculturated, and more ethnically identified coethnic peers. With a research team composed mostly of Asian American students, I interviewed respondents about the use of "FOB" and related terms. Our analysis uncovered a definition of "FOB" grounded in anti-Asian stereotypes disseminated in the white-dominated society and the glorification of whiteness and Americanness (Pyke and Dang 2003). The composite sketch of a "FOB" that emerged in the interviews was a socially befuddled "nerd" who is inept, too traditional, patriarchal, and slow to adapt to American society. Many respondents admitted using the term to derogate coethnics and to avoid social contact with those so-labeled, lest they be assumed to be a "FOB" as well. Entire peer groups enlisted the identity term to ridicule less-assimilated coethnics, distance themselves from the negative stereotype of Asians, and construct a positive self-identity. It was a way of saying, "I'm not a 'FOB.' Those are the real 'FOBs' over there." This strategy of resisting the imposition of negative stereotypes by imposing them on other members of one's subordinated group and then distancing oneself from those "others" is known as "defensive othering" (Anzaldúa 1993; Schwalbe et al. 2000). Defensive "othering" is not absolute resistance, however, as it fails to challenge the derogatory stereotypes, instead suggesting that the stereotypes are true, just not true of oneself.

As other dimensions of internalized racial oppression emerged in the data (see Pyke and Johnson 2003), my project became more intensely focused on this concept, which I was surprised to find largely absent in the race literature. My surprise was due in part to my familiarity with the study of internalized class and gender oppression in the sociology and feminist literatures (see Bordo 1993; Pyke 1996; Seccombe 1998). I had expected to find these theoretical understandings of oppression shared in the study of racial inequality. It was at this time that I learned I was treading on sensitive and highly volatile terrain (see hooks 1995, 2003; Russell, Wilson, and Hall 1992). Some have suggested that attention to internalized racism violates "a politics of knowledge." Specifically, they argue that attention to complicity rather than resistance contributes to a negative characterization of the oppressed as mere fools who lack agency. They worry that such attention undermines efforts to dismantle racial hierarchies. Others acknowledge that internalized racism probably is a problem, but they fear attention to it will expand to a negative focus on how the oppressed keep themselves down (Jones 1994). Some worry that internalized racism will be used to suggest inherent deficiencies among the oppressed and to blame them for their oppression. History provides good reason for such concern. In the 1930s, when psychologists studied internalized racism among blacks as indicated by measures of self-esteem, their initial concern with psychological oppression shifted into a problem of black psychopathology. Internalized racism was recast as reflecting a black proclivity toward self-hatred rather than a problem of white racism (for a review, see Baldwin 1979).

I had to grapple with these issues, especially in relation to the impact of my whiteness on this research. Postcolonial and third world feminisms had pointed out the shortcomings of white women's representations of nonwhite, non-Western females (Mohanty 2002). I worried that my analysis would be received with suspicion and discounted as a white woman's perspectival (mis)reading and (mis)representation of Asian "others" shaped by my own investment in whiteness rather than an elaboration of the far-reaching and insidious character of white racism. On the other hand, I was not comfortable with reductionist and essentialist assumptions about studying "others," for, to some extent, we are always outsiders to those we study (Naples 2003). I drew confidence from the work and words of other white antiracist scholars such as Julie Bettie, a feminist sociologist who introduces her study of Mexican American girls with a thorough examination of these issues. She concludes that outsiders politically committed to studying domination so as to eliminate it can do so well enough to be of service to the oppressed (2003, 25).

My research began out of a commitment to the majority of my students who are Asian American, and was conducted in close collaboration with Asian American undergraduate research assistants, many of whom initially participated in the project as respondents. Thus, I enjoyed many opportunities to check my interpretations against the understandings of my students and research assistants, and to incorporate their feedback. In fact, I was encouraged in this research by Asian American research assistants and students who found internalized racial oppression to be useful in understanding their own thought patterns and experiences. Some explained that the concept gave a name to a problem they did not previously understand but that had troubled them. I recall two Asian American students, a man and a woman, who attended the conference that gave birth to this volume during which a few scholars criticized my analysis of internalized racial oppression, arguing that it violates "a politics of knowledge" and presents Asian Americans as "dupes." They suggested I focus on resistance instead. Two days later, these students visited my office urging me not to heed the advice of these critics, with whom they were in vehement disagreement. Recounting their own experiences with internalized racial oppression, the students argued in favor of the concept's relevance in their lives. I also received encouragement from race scholars in my discipline who, acknowledging the political difficulties and discomfort aroused by the study of internalized racial oppression, suggested strategies for mitigating them.[2] However, before coming back to this research, I needed to examine more closely the taboo on the study of internalized racism that has rendered it, in the words of Stuart Hall (1986), one of the least understood aspects of racism. The rest of this chapter is devoted to that effort.

Reasons for the Taboo on Internalized Racism

Identity Politics and Essentializing Race

To understand why the mere mention of internalized racial oppression inspires such aversion, we need to consider some of the factors underlying what I view as a tendency to fetishize resistance in contemporary scholarship. The social and civil rights movements of the 1960s and 1970s and the rise of identity politics had a profound effect on scholarship. In sociology, functionalism was pronounced dead, Marxism was embraced, and feminist and critical race theories were on the rise. Culture of poverty approaches, like the 1966 Moynihan Report, blaming the values and attitudes of blacks and Mexican Americans for not achieving economic and educational parity with whites came under attack and were replaced by social structural explanations attributing the economic and social disenfranchisement of racial minorities to systems of inequality (Roschelle 1997). Many scholars considered the impact of their work beyond the ivory tower, prompting scholarship concerned with equality and struggles for social justice. Understandably, their attention turned to resistance. Resistance narratives are intuitively appealing to scholars committed to struggles against domination for several reasons. Accounts of resistance accord agency to the subjugated and the ability to wrestle power and foment change from *within* systems of domination, providing a refreshing alternative to tendencies to theorize an overdetermined subject. Tales of resistance are also appealing because they exalt the subjugated, boost morale, inspire oppositional politics, and are important resources in identity politics. These factors contribute to what I regard as a hegemony of the resistance narrative in today's scholarship.

To understand this dynamic, we must consider the role of identity politics. Identity politics presumes that members of an oppressed group share certain fundamental experiences with subjugation that shape a collective knowledge and the formation of group-based political strategies. In this political context, scholars and activists conceptualized a seemingly unified race consciousness among members of racialized ethnic groups, implying a core constitutive race-based political perspective. Even though scholars acknowledge that racial categories and their meanings are socially constructed, there nonetheless remains a stubborn tendency to essentialize race with the presumption that those who share certain racial biological markers also share racial attitudes and perspectives that coalesce around experiences with racism (Glenn 1999). Claims of an "expert" situational, standpoint, or essentialized knowledge of oppression are central to identity politics. While it stands to reason that many members of an oppressed group will develop some shared understandings of their subjugation, identity politics assumes that such an understanding includes an acute awareness of the contours and mechanisms of oppression, resulting in collective and individual strategies of resistance. As a result, whether intended or not, we have constructed a nonwhite racial subject for whom agency is synonymous with resistance. This assumption is referred to by Chandra Mohanty (2002, 208) as "I am, therefore I resist." She counters that simply being a member of an oppressed group is not "sufficient ground to assume a politicized oppositional identity" (208).

Postmodern conceptualizations of power read agency and resistance as favorable forces to be found wherever there is domination. That is, agency and resistance, which are treated as one and the same, depend upon domination. This understanding easily expands into the assumption that more domination produces more opportunities for agency. The result is doublespeak: domination creates agency. There are many examples of this kind of thinking in scholarship, particularly in analyses that examine several axes of domination simultaneously. One example is an examination of the changing conditions for Uighur Muslim women in Xinjiang, China, after the heavy inmigration of the Han-Chinese, whose dominating presence transformed the indigenous, previously homogeneous population into a religious and ethnic minority (Obol 2005).

Sadat Obol argues that Uighur women, who earlier endured only gender oppression, found new openings for agency and resistance to patriarchy when religious and ethnic domination was added to the mix. Obol concludes, "In the process of this discussion, one can see that the marginality focused upon is more complex than that of simple oppression. It is largely oppressive, but ironically it can simultaneously be partially liberating. It does this by creating new ways of thought and new avenues of agency. That is, the triple marginality of Uighur women in post-Migration Xinjiang creates a dialectic of negative and positive consequences that allow for the possibilities of new avenues for human agency" (2005, 204). While I do not disagree that the domination of Han-Chinese set into play changes in Uighur gender relations that had some liberatory effects for latter-generation females, I am deeply troubled by this tendency to fetishize resistance and agency and by the recasting of domination as a positive force, particularly when there is a failure to consider the role of complicity and internalized oppression in these dynamics. Do not the oppressors offer rewards to the subjugated like the illusion of power as well as some token liberatory gains in order to win their compliance and consent to oppression? More importantly, who benefits most from the hegemony of the resistance narrative, the oppressed or the oppressors? Feminist philosopher Susan Bordo (1993) suggests that the overuse of the rhetoric of resistance benefits the oppressors by mystifying and normalizing domination and complicity.

As a result of this tendency to see only resistance among the subjugated, we have undertheorized the ways the racially subjugated collude in sustaining racism. The result is great difficulty accounting for members of a racially subjugated group who eagerly embrace the ideas and values of the oppressors. They are regarded as little more than freakish individuals whose attitudes and behavior bear no similarities or connection to the rest of the group. Take, for example, the way prominent individuals who undermine antiracist projects and display white supremacist attitudes (i.e., internalized racism), such as the aforementioned Supreme Court Justice Clarence Thomas and former University of California regent Ward Connerly, are discounted as aberrant racial sellouts who are not "really" black (or Latino or Asian). They are symbolically expelled from the group, as their presence would undermine the claim of identity politics to a core-constitutive, race-based knowledge. Their ouster eliminates the need to explain their behavior within the context of the racial group, and internalized racism does not have to be acknowledged.

The conceptualization of racial attitudes as flowing directly and rather simply out of racial categories that mark shared experiences and perspectives elides internal racial variation and slips into essentialism. This essentialism undergirds the misconstrual of internalized racism as an inherent weakness, ignorance, or pathology of the racially oppressed, that is, as a derogatory statement about the essence of the group. This conceptual context limits projects of racial uplift to positive stories of the oppressed, especially accounts of their resistance in the face of widespread, overlapping, and insidious forces of oppression. Like the construction of a "model minority" stereotype that denies the ongoing oppression of Asian Americans, I see in these resistance narratives the construction of what I refer to as a "model resister" stereotype. The model resister stereotype serves as a symbol of freedom, celebrates successful advances against racism, and is an endorsement for continued political mobilization. However, it is a distortion.

While symbols of resistance can be important political resources, we need to recognize their limits and what their overuse can obstruct from view. As Edward Said (1993, 310) notes, "What invariably happens at the level of knowledge is that signs and symbols of freedom and status are taken for the reality." In the present case, symbols of agency and resistance are invoked in the construction and celebration of a positive oppositional identity. Though there are theoretical and political locations where such a focus is appropriate, the hegemony of the resistance narrative and concomitant myth of the model resister exceed their positive function at the moment they shut down inquiry into how the oppressed are brought into compliance with structures of domination and collude in the reproduction of inequality. In the words of Said (1993, 310), the result is an "impoverishing politics of knowledge."

Race scholarship's neglect of internalized racial oppression and the factors contributing to it become more apparent when we consider the attention feminist scholarship has accorded internalized gender oppression. Attempts by predominately white, middle-class feminists in the 1970s and 1980s to assert a unified core-constitutive perspective among women—and hence an identity politics—were relatively short lived. This political strategy was untenable due to the omission of women of color and third-world feminisms, as well as the inherent middle-class and heterosexual biases of the movement. When feminists were confronted with a backlash movement among the far right, including large numbers of women engaging antifeminist, antiabortion rhetoric, not only did they have to acknowledge the diversity of experiences and perspectives among women, but they also had to explain those women who invest in male dominance and actively oppose gender equality. Hence feminist scholars were forced to grapple with the notion of internalized oppression.

Since then, women's internalization and reproduction of gender oppression has been a central feature of feminist scholarship, framing investigations into women's beauty practices (see Bordo 1993), family relationships (see Pyke 1996), and so on. In contrast, race scholars were never confronted with a mass movement of nonwhites opposed to antiracist policies and organizations in support of white supremacy. Hence race scholars and activists have not had political cause to draw attention to internalized racial oppression, and have been better able to engage a race-based identity politics. And, unlike feminist scholars who had to acknowledge a diversity of viewpoints among women, there is perhaps a tendency among race activists and scholars of color engaged in resistance struggles to draw on their personal experiences with racial oppression and to overgeneralize their experiences with racism to all members of their racial-ethnic group. These dynamics help to explain what Evelyn Nakano Glenn (1999, 4) describes as the greater tendency to essentialize race than gender in the race and feminist literatures, despite gender's deeper roots in biology.

Resistance and Complicity

Another factor slowing the study of internalized racism is the theoretical treatment of resistance and compliance as mutually exclusive forces, a result of the Western epistemological penchant for simplistic dichotomies (Collins 1990). Such binary thinking has not only delayed understanding of how these dynamics are intertwined, as in the Du Boisian idea of twoness, but has also led scholars to regard acts of resistance as a higher social order than those of complicity. Resistance is idealized as active, empowering, wise, logical, and masculine, while complicity is derogated as passive, ignorant, weak, gullible, self-defeating, pathological, and feminine. Indeed, that internalized oppression has been acknowledged in feminist scholarship but ignored in much of the race literature further encourages its association with femininity. In this framework, the oppressed who internalize structures and cultures of domination are regarded as foolish, unaware dupes. Those who engage in resistance, on the other hand, are presented as knowing, rational actors. They become positive and powerful representatives of an identity group.

The binary model of resistance and complicity obscures the dependency of some acts of resistance on complicity. In order to acquire informal power and successfully resist certain oppressive practices, the oppressed are typically required to comply with larger structures of inequality. Similarly, simplistic either/or models overlook the complex nature of inequality and the ways an individual can resist one aspect of oppression while internalizing and reproducing another. Additionally, what might feel and look like an act of resistance can constitute the reproduction of inequality. Such is the case with the practice of distancing I referred to earlier, whereby the oppressed attempt to insulate themselves from negative stereotypes associated with their group by suggesting such stereotypes are true, but simply not true of themselves. Hence the subjugated can be both acutely aware of the problem of inequality and contest it in a variety of forms, yet buy into and reproduce the controlling imagery and myths generated about their group. This highlights the difficulties involved in analytically distinguishing resistance and complicity, for they are not so easily parsed. To conceptualize these dynamics as opposing forces is to oversimplify matters and undermine the accumulation of knowledge that promotes equality.

White Racism Benefits Most

The reluctance to study internalized racial oppression is tied to the historic tendency of whites to misconstrue it as a problem emanating from people of color rather than as a white problem—that is, a problem of white racism. Hence when race scholars adopt the view that people of color do not internalize racism or invest in white supremacy unless they are weak, feeble-minded, and inferior, they reiterate the derisive perspective of the oppressors. For this reason, I submit that the inattention to internalized racism can be considered, in and of itself, an example of internalized racial oppression. Oppression generates self-doubt and shame among the subjugated as well as an ever-present concern with how the dominant group perceives the subordinated. Indeed, the subjugated's quest for equality and an end to oppression often rotates around the pursuit of the dominant group's approval and respect. This public relations campaign designed for the white gaze mandates the suppression of all information that could be negatively interpreted, including accounts of internalized oppression. Further, while seeming to serve the subjugated, the silence surrounding internalized racial oppression actually benefits white racism and white privilege. In the following passage, bell hooks eloquently makes a similar point:

> Emphasis on racial uplift, though crucial to efforts to intervene on and challenge white supremacy, nevertheless created a culture of shame wherein any aspect of black life that could be seen as evidence of mental disorder, of pathology, had to be hidden or viewed as utterly aberrant. It is this untalked-about culture of shame that has made it practically impossible for African Americans to acknowledge the ways in which living in a white supremacist society and being the constant targets of racist assault and abuse are fundamentally psychologically traumatic. For black folks to acknowledge that we are collectively wounded by racial trauma would require severing our attachment to an unproblematized tradition of racial uplift where that trauma had been minimized in the effort to prove that we were not collectively dehumanized by racist oppression and exploitation. This desperate need to "prove" to white folks that racism had not really managed to wreak ongoing psychological havoc in our

lives was and is a manifestation of psychological trauma, an over-reactive response. (1995, 134)

Why We Ought to Study Internalized Racism

In concluding my argument, I briefly outline the following seven reasons why race scholars ought to study internalized racial oppression:

1. It is only through the study of dynamics of internalized oppression, complicity, and the inculcation of white supremacist thinking among the racially subordinated that we can understand the subtle, everyday mechanisms that maintain and reproduce racial inequality. Race scholars thus need to carve out a conceptual and empirical space for considering internalized oppression.
2. The dominance of resistance narratives and a failure to sympathetically examine dynamics of internalized racial oppression result in shaming and blaming those who display some aspect of internalized racism or complicity. Studying how systems of racial domination encourage or at times require the racially oppressed to adopt stances, values, and practices promoting white supremacy will enable the development of more compassionate and effective strategies for responding to situations in which such dynamics emerge.
3. Studying internalized racism will undermine the tendency to cast the racially subordinated as possessing an innate or essentialized talent for recognizing and resisting racism, and challenge images that glorify the oppressed as possessing superhuman skills, endurance, and strength with which to resist the trauma racism inflicts on their bodies and minds. Moving beyond these essentialized notions of race will make it easier to behold racial categories as social devices designed to oppress people of color while according dominance and privilege to white folks.
4. The lack of attention to internalized racism results in white people's ignorance of the problem, freeing whites from having to assume responsibility for some of racism's most insidious and damaging consequences. This results in an underestimation of the extent to which white racism continues to be a problem and feeds the myth of a color-blind society. Consideration of internalized racism directs attention to the ongoing problems of a racially stratified society.
5. Studying internalized racism is integral to the ongoing development of critical white studies. We cannot fully understand the psychological benefits accorded to whites by a society that glorifies and privileges their racial group without shedding light on the injurious effects of internalized

racism. By keeping the problem in a dark corner of race scholarship and failing to elucidate its dynamics, we inadvertently obscure an important mechanism by which white privilege is produced and maintained. Indeed, I suggest that the lack of attention to internalized racism contributes to white supremacy and the invisibility of white privilege.

6. When we target internalized racism in our empirical research and follow its dynamics closely, we can begin to learn how it is intertwined with resistance. For example, we might find that complicity sometimes provides the illusion of power and resistance, or that resistance and empowerment dwell beneath actions, attitudes, and collective practices of compliance. We also will be able to assess the extent to which the interdependency of resistance and internalized oppression undermines the success of resistance or limits the reproductive qualities of complicity.
7. Ignoring internalized racism does not make it go away. Talking about it, bringing it out into the open, giving it a name, and seeing it as a negative consequence of racism can have tremendous consciousness-raising benefits and lead to effective strategies of resistance. In an e-mail I recently received from a former student upon her graduation, she wrote, "Learning about internalized racism has definitely allowed me to understand the thoughts that I never knew how to explain before. . . . This has given me so much strength and, even more so, pride in who I am as a Filipina-American." As Audre Lorde wrote, "The true focus of revolutionary change is never merely the oppressive situation that we seek to escape, but that piece of the oppressor which is planted deep within us" (1984, 123).

Notes

1. Much of this chapter is from a forthcoming book tentatively titled *The Hidden Injuries of Racism: Internalized Racial Oppression and Asian Americans.*
2. Most suggestions concerned the term I engage to describe this phenomenon. Some alerted me to the negative connotation of the term "self-hatred." Although used by bell hooks and Malcolm X, the concept of "self-hatred" suggests the oppressed internalize an absolute, unmitigated self-loathing without any contradictions or countervailing feelings of self-love and pride. Hence it usage can be particularly explosive. Others suggested my use of "internalized racism" was problematic as it linked "racism" with people of color and thus could be easily misunderstood. Another scholar suggested I use the DuBoisian notion of "twoness," which I found helpful in elaborating aspects of internalized racial oppression but too vague and ill-fitting a concept for the many dimensions I was observing in my empirical data. In the end, I chose to use "internalized racial oppression," though I revert to "internalized racism," which is commonly used

among psychologists today. Regardless of the term, there are some for whom this topic will remain discomforting and most unwelcome.

References

Anzaldúa, Gloria. 1993. En rapport, in opposition: Cobrando cuentas a las nuestras. In *Feminist Frontiers III*, ed. Laurel Richardson and Verta Taylor, 508–12. New York: McGraw-Hill.

Baldwin, Joseph A. 1979. Theory and research concerning the notion of black self-hatred: A review and reinterpretation. *The Journal of Black Psychology* 5:51–77.

Barlow, Andrew. 2003. *Between fear and hope: Globalization and race in the United States*. New York: Rowman and Littlefield.

Bettie, Julie. 2003. *Women without class: Girls, race, and identity*. Los Angeles: University of California Press.

Bonilla-Silva, Eduardo. 2001. *White supremacy and racism in the post–civil rights era*. Boulder: L. Rienner.

Bordo, Susan.1993. Feminism, Foucault, and the politics of the body. In *Up against Foucault*, ed. Caroline Ramazanoglu, 170–202. New York: Routledge.

Brodkin, Karen. 1998. *How Jews became white folks and what that says about race in America*. New Brunswick, NJ: Rutgers University Press.

Butler, Cleve, Eugene Tull, Earle C. Chambers, and Jerome Taylor. 2002. Internalized racism, body fat distribution, and abnormal fasting glucose among African-Caribbean women in Dominica, West Indies. *Journal of the National Medical Association* 94:143–48.

Collins, Patricia Hill. 1990. *Black feminist thought*. New York: Routledge.

Du Bois, W. E. B. 1903/1989. *The souls of black folk*. New York: Penguin.

Fanon, Frantz. 1963. *The wretched of the earth*. New York: Grove Press.

———. 1967. *Black skin, white masks*. New York: Grove Press.

Fortes De Leff, Jacqueline. 2002. Racism in Mexico: Cultural roots and clinical interventions. *Family Process* 41:619–23.

Frankenberg, Ruth. 1993. *White women, race matters*. Minneapolis: University of Minnesota.

Freire, Paulo. 1968/1970. *Pedagogy of the oppressed*. New York: Continuum.

Glaser, Barney G., and Anselm L. Straus. 1967. *The discovery of grounded theory*. New York: Aldine.

Glenn, Evelyn Nakano. 1999. The social construction and institutionalization of gender and race. In *Revisioning gender*, ed. Myra Marx Ferree, Judith Lorber, and Beth B. Hess, 3–43. Thousand Oaks, CA: Sage.

Gramsci, Antonio. 1971. *Selections from the prison notebooks of Antonio Gramsci*. Ed. and trans. Quintin Hoare and Geoffrey Nowell Smith. New York: International Publishers.

Hall, Stuart. 1986. Gramsci's relevance for the study of race and ethnicity. *The Journal of Communication Inquiry* 10:5–27.

Heldke, Lisa, and Peg O'Connor. 2004. *Oppression, privilege, and resistance: Theoretical perspectives on racism, sexism, and heterosexism*. San Francisco: McGraw Hill.
hooks, bell. 1995. *Killing rage: Ending racism*. New York: Henry Holt.
———. 2003. *Rock my soul: Black people and self-esteem*. New York: Atria.
Hunter, Margaret L. 2005. *Race, gender and the politics of skin tone*. New York: Routledge.
Jones, Lisa. 1994. *Bulletproof diva: Tales of race, Sex, and Hair*. NY: Anchor Books.
Lipsitz, George. 2006. *The possessive investment in whiteness: How white people profit from identity politics*. Philadelphia: Temple University Press.
Lipsky, Suzanne. 1987. *Internalized racism*. Seattle: Rational Island Publishers.
Lorde, Audre. 1984. Sister/outsider. Freedom, CA: Crossing Press.
Kandiyoti, Deniz. 1988. Bargaining with patriarchy. *Gender & Society* 2:274–90.
Kaw, Eugenia. 1993. Medicalization of racial features: Asian American women and cosmetic surgery. *Medical Anthropology Quarterly* 7:74–89.
Kenny, Michael. 2004. *The politics of identity: Liberal political theory and the dilemmas of difference*. Malden, MA: Polity.
Memmi, Albert. 1965. *The colonizer and the colonized*. Boston: Beacon Press.
Mohanty, Chandra T. 2002. Cartographies of struggle: Third world women and the politics of feminism. In *Race critical theories*, ed. Philomena Essed and David Theo Goldberg, 195–219. Malden, MA: Blackwell.
Naples, Nancy. 2003. *Feminism and method*. New York: Routledge.
Obol, Sadat. 2005. Marginalizing the majority: Migration and the social construction of identity among Uighur Muslim women in China. In *Marginality, power and social structure: Issues in race, class, and gender analysis*, ed. Dennis Rutledge, 191–206. Amsterdam: Elsevier.
Omi, Michael, and Howard Winant. 1986. *Racial formation in the United States*. New York: Routledge.
Osajima, Keith. 1993. The hidden injuries of race. In *Bearing dreams, shaping visions: Asian Pacific American perspectives*, ed. Linda Revilla, Gail Nomura, Shawn Wong, and Shirley Hune, 81–91. Pullman: Washington State University Press.
Pyke, Karen. 1996. Class-based masculinities: The interdependence of gender, class, and interpersonal power. *Gender and Society* 10: 527–49.
———. 2000. "The normal American family" as an interpretive structure of family life among children of Korean and Vietnamese immigrants. *Journal of Marriage and the Family* 62:240–55.
Pyke, Karen, and Tran Dang. 2003. "FOB" and "whitewashed": Identity and internalized racism among second generation Asian Americans. *Qualitative Sociology* 26:147–72.
Pyke, Karen, and Denise Johnson. 2003. Asian American women and racialized femininities: "Doing" gender across cultural worlds. *Gender & Society* 17:33–53.
Rasmussen, Birgit Brander, Eric Klinenberg, Irene J. Nexica, and Matt Wray, eds. 2001. *The making and unmaking of whiteness*. Durham, NC: Duke University Press.
Roschelle, Anne R. 1997. *No more kin: Exploring race, class and gender in Family networks*. Thousand Oaks, CA: Sage.

Russell, Kathy, Midge Wilson, and Ronald Hall. 1992. *The color complex*. New York: Harcourt Brace Jovanovich.

Sa'ar, Amalia. 2005. Post-colonial feminism, the politics of identification, and the liberal bargain. *Gender and Society* 19:680–700.

Said, Edward. 1993. The politics of knowledge. In *Race, identity, and representation in education*, ed. Cameron McCarthy and Warren Crichlow, 306–14. New York: Routledge.

Sandler, Kathe. 1993. A question of color. Film Two Productions. Writer, director, and producer.

Schwalbe, Michael, Sandra Godwin, Daphne Holden, Douglas Schrock, Shealy Thompson, and Michele Wolkomir. 2000. Generic processes in the reproduction of inequality: An interactionist analysis. *Social Forces* 79:419–52.

Seccombe, Karen. 1998. "They think you ain't much of nothing": The social construction of the welfare mother. *Journal of Marriage and the Family* 60:849–65.

Semmier, Pamela Lucey, and Carmen Braun Williams. 2000. Narrative therapy: A storied context for multicultural counseling. *Journal of Multicultural Counseling and Development* 28:51–62.

Taylor, Jerome. 1990. Relationship between internalized racism and marital satisfaction. *The Journal of Black Psychology* 16:45–53.

Taylor, Jerome, and Beryl B. Jackson. 1991. Evaluation of a holistic model of mental health symptoms in African American women. *The Journal of Black Psychology* 18:19–45.

Thompson, Maxine S., and Verna M. Keith. 2001. The blacker the berry: Gender, skin tone, self-esteem, and self-efficacy. *Gender & Society* 15:336–57.

Watts-Jones, Dee. 2002. Healing internalized racism: The role of a within-group sanctuary among people of African descent. *Family Process* 41:591–601.

Woodson, Carter G. 1933/1990. *The mis-education of the negro*. Nashville: Winston-Derek.

Winant, Howard. 1995. Symposium: On West and Fenstermaker's "doing difference." *Gender & Society* 9:491–513.

Yeatman, Anna. 1993. Voice and the representation in the politics of difference. In *Feminism and the politics of difference*, ed. Sneja Gunew and Anna Yeatman, 228–45. San Francisco: Westview.

CHAPTER 6

Poetry and Cultural Change: Charles Reznikoff

Steven Gould Axelrod

In 1920, Charles Reznikoff, the son of Jewish-Russian immigrants, published the following short, untitled poem:

> Her work was to count linings—
> the day's seconds in dozens.[1]

When I first read this poem, I did not get it. I asked my wife Rise what she made of it. Rise's grandparents, like my own, were Jewish immigrants from Eastern Europe. Her father had spent his life as a cutter of ladies' garments, a member of the International Ladies' Garment Workers Union. She told me that "seconds" are pieces that have mistakes in them; they must be discarded or sold at discount. Reflecting her father's perfectionism, she said that the poem indicated that the quality of the work in this shop was shoddy. There were dozens and dozens of seconds that needed to be counted. The thing I noticed in the poem was the tedium of the young woman's work life: "Her work was to count linings— / the day's seconds in dozens." Surely a double meaning exists in that last line. The "seconds" are not simply the imperfectly cut linings but also the clock's seconds, ticking off remorselessly as the young woman sits there counting garment linings. I live a different, more fortunate life, but I feel that I am one step away from her—literally and figuratively.

This, then, is a very short poem, written by a son of poor Jewish immigrants, describing the painfully monotonous, impoverished life of another immigrant or child of immigrants. This young woman worked long hours for low wages in the newly unionized environment that followed the disastrous Triangle Shirtwaist Company fire of 1911, one of the pivotal tragedies in American history.[2] Yet it is fair to say that such simple poems ultimately transformed U.S. and global poetic culture. The process of that transformation was a gradual one. Reznikoff wrote poetry in obscurity for over a decade, generally publishing his poems at his own expense while working menial jobs selling hats or writing case abstracts for legal reference books.[3] As he continued to write and to publish, he began to exert an influence on other poets. This impact became palpable in February 1931, when Louis Zukofsky published his landmark "Objectivists" issue of *Poetry* magazine.[4] The issue featured six short poems by Reznikoff, including the following:

> Rooted among roofs, their smoke among the clouds,
> Factory chimneys—our cedars of Lebanon. (Poems I:115)

Such poems looked intently and concisely at the urban environment, often in a mood of quiet melancholy. This particular poem notably defers its subject—factory chimneys—through two subordinate clauses (and half the poem), in order to achieve suspense followed by the theatrical flourish of revelation. Only in the poem's final words do the factory chimneys come into focus as the urban scene's ironic equivalent to the cedars of Lebanon, praised so highly in the Hebrew Scriptures.[5]

In *Poetry*, Reznikoff's work appeared alongside that of William Carlos Williams and such younger poets as Basil Bunting, George Oppen, Carl Rakosi, Kenneth Rexroth, and Zukofsky himself. The issue also included Zukofsky's manifesto, "Sincerity and Objectification: With Special Reference to the Work of Charles Reznikoff," which explained the new "objectivist" aesthetic. Zukofsky asserted that the verbal qualities of Reznikoff's shorter poems "do not form mere pretty bits," but rather suggest "entire aspects of thought."[6] We can sense what Zukofsky meant in the striking, paradoxical visual images contained in Reznikoff's phrases "rooted among roofs" and "smoke among the clouds." Zukofsky argued that not even Reznikoff quite attained Ezra Pound's level of "objectification," which referred to the patterning of words in an autonomous sonic and semantic arrangement.[7] But he added that Reznikoff had reached a superlative level of "sincerity"—that is, his "care for significant detail and precision."[8] He quoted, as an example, a Reznikoff poem about preparations for a Passover Seder, probably the first time the word "Passover" had ever appeared in *Poetry* magazine. In an endnote to the essay, Zukofsky quoted Pound himself praising Reznikoff and speculating whether "the next wave of literature will be Jewish."[9] Reznikoff at this instant became somebody real, somebody significant in poetic history—or at least he seemed to have become so. Thanks to Zukofsky's tactical brilliance, four Jewish experimental poets—Reznikoff, Oppen, Rakosi, and Zukofsky himself—momentarily became significant figures in the Pound Era.[10] It was the first of several transitory legitimations that would mark Reznikoff's difficult career.

Zukofsky, himself the son of working-class immigrants from Russia, might be expected to find Reznikoff's work resonant. Yet Reznikoff's influence on other poets became both broad and deep. Here, for example, is an untitled poem from the late 1930s by Lorine Niedecker, who discovered her poetic vocation upon reading the "Objectivists" issue of *Poetry* in a northern Wisconsin public library:

> Young girl to marry,
> winds the washing harry.[11]

In place of urban factory life, this poem gives us rural domesticity. But like Reznikoff, Niedecker is using a concentrated style to evoke the everyday existence of people around her. Moreover, there is a social sympathy for the poor young girl of this poem that reminds one of Reznikoff's sensitivity to his garment worker. Niedecker's young girl marries, and her washing is harried—plagued or troubled by winds. On the one hand, she has entered a life of drudgery, repetitively doing laundry in a way that is analogous to the numbing factory work of Reznikoff's garment worker. On the other hand, those harried or plagued linens, buffeted in the wind, evoke the young girl herself—just as, one could say, those seconds that Reznikoff's garment worker repetitiously counts become an evocative image of *her*, forced to live a second-hand, second-rate, discounted, and discardable life.

The poetic history I am tracing here has yet other chapters. In the 1950s and 1960s, the Beat movement adapted Reznikoff's often gritty scenes of working-class life to a new, exuberant, outcast style. Allen Ginsberg first encountered Reznikoff through his association with Zukofsky and Williams, and he later taught courses on the poet, whom he valued for his power of "direct observation" and his "grounding in and acceptance of existence."[12] One can sense Reznikoff's influence in the "poverty and tatters" of the cold-water flats of Ginsberg's "Howl" and in the immigrant family interiors of "To Aunt Rose" and "Kaddish."[13] One can also trace a line from Reznikoff to the urban fantasias of the New York poets circa 1950 to 1980. Frank O'Hara's poetry, for example, accumulates telling details of city life, such as an old man "on the sidewalk" drinking beer, or a photo of Billy Holliday glimpsed in a newspaper.[14] Moreover, the impact of Reznikoff's later documentary texts, such as *Testimony* and *Holocaust*, may be felt on several generations of "material word" poets, ranging from Muriel Rukeyser to Susan Howe.[15] Ron Silliman argues that the work of Reznikoff and other objectivists had a "resurrection" in the early 1960s that has transformed poetic practice ever since.[16] Reznikoff's immanence now pervades the work of postmodern poets around the world.[17]

Reznikoff's continuing influence is clearly evident, for example, in the work of the language poets, an avant-garde movement with a worldwide impact that began in the 1980s. Language poetry looks in some ways like the opposite of objectivism. Instead of hard-edged visual imagery—garment linings, factory chimneys, or wet laundry hanging out to dry—language poetry highlights the impermeability of both language and subjectivity. Such poetry is so opaque that it is often difficult to discern a physical object or a social condition in it. Yet the language poets looked to the objectivists as their precursors, just as the younger objectivists looked to Reznikoff. The language poets found something useful in the objectivists' simplicity and spontaneity. Charles Bernstein, for example, begins his playful poem, "Of Time and the Line," by contrasting comedian George Burns, who "weaves lines together," with Hennie Youngman, "whose lines are strict- / ly paratactic."[18] It is initially hard to see any lineage (if I may use that term) between Reznikoff's garment worker and Bernstein's musings on the word "line"; and it is hard to see a connection between Reznikoff's precise visual observation and implied social critique and Bernstein's happy-go-lucky involvement with American popular culture. But Burns and Youngman both proffer "lines," as does the garment industry, and as do the poets. Moreover, Burns and Youngman, like Reznikoff, were the children of Jewish immigrants from Eastern Europe. In his essay "Reznikoff's Nearness," Bernstein has observed, "[Reznikoff's] parents (like my own grandparents) came from Russia, sometime after [the pogroms of] 1881."[19] Burns and Youngman integrated their brands of *Yiddishkeit* into American humor, just as Reznikoff and Bernstein interpellated their distinctive discourse into American poetry.

The line of descent becomes even clearer as Bernstein's poem continues. Bernstein writes that his father pushed a "line of ladies' dresses"—not down the street in a pushcart, but rather upstairs in "a fact'ry / office." His mother was more concerned with "her hemline." Bernstein's poem, like Reznikoff's, locates itself in a garment factory. Yet Bernstein's speaker tells us that his father does not work in the "fac'try," but instead owns it. His mother does not sew hems, but cares about changes in hemline fashion. There is both continuity and rupture between Reznikoff and Bernstein. Reznikoff never did succeed financially. On the day he died, he said to his wife, "You know, I never made money but I have done everything that I most wanted to do."[20] His inheritor, Charles Bernstein, alludes instead to familial financial success. But to some degree, he still retains the perspectives of the garment worker and the man with the pushcart. He observes that

> The lines of an imaginary are inscribed on the
> social flesh by the knifepoint of history.[21]

He thus remains faithful to Reznikoff's socially critical position. Moreover, the poets and the cited comedians retain formal contiguities as well. Youngman's "paratactic" style of comedy foreshadows Bernstein's own poetic parataxis. Neither Youngman nor Bernstein try to provide a master narrative of the world. They provide discrete glints of insight, much as Reznikoff did.

Let us now look at some of Reznikoff's other poems. This is not simply a glance at a lost social past, though it is that, too. It is also an encounter with the present—and in two senses. First, Reznikoff lives on in the way I have been suggesting, as an influence on various avant-garde movements, all of which have global associations. The immigrant's son with a clear eye, a verbal gift, and no talent for making money transformed a century of U.S. poetry and exerted an impact on world poetry as well. Second, Reznikoff survives in his own voice. Admittedly, acknowledgment has come sporadically, despite Zukofsky's advocacy in 1931. By midcentury, Reznikoff had "virtually disappeared from the American literary scene," perhaps because of his "unfashionable Yiddish and Jewish background," [22] though he actually spoke Yiddish poorly and did not write in the language at all. His poetry appeared in neither of the comprehensive midcentury anthologies.[23] But in anthologies currently circulating, he receives representation ranging from ample to generous.[24] In Europe and elsewhere, he is increasingly regarded as a modernist master whose work has shaped generations of postmodernist poets. For many readers and writers, Reznikoff provides haunting images of the melancholy of migration as well as an intimation of the complex and sustaining possibilities of diasporic fantasy.

Charles Reznikoff was born in the Jewish ghetto of Brownsville in Brooklyn, New York, in 1894. He was the eldest child of a tailor and a seamstress, individuals with very limited English, who had fled the anti-Jewish massacres in Russia of the 1880s. As Milton Hindus noted, these immigrants "seemed to be escaping from something in the old country rather than seeking something in the new one."[25] Except for a year at the University of Missouri School of Journalism and a later sojourn in Los Angeles as an editorial assistant to his friend Albert Lewin at Paramount Studios, Reznikoff lived all his life in New York City, dying there in 1976. He wrote luminous poems detailing the lives of the underprivileged, immigrants, and the working poor. The poems pay passionate attention to such people. They unerringly locate the transformative moments of perception and grace embedded in even the most difficult lives. They testify to the power of poetic language to preserve the memory and confirm the value of such lives. The poems insist that we *see* every worker, every marginalized or previously unrepresentable subject. Reznikoff said of his poems, "I believe in writing about the object itself, and I let the reader, or listener, draw his own conclusions."[26] He sought to inscribe "the pithy, the necessary, the clear, and plain."[27] All his early New York poems, growing out of daily long walks through the city, present fragments of working-class life observed on the streets, in public places, in factories, and in tenement buildings. The poems evoke "the thicks and thins of an urban 'text'" written by the city's denizens as they go about their daily lives.[28]

Reznikoff was a lonely man in almost every sense. His novel, *The Manner Music*, describes its autobiographical protagonist as being "wrapped up in his thoughts,"[29] and his poems recurrently depict their speaker as being "apart and alone" (*Poems* II:27). Reznikoff loved to read, to walk, and to write. As his letters reveal, he was not on particularly intimate terms with his best friend, Albert Lewin, or even his own wife, Marie Syrkin.[30] In her frank memoir of their marriage, Syrkin recalls him as "a solitary figure" and ruefully observes of their very best time together, "We got along almost happily."[31] He had no children and wanted none. Detached at the workplace, he quit or was fired from every job he held. He never traveled out of the United States, even to accompany his wife. Nor was he particularly interested in other poets. He once commented, "When I consider what all magazines publish, I feel it no honor to appear in them" (*Letters* 22), a revealing dismissal of all the other poets of his time. As a Jew who did not assimilate in the manner of Gertrude Stein or Nathanael West, Reznikoff was rejected by the mainstream and avant-garde journals and presses of his time. He published regularly only in the intellectual Jewish monthly, *the Menorah Journal*. In the early years and even toward the end of his career, his poems appeared in self-published books. After the triumph of being discovered by Zukofsky in 1928 and being honored in the "Objectivists" issue of *Poetry* in 1931, he did become friendly with Zukofsky, Oppen, and Rakosi. But even those relationships seem thin and remote. Reznikoff lived within himself and through his eyes and ears. He liked walking up and down the city streets, in a kind of working-class *flânerie* or "wandering compulsion,"[32] witnessing and absorbing. He was, as Eliot Weinberger remarked, "the perfect passerby."[33]

Yet Reznikoff's artistry did not derive entirely from his experience as a lone nomad moving through urban space. A well-read and cultured man, he also incorporated the numerous transnational artistic and intellectual projects circulating around him. He revered the high modernist ethos of T. S. Eliot and Pound, and he felt "very much influenced by Pound."[34] He must have felt pleased when Pound sent word through Zukofsky that he liked

Reznikoff's poetry,[35] and he was elated on another occasion to attend a lecture by Eliot (*Letters* 195). Typical of Reznikoff, however, he made no effort to correspond with Pound or to speak with Eliot after the lecture. Reflecting the conventional avant-garde judgment of his era, Reznikoff observed, "Other than Pound, I know no one except T. S. Eliot who is genuine," though he added that there was still "much to be done," presumably by a poet such as himself (*Letters* 201). This comment is discouraging, because it shows Reznikoff writing off the other poets who might have supported or taught him, poets with immigrant backgrounds or transnational interests similar to his own, such as Sadakichi Hartmann, Gertrude Stein, Amy Lowell, Yone Noguchi, Mina Loy, William Carlos Williams, H. D., Claude McKay, Langston Hughes, and Countee Cullen. Nevertheless, Reznikoff read many of those poets in the pages of *Poetry, Dial, Pagany, Contact*, and *The New Freeman*, even if he could not bring himself to speak favorably of them. Unable to get his own poetry accepted with any regularity by the avant-garde poetry journals, he must have felt the sting of neglect and envy, which prevented him from acknowledging any but the two recognized masters of the era, Pound and Eliot.

Yet all these poets contributed, in one way or another, to Reznikoff's growing interest in African, Asian, and Native American cultures. He showed a particular fascination with East Asian and Native American arts, attending exhibits and performances of such work with great enthusiasm (*Letters* 43, 83, 101, 105, 109, 208). His bookshelves "were crowded with Haikus and Chinese poets."[36] He sought to import something of what he read and saw into his own writing. He identified his own poetic practice with that of the Sung Dynasty poet, Wei T'ai, who remarked, "Poetry presents the thing in order to convey the feeling. It should be precise about the thing and reticent about the feeling."[37] Reznikoff felt that free verse "in its essence, a lot of it is what the Chinese did."[38] He recognized that "condensation," of the sort observable in East Asian and Native American texts, was "right up [his] alley" (*Letters* 298). He attempted to center his own poetry, above all, on "the seeing eye, 'the haiku spirit'" (*Letters* 185).

Reznikoff's poetry both reflected and swerved from the East Asian, Native American, and modernist texts then being disseminated. In this deterritorialized moment of cultural reorganization, the new poetry emphasized verbal economy, the sensuous perception of natural objects, and an inward response. We can see this set of qualities at work, for example, in the following Chippewa song, which was translated into English by ethnomusicologist Frances Densmore and published in 1910:

> As my eyes search the prairie
> I feel the summer in the spring.[39]

Such songs pay close attention to sense imagery, landscape, and the changing seasons. We detect an analogous poetic at work in the opening lines of the poem that initiated the imagist movement in 1913, H. D.'s "Hermes of the Ways":

> The hard sand breaks,
> and the grains of it
> are clear as wine.[40]

With those precise visual images surprisingly juxtaposing sand and wine, imagism was born. We observe a similar kind of poetic renewal, Japanese rather than Greek in tone, in Sadakichi Hartmann's "Haikai" of 1915:

> White petals afloat
> On a winding woodland stream—
> What else is life's dream![41]

Even Pound's two-line, haiku-like "In a Station of the Metro" of 1913, which evokes the urban milieu in its title and first line, returns to a more traditional image of nature in the second line:

> Petals on a wet, black bough.[42]

Influenced by Ernest Fenellosa's study of Chinese poetry as well as the experiments of H. D. and perhaps Hartmann, Pound advocated "direct treatment of the 'thing,'" using "no word that does not contribute to the presentation," and a rhythm "in the sequence of the musical phrase, not in sequence of a metronome."[43]

In a similar spirit, Reznikoff declared himself interested in "emotional objects only" (*Letters* 37), and he, too, sought the virtues of verbal concentration and musical rhythm. But his poems tended to have "things" rather than a single "thing" in them; he wrote, "My own belief is to name and to name and to name."[44] And his subjects were metropolitan, social, dynamic, and working class—not the isolated natural objects found in other modernist poems. For example, Reznikoff evokes the end of the work day in this untitled poem, first published in 1918:

> The shopgirls leave their work
> quietly.
> Machines are still, tables and chairs
> darken.
> The silent rounds of mice and roaches begin. (Poems I:15)

The poem evokes the low-paying, labor-intensive, vermin-infested world of garment and millinery-piece work, a sweatshop staffed largely by immigrant women and their daughters. Although condensed and sequenced in musical phrases (note the emphasis on "quietly" and "darken" and the deemphasis of "begin"), the poem does not immediately provide a single image as precise as H. D.'s clear grains of sand or Pound's broken petals.

The sensory imagery is deferred and oblique, initially dependent on a series of understated contrasts. The poem notes the hush of the departing shopgirls (who are otherwise unmarked in terms of appearance, age, or national origin), the implied clatter and activity of the sewing machines before they become "still," and the implied brightness of the workplace before it is darkened by nightfall and quitting time. Finally, the first really striking image of the poem appears: mice and roaches. It is as if the night shift has begun, the female workers replaced by vermin whose monotonous rounds mimic and mock the workers' repetitive, voiceless labor. This is a poem of sensory absence: departing bodies, muteness rather than speech, and a focus on common vermin rather than a stable, beautiful object (a grain of sand or a petal). Reznikoff's poem does not seek in any way to invoke or manufacture a concept of "Americanness." Nor does it protest in any stereotypical way. Its skepticism toward capitalism and the standard national narratives, however, is implicit and powerful. It twists its global influences—transmitted through translations, exhibits, and performances and through modernist imitations—into something new. The son of immigrants has invented an imagism of factories, urban spaces, and immigrant life.

Another poem from 1919 suggests the interior lives of female workers as follows:

> In the shop, she, her mother, and grandmother,
> thinking at times of women at windows in still streets,
> or women reading, a glow on resting hands. (Poems I:22)

Here we see the triangular unity of the young woman, her mother, and her grandmother, all of them thinking the same thought. Their lack of upward social mobility is painfully indicated by the fact that all three generations perform exactly the same manual labor. The three women find a moment of tranquility by imagining a very different kind of woman, looking out the window or quietly reading—a woman finding sustenance in her own intellectual, emotional, and spiritual life, a woman with time to spend nourishing her inner self. The three women are conjuring an image of what they themselves precisely are not, what circumstances do not allow them to be, yet what they could be. And here is yet another worker poem from 1919:

> The girls outshout the machines
> and she strains for their words, blushing.
> Soon she, too, will speak
> their speech glibly. (Poems I:29)

In this poem, a shy, young initiate feels out of place and self-conscious in the noisy factory. She can barely make out the words of her seasoned co-workers as they "outshout" the clattering machines. The poem foresees, however, that she, too, will soon lose her youthful timidity and begin shouting casually, a transformation telegraphed in the lines' end words, "blushing," "speak," and "glibly." We encounter in all these poems the empathic realism that informs so much of Reznikoff's work.

Even when Reznikoff does evoke a natural scene, it is with a distinct difference. Here, for example, is a two-liner from 1920:

> They have built red factories along Lake Michigan,
> and the purple refuse coils like congers in the green depths. (Poems I:29)

With its scintillating color contrasts of red, purple, and green, this poem shares the visual intensity of imagist poems by Hartmann, Noguchi, Williams, Pound, and H. D. The final simile, too—"like congers in the green depths"—evokes an animal prized in Japanese culture and art, the eel, and represents it in what Reznikoff would call "the haiku spirit" (*Letters* 185). Yet this poem is not simply an example of imagism with a haiku influence; it is also industrial imagism, environmentalist imagism, and protest imagism. "They"—the puissant corporate forces made pronominally distinct from "us"—have constructed brick factories on Lake Michigan, disrupting the natural scene and the coherence of the landscape. The industrial wastes may resemble eels, but the simile only underscores that they are in fact unnatural. The waste products pollute the lake, just as the factories abolish the wilderness—ethical contrasts communicated through the violent juxtaposition of dissimilar color adjectives (red, purple, green) and nouns (lake, factories, refuse, congers).

In all these poems, Reznikoff brings an imagist aesthetic, influenced by Asian and Native American sources, into an immigrant Jewish poetic tradition strong on social commentary. Between the end of the Civil War and the beginning of World War I, about two million Jews immigrated to the United States, most fleeing pogroms in Russia and Eastern Europe.[45] These newcomers represented 15 percent of European Jewry and nearly 8 percent of all the immigrants to the United States. These men, women, and children made their way in the new land by working in factories and shops or as peddlers. One of my own grandfathers, for example, worked with sheet metal for Ford, possibly in the very factory Reznikoff's Lake Michigan poem describes. In 1890, no less than 60 percent of all Jews working in New York City labored in the garment industry.[46]

Many Jewish poets besides Reznikoff wrote poems about these workers and their conditions. For example, Morris Rosenfeld's "Memorial to Triangle Fire Victims," composed in Yiddish, laments the 1911 Triangle Shirtwaist Company fire in New York, in which 146 Jewish and Italian female workers suffocated from smoke inhalation, burned alive, or jumped to their deaths. In Leon Stein's translation, one passage reads,

> Only hell's fire engulfs these slave stalls
> And Mammon devours our sons and daughters.
> Wrapt in scarlet flames, they drop to death from his maw
> And death receives them all.[47]

Reznikoff's poetry differs from this tradition of Jewish social verse in its adoption of modernist attributes. As Reznikoff once wrote, echoing Paul Verlaine, "We will wring the neck of rhetoric" (*Letters* 186)—even if, in this case, the rhetoric is that of his fellow Jewish poets. Yet within American Yiddish poetry itself, modernist strictures were beginning to be felt, as in the *In Zich* manifesto of 1920, which proposed that Yiddish poetry present life "as it actually is, with precision."[48]

Although Reznikoff spoke of himself as apolitical in his later years, his poems always brim with a passion for social justice, as do many of the texts of his Yiddish-writing peers. He allied himself with progressive elements in Jewish culture and, as time went on, with Judaism as a spiritual "discipline" if not as an organized religion.[49] In several letters in 1929, he mused, "We may look to the rabbis to be at most guardians, but not creators," and wrote, "The land that we Jews hold in common—free of any mandatory power—is ideas expressed in words" (*Letters* 67, 69). For Reznikoff (as for Wallace Stevens), poets were to assume rabbinical functions, guiding readers toward a better world through words. Even more radically, he looked forward to a condition that has been termed "diasporic consciousness" or "diasporism,"[50] a postcolonial sense that nomadic contingency is a positive resource and that language itself is the ultimate homeland. Thus, Reznikoff put Jewish social thought into conversation with modernist aesthetic values, generating an innovative poetics that would inspire, as we have seen, the future of poetry.

Reznikoff wrote many poems about immigrants from places such as Germany, Italy, Spain, Greece, China, and Puerto Rico, and many poems about African Americans. But he also wrote frequently about Jews, particularly immigrants and the children of immigrants. These poems typically encapsulate the lives of individuals, their hopes and failures, in a few telling lines:

In a month they would be married.
He sang a song to himself in which her name was the only word.
His mother was waiting up for him. She said, "I was told today that her mother died
 an epileptic,
and her brother is an idiot in a home somewhere. Why didn't she tell you?"
He thought of hugging her narrow shoulders, comforting her;
of noting their children's quirks and screeches fearfully—
how the moonlight had been glittering in her eyes. (Poems I:57)

Here we see three people's lives being changed and probably ruined in a single moment. Focus never veers from what is actually there to be described: the young man's song, his mother's words, his subsequent thoughts. The moment, evoked with the poet's characteristic "restraint and understatement,"[51] functions as a synecdoche for the characters' complex interrelationships. And then even the moment is further reduced to a single verb tense; the drama of three lives is ultimately concentrated into something as apparently simple and innocent as a past perfect copula, "had been."

Reznikoff also zeroes in on the experience of anti-Semitism, which he observed all around him and had experienced personally at the age of twelve, when he moved with his family to a Brooklyn neighborhood in which they were "the only Jews for blocks" (*Poems* II:153). Reznikoff evokes such an experience in this untitled poem of 1921:

It had long been dark, though still an hour before supper-time.
The boy stood at the window behind the curtain.
The street under the black sky was bluish white with snow.
Across the street, where the lot sloped to the pavement,
boys and girls were going down on sleds.
The boys were after him because he was a Jew.
At last his father and mother slept. He got up and dressed.
In the hall he took his sled and went out on tiptoe.
No one was in the street. The slide was worn smooth and slippery—just right.
He laid himself on the sled and shot away. He went down only twice.
He stood knee-deep in snow:
no one was in the street, the windows were darkened;
those near the street-lamps were ashine, but the rooms inside were dark;
on the street were long shadows of clods of snow.
He took his sled and went back into the house. (Poems I:45–46)

The Jewish boy of this poem is relegated to the margins by his anti-Jewish neighbors. He must play at night, and he can be a happy boy only at night. Ethnic and religious prejudice isolate him from others—not simply from the neighborhood children and their parents but also from his own parents, from whom he is distanced by his secret life. Stephen Fredman comments that through understatement and narrative jumping, the poem conveys "a range of compelling emotions: loneliness, furtiveness, fear, desire, and exhilaration. In the social landscape portrayed by the poem, 'it had long been dark, though still an hour before suppertime,' for the wintry darkness of social exclusion has stained the entire day."[52] The darkened windows of the neighboring houses suggest that "for the Jewish boy, the mentality of anti-Semitism is opaque; he cannot penetrate the consciousness that sees him as Other."[53] Fredman also sees the poem as an allegory of Reznikoff's isolation within the poetic community.[54] Feeling that "the boys were after him because he was a Jew," Reznikoff wrote poetry in the shadows, able to publish only in *the Menorah Journal.*

Beyond evoking his own experience as a Jewish boy and perhaps as a Jewish poet, this poem participates in patterns of awareness common in the poetry of diasporic minorities. As Ranen Omer-Sherman has stated, "Reznikoff's poetry responds to Jewish traditions that strain against coercive narratives of nationalism. He drew from these traditions in ways that helped illuminate other marginal identities."[55] For example, consider in this context an understated poem by an anonymous Japanese immigrant to the United States in the early decades of the twentieth century:

> Just for a while
> Meeting up with a person
> Who was anti-Japanese,
> I scraped against a spirit
> Dissonant with mine.[56]

Or ponder the following poem written by an anonymous migrant from India in about 1920:

> Some push us around, some curse us.
> Where is your splendor and prestige today?
> The whole world calls us black thieves,
> The whole world calls us "coolie."
> Why doesn't our flag fly anywhere?
> Why do we feel low and humiliated?
> Why is there no respect for us in the whole world?[57]

One especially illuminating detail in this latter poem is the portability of the derogatory comment. This South Asian poet complains that whites call his people "black thieves" and "coolie," thus ascribing to them stereotyped identifications as African Americans and Chinese. Each marginalized group becomes, in the white supremacist view, indistinct from the others and therefore a potential metonym for the others. In an obverse fashion, the Jewish boy in Reznikoff's poem symbolically reaches out to other marginalized identities. Pushed around and "humiliated," like the Indian American just quoted, he is associated with darkness, blackness, shadows, and night—frequent tropes for African Americans in both black and white discourse. Moreover, he initially hides in his house "behind the curtain," evoking both female and queer identity (as in Section 11 of Walt Whitman's "Song of Myself").

Now consider "Incident," a poem Countee Cullen published in 1925, four years after Reznikoff's poem.[58] In this poem, an African American speaker recalls a childhood visit to Baltimore, during which he encountered racism for the first time. The visiting eight-year-old boy smiles at a white boy of the same age, but the white child, instead of returning the smile, sticks out his tongue and calls the visiting boy "Nigger." Cullen's speaker concludes that he saw the whole of Baltimore from May until December, but "of all the things that happened there / That's all that I remember." The incident becomes a hole that swallows up surrounding memories, a psychic injury that will not heal.

Like Reznikoff's Jewish boy, who is excluded from white citizenship by the threat of violence, Cullen's autobiographical speaker discovers his own exclusion from white citizenship. He passes from a state of heedless innocence, which assumes a universality of rights and privileges, into the traumatizing experience of racial hierarchy. Placing these contemporaneous poems by Jewish American, South Asian American, and African American poets on the same plane allows us to recognize the ways in which all their subjects fall out of the project of white subjectivity, however much some of them might wish to participate in it. Such a comparison also suggests some of the asymmetries governing racialized subjects. Reznikoff's protagonist finds ways around the system that excludes him, whereas no such stratagem can alter the situation of Cullen's African American speaker. Years after his childhood visit to Baltimore, his memory contracts to one painful event—his initiation into bigotry. We can see from such juxtapositions that Reznikoff's poems do more than look forward to future avant-garde projects. They also look sideways, at the many varieties of diasporic poetry. They join with those parallel discourses as alternative modes of social representation, glimpses into the varieties of both exclusionary experience and deterritorialized subjectivity.

Let me close with one of Reznikoff's last poems, published in 1969 when he was seventy-five years old. It is a collage based on the Talmud—the ancient book of Jewish law and moral instruction. The poem shows Reznikoff finding contemporary illumination within the traditions of Jewish wisdom discourse as follows:

> If the ship you are traveling on is wrecked,
> a plank may come floating your way;
> and on it you may ride wave after wave
> until you walk again on dry land. (Poems II.194)

Reznikoff alludes here to his parents' experience of coerced immigration and to his own ceaseless marginality and mobility. He suggests that his life story—and that of others around him—arose out of catastrophic change ("wrecked") and random happenstance ("may"). Riding waves of those painful, unpredictable experiences, his speaker has the good fortune to arrive on solid ground at last. He models what Jonathan Boyarin calls "*nakhnu-ma*, survival and presence through absence and loss."[59] In one sense, this poem is a parable of immigration, the story of a dangerous crossing between dissimilar cultural spaces. In another sense, the poem figures a creator's struggle for artistic accomplishment. And, in yet another sense, the poem commemorates the dangers and blessings of everyday life.

Notes

1. Charles Reznikoff, *Poems 1918–1975: The Complete Poems of Charles Reznikoff*, ed. Seamus Cooney (Santa Rosa, CA: Black Sparrow Press, 1989), I:29. This volume reprints Reznikoff's previous two volumes of collected poems, *Poems 1918–1936* and *Poems 1937–1975*, retaining separate pagination for each. Further references to Reznikoff's *Poems 1918–1975* will be cited parenthetically in the text as *Poems*, with pagination indicated by the mark I or II. Grateful thanks for helpful comments on earlier versions of this essay are due to Jeremiah B. C. Axelrod, Rise B. Axelrod, Emory Elliott, Grace Hong, Lisa Lowe, and Camille Roman.
2. The 1911 Triangle Shirtwaist Company fire in New York City was one of the worst industrial fires in U.S. history. Eight hundred low-paid workers, mostly Jewish and Italian American women, were trapped in the building, and 146 of them died. The fire, which followed an unsuccessful strike by shirtwaist makers for safer working conditions, had the effect of strengthening the union movement and initiating governmental regulations of safety. See Leon Stein, *The Triangle Fire* (Ithaca, NY: Cornell University Press, 2001; originally published, 1962); and David von Drehle, *Triangle: The Fire that Changed America* (Boston: Atlantic Monthly Press, 2003).

3. Milton Hindus, Introduction to *Charles Reznikoff: Man and Poet* (Orono: National Poetry Foundation, University of Maine, 1984), 23–27.
4. *Poetry: A Magazine of Verse* 37, no. 5 (February 1931).
5. For example, Psalms 104:16: "The trees of the LORD are full of sap; the cedars of Lebanon, which he hath planted." See also Judges 9:15 and Ezekiel 27:5.
6. Louis Zukofsky, "Sincerity and Objectification: With Special Reference to the Work of Charles Reznikoff," *Poetry* 37, no. 5 (February 1931): 273.
7. Ibid., 276.
8. Ibid., 283.
9. Ibid., 285.
10. Nevertheless, forty years later, Reznikoff had virtually disappeared again. In Hugh Kenner's account of the period, *The Pound Era* (Berkeley: University of California Press, 1971), Reznikoff rated only one mention, in a list of poets who had "grasped" Pound's principle (404).
11. Lorine Niedecker, *Collected Works*, ed. Jenny Penberthy (Berkeley: University of California Press, 2002), 90.
12. Allen Ginsberg, "Reznikoff's Poetics," in *Charles Reznikoff: Man and Poet*, ed. Milton Hindus (Orono: National Poetry Foundation, University of Maine, 1984), 141.
13. Allen Ginsberg, *Collected Poems 1947–1997* (New York: HarperCollins, 2006), 134–41, 192–93, 217–35.
14. Frank O'Hara, *Collected Poems*, ed. Donald Allen (1971; repr., Berkeley: University of California Press, 1995), 371, 325.
15. Charles Reznikoff, *Testimony* (New York: Objectivist Press, 1934), revised as *Testimony, Volume 1: The United States (1885–1915) Recitative* (Santa Barbara, CA: Black Sparrow Press, 1978); Charles Reznikoff, *Holocaust* (Los Angeles: Black Sparrow Press, 1975). On the relationship of Reznikoff to Rukeyser and Howe, see Michael Davidson, *Ghostlier Demarcations: Modern Poetry and the Material Word* (Berkeley: University of California Press, 1997), 150–70.
16. Ron Silliman, *The New Sentence* (New York: Roof, 1995), 136.
17. This is perhaps especially true in France and Poland. See *Europe, revue littéraire mensuelle* (Paris), June–July 1977 (objectivist poetry issue); *Literatura Na Swiecie* (Warsaw) December 12, 1982 (Reznikoff issue); Serge Fauchereau, *Lecture de la poésie américaine* (Paris: Somogy, 1998); Genevieve Cohen-Cheminet, "Charles Reznikoff: New World Poetics," in *Strategies of Difference: Case Studies in Poetic Composition*, ed. Pierre Lagayette (Minuit, 1969; repr., Madison, NJ: Fairleigh Dickinson University Press, 1998), 122–45; Piotr Sommer, ed. *Artykuly pochodzenia zagranicznego* (Gdansk, Poland: Marabut, 1996); and Piotr Sommer, *Po stykach* (Gdansk, Poland: slowo/obraz terytoria, 2005).
18. Charles Bernstein, "Of Time and the Line," in *Rough Trades* (Los Angeles: Sun & Moon Press, 1991), 42.
19. Charles Bernstein, "Reznikoff's Nearness," in *My Way: Speeches and Poems* (Chicago: University of Chicago Press, 1999), 147.
20. Marie Syrkin, "Charles: A Memoir," in *Charles Reznikoff: Man and Poet*, ed. Milton Hindus (Orono: National Poetry Foundation, University of Maine, 1984), 65.

21. Bernstein, "Of Time," 42.
22. Hindus, Introduction, 15. Rachel Blau Duplessis and Peter Quartermain, Introduction to *The Objectivist Nexus: Essays in Cultural Poetics* (Tuscaloosa: University of Alabama Press, 1999), 14.
23. F. O. Matthiessen, ed., *The Oxford Book of American Verse* (New York: Oxford University Press, 1950). Albert Gelpi, ed., *The Poet in America: 1650 to the Present* (Lexington, MA: D. C. Heath, 1973).
24. Cary Nelson, ed., *Anthology of Modern American Poetry* (New York: Oxford University Press, 2000), 354–70; *American Poetry: The Twentieth Century, Volume 2, E. E. Cummings to May Swenson* (New York: Library of America, 2000), 42–56; Jahan Ramazani, Richard Ellmann, and Robert O'Clair, eds., *The Norton Anthology of Modern and Contemporary Poetry, Volume 1: Modern Poetry* (New York: W. W. Norton, 2003), 537–45; Steven Gould Axelrod, Camille Roman, and Thomas Travisano, eds., *The New Anthology of American Poetry, Volume 2: Modernisms 1900–1950* (New Brunswick, NJ: Rutgers University Press, 2005), 488–507.
25. Hindus, Introduction, 17.
26. Charles Reznikoff, *By the Well of Living and Seeing: New and Selected Poems, 1918–1973* (Santa Rosa, CA: Black Sparrow Press, 1974), 172.
27. Ibid., 172.
28. Michel de Certeau, *The Practice of Everyday Life*, trans. Steven Rendall (Berkeley: University of California Press, 1984), 93.
29. Charles Reznikoff, *The Manner Music* (Santa Barbara, CA: Black Sparrow Press, 1977), 21.
30. Charles Reznikoff, *Selected Letters 1917–1976*, ed. Milton Hindus (Santa Rose, CA: Black Sparrow Press, 1997), 125–26, 144–45, 211, 227–28, 234–35, 249, 286, 290. Further references will be cited parenthetically as *Letters*.
31. Syrkin, "Charles," 43, 59.
32. John Bowlby, *Loss: Sadness and Depression* (New York: Basic Books, 1980), 343.
33. Eliot Weinberger, "Another Memory of Reznikoff," in *Charles Reznikoff: Man and Poet*, ed. Milton Hindus (Orono: National Poetry Foundation, University of Maine, 1984), 77.
34. Janet Sternburg and Alan Ziegler, "A Conversation with Charles Reznikoff," in *Charles Reznikoff: Man and Poet*, ed. Milton Hindus (Orono: National Poetry Foundation, University of Maine, 1984), 130.
35. Zukofsky, "Sincerity and Objectification," 285.
36. Syrkin, "Charles," 60.
37. L. S. Dembo, "Charles Reznikoff: A Talk," in *Charles Reznikoff: Man and Poet*, ed. Milton Hindus (Orono: National Poetry Foundation, University of Maine, 1984), 97.
38. Reinhold Schiffer, "The Poet in His Milieu," in *Charles Reznikoff: Man and Poet*, ed. Milton Hindus (Orono: National Poetry Foundation, University of Maine, 1984), 116.
39. Axelrod, Roman, and Travisano, eds., *New Anthology, Volume 2*, 11.

40. H. D. [Hilda Doolittle], "Hermes of the Ways," *Complete Poems 1912–1944* (New York: New Directions, 1983), 37.
41. Sadakichi Hartmann, "Haiku 1," *Tanka and Haikai*, in *The New Anthology of American Poetry, Volume 1: Traditions and Revolutions, Beginnings to 1900, ed.* Steven Gould Axelrod, Camille Roman, and Thomas Travisano (New Brunswick, NJ: Rutgers University Press, 2003), 676. Poem originally published, 1916.
42. Ezra Pound, "In a Station of the Metro," in *Personae: Collected Shorter Poems* (New York: New Directions, 1971), 109.
43. Ezra Pound, "A Retrospect," in *Literary Essays of Ezra Pound*, ed. T. S. Eliot (New York: New Directions, 1935), 3. Originally published, 1918.
44. Dembo, "Reznikoff," 98.
45. Arthur Hertzberg, *The Jews in America: Four Centuries of an Uneasy Encounter, A History* (New York: Simon and Schuster, 1989), 152–53.
46. Ronald Takaki, *A Different Mirror: A History of Multicultural America* (Boston: Little, Brown, 1993), 288.
47. Axelrod, Roman, and Travisano, eds., *New Anthology, Volume 2*, 30.
48. Irving Howe and Eliezer Greenberg, eds., *A Treasury of Yiddish Poetry* (New York: Holt, Rinehart and Winston, 1969), 41.
49. Dembo, "Reznikoff," 105.
50. Jonathan Boyarin and Daniel Boyarin, *Powers of Diaspora: Two Essays on the Relevance of Jewish Culture* (Minneapolis: University of Minnesota Press, 2002), 4–5, 26–27; Ranen Omer-Sherman, *Diaspora and Zionism in Jewish American Literature: Lazarus, Syrkin, Reznikoff, Roth* (Hanover, NH: University Press of New England, 2002), 111.
51. Milton Hindus, *Charles Reznikoff: A Critical Essay* (Santa Barbara, CA: Black Sparrow Press, 1977), 19.
52. Stephen Fredman, *A Menorah for Athena: Charles Reznikoff and the Jewish Dilemmas of Objectivist Poetry* (Chicago: University of Chicago Press, 2001), 19.
53. Ibid., 19.
54. Ibid., 20.
55. Omer-Sherman, *Diaspora and Zionism*, 115.
56. Axelrod, Roman, and Travisano, eds., *New Anthology, Volume 2*, 28.
57. Ibid., 543.
58. Countee Cullen, "Incident," in *My Soul's High Song* (New York: Doubleday, 1990), 90.
59. Boyarin and Boyarin, *Powers of Diaspora*, 12.

CHAPTER 7

Veneration and Violence
Pedagogical Forces in Chicana Literature and Visual Art

Tiffany Ana Lopez

The seeds of my ongoing engagements with matters of cultural production and social change are rooted in my growing-up years, experiencing violence and Catholicism in a Mexican American family. My father was the son of Mexican immigrants who had come to the United States to work in agriculture as field laborers and stayed to better their family's future. My mother was the daughter of poor whites who had moved into the heart of the California desert, living the hardscrabble life of those who had migrated west during the dustbowl era. Neither ever spoke in detail about their family histories. Both turned to the church to guide and direct them through their frustrations and struggles. Economic pressures always took center stage and were made to stand in for other tensions that merged together and exploded.

The violence enacted against my siblings and me constituted a passing on of the wounds my parents felt they could never heal from their own personal, familial, and financial burdens. So they took us to Catholic churches and schools. In those spaces, the physical violence at home was further punctuated, the words and images set forth by our teachers and preachers instructing in ways that both supplemented and confused. Though spiritually inspired by stories of the Virgin Mary, I got punished for my questions ("Why do we never see her body?") and set up for a sense of inadequacy as a woman. Her exemplary characteristics of being female—maternal, selfless, sexless, compassionate, overflowing with unconditional love, perpetually gazing downward, holy, and without any demands, questions, or expectations—loomed large as impossibly and inimitably normative. My brother was eventually crippled by the failure of our mother to live up to this image and the ultimate credo to put thy father above all else.[1] I survive by rebelling and relocating myself within the landscape of counterdiscourse forged by Chicana writers and artists: making *familia* from scratch, touching the wound in order to heal, and unraveling women from the ball of yarn.[2]

This chapter works from these juncture points to explore the ways myths and icons inform violence and social change as they circulate from one cultural location to the next. It focuses on the pedagogical force of enduring icons of Chicana literature and visual culture, La Virgen de Guadalupe, La Llorona, and La Malinche—what Alicia Gaspar de Alba describes as "the female trinity of Chicana identification" (Gaspar de Alba 1998, 139)—with an emphasis on their roles in the various intersecting forms of violence performed on the construction of Chicana identity, and the counternarratives produced by Chicana writers and artists that signal a critical discourse designed to celebrate what is most productive about enduring female icons while also grappling with what is violent and traumatic.

Diana Taylor writes, "For Mexicans, Mexican Americans, and Chicanas, the feminine gender is always dual, always liminal, always the mirroring of the defied mother (Malinche) and the Virgin" (Taylor 2003, 90). These icons so consistently and forcefully permeate discussions about Chicanas and social struggle because they are intertwined with the histories of violence that define female identity and culture, from the colonization of land to the subjugation of body.[3] The ongoing case of the hundreds of women that continue to disappear and are murdered in the border town of Ciudad Juarez powerfully illustrates the importance of bringing together in conversation matters of violence and the power of enduring female icons; both historically shape thinking about women and the ways they are, and consequently are not, valued. As Rosa Linda Fregoso emphasizes in her discussion of the making of social identities on the borderlands, "Feminicide in Juarez makes evident the reality of overlapping power relations on gendered and racialized bodies as much as it clarifies the degree to which violence against women has been naturalized as a method of social control."[4]

Myths and icons play a significant role the process of naturalization. If women are principally venerated as mythic figures and icons, it becomes quite easy to discount the vast majority of women existing outside the sanctioned frames of reverence and respect. As imagined subjects, they are tethered to a field of reference that values them in highly limited ways. Women find themselves looking at a mirage, the promise of participatory equality or social capital always in sight but never fully substantiated. It is significant that in the many cases and accounts of the murdered women of Juarez, investigatory questions about the ongoing horrific violence targeted toward women as a group are always countered by accusations by the police and other official spokesmen of the patriarchal social order that the victim was probably somewhere she should not have been, with people she should not have been seeing, doing something she should not have been doing. If they are not virgins, then they are whores; if not mothers at home, then loose women on the streets; if not venerated, then violated.

Fixing women into such narrow and rigid paradigms as the virgin/whore dichotomy has the potential to lead to trauma and violation because of the tensions created about identity performance. To be cast in the role of the virgin is to be set up for moral failure; to be cast as a whore is to be designated for scapegoating at best, and physical attack at worst. La Virgen de Guadalupe, La Malinche, and La Llorona comprise paradigmatic visual icons and narrative subjects in Chicana art and literature because they form such a powerful springboard for critical engagement with issues of identity, politics, and culture.[5] Notably, these icons portray the female as central in making and breaking familial and social formation. Even more significant, they are never positioned as representing a complex or fluid range of life forces.

As Alicia Arrizon argues, "A woman is a grandmother, a mother, or a future wife, each of whom will follow the same path, but she is never a lesbian or a single mother enduring the hardships of society" (Arrizon 1999, 80). In her analysis of patriarchal oppression and its manifestations within Chicano culture, Yolanda Broyles-Gonzalez emphasizes the inability to accept women as occupying varied and infinite roles as "a form of blindness that prevents many from perceiving the vast spectrum of experiences that in reality make up womanhood." The final point of her readings is that "maintenance of male power *needs* a fragmented (i.e., nonthreatening) image of women" (Broyles-Gonzalez 1994, 144). The ability of enduring female myths and icons to so restrict the social imaginary effectively fuels the structures of patriarchy. Chicana art and literature attempt to look inside the working of the machine. Eden Torres best observes, "Our political rhetoric does not always reveal the scars we carry in our hearts heavy with this history, but our literature tells the story" (Torres 2003, 12).

The Virgin Mary is most venerated for being a spiritual mother;[6] a more racially and culturally specific syncretized version of this symbol, La Virgen de Guadalupe, is revered for speaking directly to the disenfranchised.[7] Also an icon of female creation, but one inextricably tied to destruction, La Malinche represents cultural betrayal defined and coded as female, her mouth and vagina marked as sites of shame for the acts of translation and sexual intercourse with the oppressor that are said to have brought about the downfall of her people.[8] Norma Alarcon's landmark essay "Chicana's Feminist Literature: A Re-vision Through Malintzin / or Malintzin Putting Flesh Back on the Object" clarifies the importance of reading such myths as La Malinche, or Malintzin, with focused attention on the culturally specific elements and how they decidedly inform registers of gender and power as follows: "Unlike Eve whose primeval reality is not historically documentable and who supposedly existed in some past edenic time, Malintzin's betrayal of our supposed pre-Columbian paradise is recent and hence almost palpable. This almost within-reach past heightens romantic nostalgia and as a consequence hatred for Malintzin and women becomes as vitriolic as the American Puritans' loathing of witches-women" (2002, 203).[9] The myth of La Llorona portrays women as figures to be feared in its telling a story of the wailing woman (in Spanish, *llorar* means "to cry") who, scorned by her male lover, throws her children into a river. After, she forever wanders the banks in search of their bodies.[10] Chicana mothers have traditionally told this story to their children as a means of control, warning, for example, "Come inside right now, or La Llorona will get you." She is a feminized and racialized version of the archetypal "Boogeyman," however one that is steeped in conflict over the female and her social roles.

As Rebolledo emphasizes in her work on representations of La Malinche and La Llorona, "the image is a negative one, tied up in some vague way with sexuality and the death or loss of children: the negative mother image" (1995, 62–63). While centering on female figures, these myths definitively capture all women within a frame of idealized heteronormative femininity positively or negatively bound to motherhood.[11] While portrayed as mothers, the Virgin Mary and La Virgen de Guadalupe get distinguished as the mothers of sons; their virginal nature also marks an enforced split between spirituality and sexuality. La Malinche and La Llorona ostensibly have daughters. But, notably, these myths position women as punished or tormented for their sexuality, their legacy to their daughters is fraught with shame and mourning. Ana Castillo explains how the good mother/bad mother, virgin/whore dyads offer a portrait that ultimately speaks to the social status of Chicanas generally. She writes, "When Our Mother is seen only as the one-dimensional Mary of modern times, instead of the great dual force of life and death, She is relegated to the same second-class status of most women in the world" (1996, 78).

These stories have great pedagogical force because they are told starting in childhood and they resonate well into adulthood, overtly and covertly outlining the points of demarcation that shape Chicanas' sense of agency and subjectivity, what is possible and accepted in their being and acting in the world. As Diana Taylor so clearly describes, "the social frameworks that enable the practice of memory regulate the conflictive ways in which Mexican, Mexican American, and Chicana women inhabit their sexuality and ethnic belonging. Yet, we cannot transfer memory outside of these frameworks" (Taylor 2003, 100). Spotlighting the legacy of such mythic structures, Cherrie Moraga writes, "There is hardly a Chicana growing up today who does not suffer under Malinche's name, even if she never hears directly of the one-time Aztec princess" (Moraga 2000, 92).

The violation such mythology performs lies in its reinforced containment of any bold attempts by women working to imagine themselves outside the fixed frames of reference. Alarcon cogently explains, "Because the myth of Malintzin pervades not only male thought but ours [Chicanas'] too as it seeps into our own consciousness in the cradle through their eyes as well as our mothers', who are entrusted with the transmission of culture, we may come to believe that indeed our very sexuality condemns us to enslavement. An enslavement which is subsequently manifested in self-hatred. All we see is hatred of women. We must hate her too since love seems only possible through extreme virtue whose definition is at best slippery" (Alarcon 2002, 203). As Chicana feminist writers and critics so often stress in their work, mothers play a pivotal role as transmitters, and hence enforcers, of familial and cultural history, as well as models of gender performance and emotional stability. Given that motherhood is the designated currency of the social capital generated by the foundational icons for Chicana identification, mother-daughter relationships thereby provide a significant launching point for critical engagement. Indeed, Moraga affirms, "It's the daughters who are my audience." She continues, stressing the importance of eventually distinguishing oneself outside the mother-daughter paradigm, "To be free means on some level to cut that painful loyalty when it begins to punish us" (Moraga 1983, vii).

To be taught in any way and at any level a disavowal of the female is, in the end, for women, to be taught a disavowal of the self. Because these female myths and icons teach a profound distancing of the female spirit, they also position the feminized as something negatively marked. In this way, misogyny and homophobia operate in tandem.[12] Exalting La Virgen as the mother of a son places the son, not the mother, in the center of the narrative frame. Moraga powerfully illustrates this in her play *Shadow of a Man*, both in its title (even when no men are present on stage, patriarchy and masculinity inform the relationships between women and the sense of female self) and in a key scene in which the mother chatters on in wonderment about her baby grandson's penis and ignores her eldest daughter who enthusiastically stands before her dangling a set of keys while seeking congratulations on obtaining her first car. The keys, a phallic symbol, contrast with the baby's penis and represent newly acquired female mobility. The mother, Hortensia, exclaims that the male baby's penis is "like a little jewel" and declares, "Mi machito. That's one thing, you know, the men can never take from us. The birth of a son" (Moraga 1994, 61), to which her daughter, Leticia, replies, "Well I don't see you getting so much credit" (Moraga 1994, 61).[13] This moment of the daughter talking back to the mother represents the practice of calling into question loyalties that diminish, marginalize, or, to use Moraga's wording, punish.

Yvonne Yarbro-Bejarano's reading of Moraga's work as follows focuses on the way she deconstructs phallocentric discourse as a means to excavate patriarchal violence: "Moraga has stated that she is merely calling power by its name. The 'dick' in her writing does not represent biological superiority but the symbol of masculine power; for women to write their female bodies as sites of power it is necessary to break down the violence perpetrated in the name of the phallus" (Yarbro-Bejarano 2001, 56). Expanding an interrogation of violence includes the analysis of cultural myths that so destructively shape the female sense of self. As phallic signifiers, they provide the linguistic glue that transverses the web of patriarchal authority and violence.

In *Shadow of a Man*, Hortensia performs the role of being first and foremost a mother of sons, which above all defines her sense of achievement as a mother. ("That's something they can never take away from us.") Though Hortensia's son Rigo never appears on stage, he occupies a substantial amount of narrative space in the play as the subject of her conversation. An infant male, Rigo's son, is figuratively and literally placed in the spotlight. It is both the subject of men and the male subject that cast a shadow on this play about the survival of women in patriarchal familial culture. When her mother reiterates such patriarchal and antifemale rhetoric as "If God had wanted you to be a man, he would have given you something between your legs" (Moraga 1994, 76–77), Leticia's declaration "I have something between my legs" (Moraga 1994, 77) sets forth a positive woman-centered counter-discourse that takes women out of the shadows by affirming female identity and celebrating female sexuality, while also insisting on the centrality of mother-daughter relationships historically eclipsed by the veneration of women as mothers of sons. However, by portraying the female characters in this play across multiple generations, including the mother, aunt, daughters, and male grandson, Moraga envisions a potential new generation that includes resistant feminist readers and boys and men as feminists in progress.[14] In her work, recovery from violence within family and nation depends on this.

In her discussion of *Shadow of a Man*, Yarbro-Bejarano reads Leticia's feminist consciousness as centered in her engagement with matters of race and class that charge the Chicano movement era politics that set the play and thus motivate her character.[15] In the pivotal scene alluded to earlier, in which Hortensia confronts Leticia for staying out late and running around on the streets "free like a man" (Moraga 1994, 76), Leticia divulges the intentional loss of her virginity and declares having done so as a feminist act. She says, "I was tired of carrying it around, that weight of being a woman with a prize. I wanted for it to be worthless. . . . Not for me to be worthless, but to know that my worth had nothing to do with it" (Moraga 1994, 78).

The scene also represents one of the many ways in which Moraga translates her focus on the legacy of La Malinche in her essay and memoir into her theater work. Leticia's verbal exchanges with her mother challenge the residue of the Malinche narrative. Leticia refuses to be stigmatized for what she says or does. She does not apologize for her radical politics or her sexual pleasure. Her mouth is not a site of shame, and neither is her vagina. Notably, Moraga employs the tradition of Chicano theater to revise female myth and illustrate the movement of her feminist pedagogy from theory into practice. In doing so, her project also expands the frame of imagining women within Chicano nationalism, to generate the possibilities of what she terms a Queer Aztlan, "a Chicano homeland that could embrace *all* of its people" (Moraga 1993, 147). Importantly, Moraga does not reject nationalism, just as she does not reject the mother, just as Chicanas do not cast aside the iconography of La Virgen de Guadalupe and the mythology of La Malinche. She understands the powerful historic role each has in shaping the Chicana and Chicano political imaginary and seeks to revise it anew.

As much as Moraga in her plays focuses on daughters, so, too, does she explore the figures of mothers. In her memoir, *Loving in the War Years/lo que nunca paso por sus labios*, rather than blame women for participating in and perpetuating patriarchal structures, Moraga looks at the gains offered to women, and how their investments and benefits fuel cultural dynamics that ultimately reveal themselves as destructive to women both individually and collectively. Moraga works from candid autobiographical examples, such as her own waiting on the men in her household out of love and respect for her mother's wishes. Recalling a phone conversation in which her mother abruptly ends talking with her daughter in order to take a call from her son, Moraga pointedly, albeit painfully, unfolds her theorizations as follows:

> Ask, for example, any Chicana mother about her children and she is quick to tell you she loves them all the same, but she doesn't. *The boys are different.* Sometimes I sense that she feels this way because she wants to believe that through her mothering, she can develop the kind of man she would have liked to have married, or even have been. That through her son she can get a small taste of male privilege, since without race or class privilege that's all there is to

> be had. The daughter can never offer the mother such hope, straddled by the same forces that confine the mother. As a result, the daughter must constantly earn the mother's love, prove her fidelity to her. The son—he gets her love for free. (Moraga 1983, 102)

This passage provides a launching point that Moraga translates in her writing across genres, as exemplified in the mother-daughter scenes from *Shadow of a Man* discussed earlier in this chapter.[16] As represented in her critical refiguring of Chicano nationalism, she consistently explores women's issues as absolutely central to matters of culture and community, and she affirms her employment of the personal as critically necessary: "Without indulging our fears, our fantasies, our fury, how then are we to land upon the truth?" (Moraga 1983, vii).[17] As her work so effectively illustrates, in writing about ourselves, we must write about our mothers. We are our *virgencitas*, ourselves.[18]

One of Moraga's original collaborators, Gloria Anzaldua, in *Borderlands/ La Frontera*,[19] observes the ways the Virgin image directs the Chicana to sever the elements of her identity into competing parts as follows: "The Catholic and Protestant religions encourage fear and distrust of life and of the body; they encourage a split between the body and the spirit and totally ignore the soul; they encourage us to kill off parts of ourselves. We are taught that the body is an ignorant animal; intelligence dwells only in the head" (Anzaldua 1987, 37). Moraga addresses this fragmentation in *Heroes and Saints* through her portrait of Cerezita, the play's leading female protagonist, born with severe birth defects from her mother's exposure to pesticide poisoning while working the fields during her pregnancy. Cerezita is missing all her limbs, her head distinct from a fully articulated body. While Moraga makes explicit that with this character she is directly referencing Luis Valdez's *The Shrunken Head of Pancho Villa*, she is also clearly drawing from nationalist visual rhetoric of the Virgen de Guadalupe.[20] Dolores views Cerezita as "como un santo" (like a saint) because of her physical disability. When she catches Cerezita reading a book on human anatomy, Dolores admonishes, "The greatest sins are committed in the mind" (Moraga 1994, 37). With these lines of dialogue, Moraga spotlights the mother's absorption of the polarizing logic of the virgin/whore paradigm.

In the spirit of El Movimiento (The Chicano Movement), Moraga uses Virgen iconography to position Cerezita as a political leader who fuels the spirit of Chicano movement necessarily revised to include women and other culturally dispossessed. Border artist Guillermo Gomez-Pena captures the ways this kind of visual grammar drawn from the vocabulary of nationalism merges the spiritual with the political as follows: "In the Chicano Movement, la Virgen was no longer the contemplative mestiza Mother of all Mexicans, but a warrior goddess who blessed the cultural and political weapons of activists and artists" (Gomez-Pena 1996, 180).

Notably, Cerezita delivers her final monologue dressed in the full regalia of the la Virgen to inspire the community in their mission to burn down the fields that are the sources of the pesticide poisoning fatally infecting the community, from its drinking water to the amniotic waters of women's wombs. Cerezita declares, "Put your hand inside my wound. Inside the valley of my wound there is a people. A miracle people. In this pueblo where the valley people lie, the river runs red with blood; but they are not afraid because they are used to the color red. . . . You are the miracle people. . . . And you will be free. Free to name this land *Madre*. Madre Tierra. Madre Sangrada. Madre . . . Libertad. The radiant red mother . . . rising" (Moraga 1994, 148). The play's closing lines emphasize the possibilities of liberation facilitated by Cerezita as both a spiritual icon and political leader. Cerezita's monologue references the female body as a wound, an image that connects her with her homeland. In *Borderlands/La Frontera*, Anzaldua describes the border as an open wound, "una herida abierta where the Third World grates against the first and bleeds" (Anzaldua 1987, 3). In this visual terrain, Cerezita symbolizes the land as the subject of colonial, economic, and environmental violence, in a near direct translation of the following point expressed elsewhere by Moraga in her essay as follows: "If women's bodies and those of men and women who transgress their gender roles have been historically regarded as territories to be conquered, they are also territories to be liberated. Feminism has taught us this" (Moraga 1993, 150).

Moraga's play stands in dialogue with other Chicana artists, writers, and critics engaged with representations of La Virgen de Guadalupe who position her as central in the lives of Chicanas and recognize her spiritual force yet also grapple with the complicated and contradictory expectations and inhabited realities set forth by her image. The Virgen de Guadalupe is presented as an icon of inspiration in ways designed to simultaneously venerate and generate, celebrating while also creating a discourse critical of the oppressive ideology that historically accompanies her image. For example, Cerezita's speech declares her own individual liberation from several intersecting forms of oppression: sexual, spiritual, physical, and generational. It is only by wearing the costume of the Virgin that Cerezita is allowed by her mother Dolores to physically leave the house. Dolores is filled with fear about how others will treat her daughter, exacerbated by a certain amount of shame she carries from believing that she did something to bring about Cerezita's disabilities. This belief is captured in her confession of having said to Cerezita's father, "Half a man makes half a baby" (Moraga 1994, 103). And it is only in the figuration of La Virgen that Dolores venerates her daughter as a community leader. Dolores personally accompanies Cerezita to the fields where Cerezita makes her final speech.

As mother and daughter, Dolores and Cerezita represent different generational positions with respect to thinking about identity, culture, and politics. Importantly, it is the icon of La Virgen that unites them in struggle. However, there is no need for conformity around her image. The people gathered together at the end of the play represent a community defined through difference, as so dramatically suggested by Cerezita. There are children, elderly, priests, queers, and a newscaster, Ana Perez, who at the beginning of the play represents the classic Malinche/sellout figure famously portrayed in *Los Vendidos*, Valdez's nationalist one-act prop play (termed "acto")[21]. As she has done with other enduring myths, Moraga has similarly revised this character into someone moved to join the social struggle of those whose stories she has witnessed. In this play that so clearly references the Chicano movement, one finds Moraga's vision for a Queer Aztlan in full practice.

Moraga's plays illustrate the centrality of women's issues to community building and the necessity for feminist consciousness—they demonstrate that we are not yet postfeminism, postracism, or post–any other term used to capture social struggle. To paraphrase Moraga, there is a danger in ranking oppressions, as they are mutually informative and cannot be parceled out. Placed in the broader context of Chicana discourse, her work also powerfully speaks the steady evolution of Chicana feminist consciousness. Since its formative years, Chicana feminism has focused on enduring female icons and myths as sources for grappling with matters of representation and the construction of Chicana identity. In her short essay "Guadalupe the Sex Goddess," Cisneros asserts, "My Virgen de Guadalupe is not the mother of God. She is God. She is a face for a god without a face, an indigena for a god without ethnicity, a female deity for a god who is genderless, but I also understand that for her to approach me, for me to finally open the door and accept her, she had to be a woman like me" (Cisneros 1996, 50).

Anna Nieto Gomez, one of the foundational voices of the Chicana feminist movement, articulates the ways Virgin mythology delimits Chicana identity and social advancement as follows:

> Marianismo, the veneration of the Virgin Mary, became the model of how to make oppression a religious obligation. . . . The veneration of the Virgin Mary defined the woman's identity as a virgin, as a saintly mother, as a wife-sex object, as a martyr. [It] has had a tremendous impact in fostering beliefs of negative existence and self-denial. . . . Church teachings have directed women to identify with the emotional suffering of the pure, passive bystander: the Virgin Mary. It is believed that through Her, the Chicana experiences a vicarious

> martyrdom in order to accept and prepare herself for her own oppressive reality (Nieto Gomez 1997, 48–49).

In the following quote, Alicia Arrizon further insists that an analysis of marianismo and machismo are mutually dependent: "These interrelated concepts define powerful cultural values—ones that strengthen the subordination of the female subject in Chicano culture" (Arrizon 1999, 80). Getting directly to the point concerning the onerous burden placed on Chicanas, Sandra Cisneros charges, "She was damn dangerous, an ideal so lofty and unrealistic it was laughable. Did boys have to aspire to be Jesus?" (1996, 48). Exploring the very real ways such icons threaten Chicanas' emotional empowerment and social advancement, in an open letter to her mother, Claudia Colindres asserts, "Putting myself first, is awfully hard, because in my brain I have it engrained that women should be like the Virgin Mary. Being docile like Mary is impossible when you have to compete for grades" (1993, 76–77). Cisneros frankly calls attention to the unacknowledged forms of violence associated with her image, the emotional burdens and physical dangers that directly stem from the impossibility of her image, writing, "What a culture of denial. Don't get pregnant! But no one tells you how not to. This is why I was so angry for so many years every time I saw la Virgen de Guadalupe, my culture's role model for brown women like me" (Cisneros 1996, 48).

In her play *Giving Up the Ghost*, Moraga illustrates the potentially grave dangers for young Chicanas taught to obey male elders without question and to be like the Virgin Mary in their practiced silence and downward glance. She also works to spotlight the destructive mythology of La Malinche by literalizing the story to illustrate how thinking about women as "the fucked one" impacts the lived reality of Chicanas. The girl protagonist, Corky, is raped by a man who enters her school under the guise of being a custodian. He calls her over to assist him and she does so "outta respect for my primo Enrique" (Moraga 1994, 26). Moraga stresses that the events take place in a classroom at a Catholic school (a space tied to colonization and patriarchy) and that the rapist declares "Soy tu papa" (I am your father) to which she recalls, "'n this gives me permission to go 'head and to not hafta fight" (Moraga 1994, 28). With these details, Moraga directs attention to the dangerous and polarizing logic of patriarchy: male protectors are simultaneously male violators and women are supposed to resign themselves to both as part of accepting patriarchal authority in total. Corky ends her retelling of the rape by crying out, "He made me a hole!" (Moraga 1994, 29), after which she disappears for the remainder of the play.

On one hand, this can be read as the result of this work being a memory play. Corky is the child persona of the adult protagonist Marisa. After surfacing this memory, Moraga leaves Marisa to grapple with the ways violence and trauma impact her sense of self, relationships, and politics. On the other hand, in this three-character play, Moraga offers a powerful visual statement in having at this very point one third of the cast disappear from the stage, which in the tradition of politicized Chicano theater that Moraga locates herself, stands in for the larger stages of Chicana/Chicano political and social struggle. The Malinche myth is shown to impact not just personal foundations but also the very groundwork of community building and social transformation.

Barbara Carrasco created her famous lithograph image *Pregnant Woman in a Ball of Yarn* (1978)[22] as a student in her early twenties in response to her brother's declaration that his young pregnant wife needed to give up her aspirations to be a college student in order to fulfill her moral obligations to motherhood. Carrasco spent the evening in furious contemplation, resulting in her graphic portrait of a naked, pregnant woman completely ensnared within a ball of yarn, her head forced to the side, her eyes and mouth violently covered in thick strands that seem to grow from her hair, her arms and legs pulled back and firmly bound, and with only her swollen breasts and belly exposed. A thick string of yarn winds down from her body like an umbilical cord leashing her to an intricately knitted baby booty, the knitting needle separate and resting apart to the right of the image. An object marking acts of creation and destruction born from the hands of women, the knitting needle simultaneously represents a tool for celebrated traditional craft and a desperate abortion instrument. Like images of the Virgen, her eyes are cast aside, her head and body distinctly separated within the ball of yarn. Carrasco's image visually literalizes the fixing of women within a world defined exclusively around motherhood.

Moraga's images of crucified dead children in *Heroes and Saints* resonate with Carrasco's lithograph. In part, Cerezita is driven by the children in her community who dig up the graves of their tiny peers, some only months old, who have died in their farming town turned cancer cluster. The small skeletal remains are then crucified and posted where others can see them. But it is not the display of the crucified dead children that is supposed to shock and outrage; rather, it is the way they have been so callously treated and imagined within the cultural economy of big business and its spin doctors that is meant to cause uproar.

Moraga portrays these as senseless acts of violence that she then employs to move audiences into a position of reading violence critically and, ultimately, participating in social change. The newscaster Ana Perez stands in for this ideal of the "critical witness," a term I use to describe those who are so moved by a work that they feel compelled to acknowledge their participation in the dynamics informing the crisis portrayed in the work, becoming actively involved in forging a path for changing those dynamics. Carrasco's *Pregnant Woman in a Ball of Yarn* also connects to the image of Cerezita in her wheelchair, trapped by her mother's expectations for her performance as daughter, woman, and disabled person (Dolores asserts, "The greatest sins are in the mind"). Carrasco's and Moraga's images resignify the Virgen icon and redefine motherhood. Together, Carrasco and Moraga represent Chicanas' vision for the ways women might serve as public mothers by employing the characteristics associated with the maternal—nurturing, compassion, selfless giving—toward community leadership.

As illustrated by the many genres that inform my readings in this chapter, Chicanas employ a wide range of intersecting epistemologies to arrive at a complex point of understanding about the foundational myths and icons that so strongly shape their identity.[23] They also illustrate the centrality of violence in these explorations. Because such personal images (particularly of the maternal) are used to charge and enforce the patriarchal structures of family, community, and nation, an analysis of the structuring of power necessitates speaking of the personal; and because the structuring of power is channeled through violence, violence must also be critically read within these contexts.

The citational footprints of this essay illustrate the absolute significance of the "female trinity" of La Virgen de Guadalupe, La Malinche, and La Llorona in the wide-ranging discussion about Chicana identity formation and attendant issues of gender, sexuality, race, and class that circulate on the dual registers of inter- and intracultural oppression. Myths and icons have been made into the very vehicles of social change. As Rebolledo states, "Mythology often functions as a collective symbolic code that identifies how we should live" (Rebolledo 1995, 49). For example, to combat social and economic violence against Mexican immigrants and Chicanos, Cesar Chavez included the image of La Virgen de Guadalupe next to the thunderbird flag on the United Farm Workers' stages of protest because she occupied such a strong place in the imaginary of the workers who defined this labor struggle.[24] Her image emblematized the politically charged act of listening to the disenfranchised while capturing the importance of spirituality and female leadership to political movement.[25] None of this was taken or employed lightly; throughout his career, Chavez worked in collaboration with labor leader Dolores Huerta and engaged in faith-based gestures, such as fasting and prayer, as part of his activist commitment.

As Amalia Mesa-Baines explains, "cultural transformation requires an expansion of aesthetic language" (Mesa-Baines 1991, 131). The writers and artists discussed thus far in this chapter illustrate some methods for expanding aesthetic language, especially by signifying foundational myths and representing enduring icons, as Moraga and Carrasco so brilliantly do in their work. This is further illustrated by the work of Yolanda Lopez, a feminist artist who has consistently challenged the visual vocabulary defining the Chicana and her place in familial, social, and cultural landscapes. Her famous series of Virgen-inspired portraits features women as artists, laborers, athletes, and activists.[26] Mesa-Baines says of Lopez's series of revised Virgen imagery, "Lopez's Guadalupes are mobile, hardworking, assertive, working-class images of the abuela as a strong, solid nurturer, mother as family-supporting seamstress, and daughter as a contemporary artist and powerful runner. . . . Lopez attests to the internal familiarity of the image and the powerful influence of her own family members" (1991, 137). In Lopez's images, women are not like the Virgen; rather, it is the Virgen who is refigured as being like women. In this way, Lopez challenges and broadens the vocabulary of her image, positioning la Virgen as more than icon, myth, or symbol, but rather as a role model directly relevant to Chicana social struggle in very material ways. As observed by Mesa-Baines, "the art in this series does not simply reflect an existing ideology; it actively constructs a new one." (1991, 137).

Such female icons represent transmission and translation—how they move a people—but also how people move these images, morphing them into different places and moments, taking what is powerful, revising what is not. We see this in Moraga's portrait of Cerezita in her wheelchair, being physically moved by others so that she may emotionally and politically move her community on to new ground. Social change depends on a public pedagogy that teaches citizens how to translate images into activism. Carrasco's *Pregnant Woman in a Ball of Yarn* is trapped within a sphere, yes, but the ball promises the possibilities of movement. Despite appearances, it is not fixed in place, for it can roll. The power of these icons to do such work is perhaps what makes them most enduring.

Chicana engagements with iconography and myth employ reverence and revision to grapple with the dual forces of cultural healing and cultural violence. These maternal icons constitute a powerful force in Chicana literary and visual culture because our mothers, for better and for worse, are our first teachers of love. Yet many of us have been made painfully aware from the outset of childhood that our mothers come nowhere near that mythological ideal of motherhood and selfless unconditional love represented by traditional Virgin iconography. There is an earth-shattering awareness of her imperfection, one that however confusingly also powerfully fuels our love. To be motherless is painfully unimaginable. We cannot abandon her, so we must revise our idea of what it is to be a mother. As the Chicana artists and writers discussed in this chapter illustrate, the many incarnations of the Virgin provide a lifeboat around which to anchor one's faith, yet her image cannot survive the duration of the journey without undergoing serious reconstruction in order to hazard the challenges and contradictions that define our lives as women struggling in a patriarchal world. We revise as a means to carve a space for ourselves that honestly venerates the love represented by our mothers but does not ignore the violations. The act of female creation begins with violence to the body. Yet, too many stories of motherhood do not honor violence as a potentially transforming element. Chicana artists and writers employ female enduring icons and myths not as a simple act of veneration, but instead as a means to undo the violence of history and representation.

Acknowledgments

Thank you to dramatist Cherrie Moraga for personal and public conversation about her work, and to artists Barbara Carrasco and Alma Lopez for ongoing personal discussion and interviews about their work and Chicana/Chicano art history. The writing of this chapter benefited from the support of a Fulbright Fellowship Senior Lectureship to Spain (2004–2005) and from work as co–principle investigator with Emory Elliott on grant project "Global Migration, Immigration and Social Transformation" under a Rockefeller Humanities Fellowship Residency Site Grant (2000–2004). Thank you to Professors Isabel Duran and Ana Anton Pacheco of the Universidad de Complutense, Madrid, and Liam Kennedy of the Clinton Institute for American Studies at University College, Dublin, for inviting me to present early versions of this chapter. Special appreciation goes to my colleagues Traise Yamamoto, Michelle Raheja, and Vorris Nunley for their inspiration and feedback on this and other work. I am also indebted to recent seminar conversations with University of California Riverside graduate students Shelley Garcia, Helen Lovejoy, Megan Stein, Laura Westengard, and Brandy Underwood, and with undergraduate Chicana research *collectiva* members Hortensia Diaz, Joelle Guzman, Sonia Valencia, and Cassandra Villa.

Notes

1. In his late twenties, my brother killed our father. In my work, I have used this and other personal experiences as a springboard for critical engagement in writing about violence. Two recent essays representing this project include "Critical Witnessing in African American and Latino Prison Narratives," (Miller 2003, 62–77) and "Emotional Contraband: Prison as Metaphor and Meaning in U.S. Latina Drama," (Fahy and King 2003, 25–40).
2. "Making *familia* from scratch" is taken from Cherrie Moraga's play *Giving Up the Ghost*; the phrase is widely cited by Chicana and Chicano critics for its articulation of the importance of redefining family outside the bounds of heteronormativity

and biology. Yvonne Yarbro-Bejarano, the authoritative critic on Moraga's work, draws the phrase "touching the wound in order to heal" from an interview with Moraga in which she discusses the ways Chicano nationalism and its theater romanticized the family as a haven from racism and class oppression without questioning or analyzing the structures of intracultural oppression maintained within the paradigm of *la familia*; Yarbro-Bejarano quotes Moraga as saying, "I feel we need to kind of touch the wounds a little bit, look at the sore spots in us" (Yarbro-Bejarano 2001, 50). Later in this chapter, I offer a reading of *Pregnant Woman in a Ball of Yarn*, the title of an art piece by Barbara Carrasco constructed to represent culturally proscribed expectations for Chicana motherhood as dangerously restrictive and ultimately performing violence on the larger Chicano community by limiting the contributions of women.

3. In *Extinct Lands, Temporal Geographies*, Mary Pat Brady focuses on the role of violence that both informs and results from the relationship between nationalism and gender for U.S. Chicanas as follows: "Chicana literature has, from its inception, contested the terms of capitalist spatial formation, including the attempts to regulate the meanings and uses of spaces, especially the use of space to naturalize violent racial, gender, sexual, and class ideologies" (Brady 2002, 6). In *Chicana without Apology*, Eden Torres reminds readers of the culturally specific elements tied to this distinct historical past that define trauma as follows: "We did not choose to leave our homelands as many immigrants have, nor elect to be absorbed into the dominant culture through forced assimilation, which is a kind of brutality against the spirit" (Torres 2003, 19).
4. Fregoso says of the phrase used to call attention to and end the violence against women in Ciudad Juarez, "'Ni una mas' stages women's visibility and invisibility in the nation as well as a confrontation with the historical and social trauma in the region" (Fregoso 2003, 1). In her analysis of filmic and journalistic representations of the murders, Fregoso argues for a refusal of readings strategies that, however seemingly urgent in tone, import an interpretive lens unable to critically magnify the complexity of the events and their complicated structures of power (i.e., patriarchy and global capitalism). She writes, "Although there is no doubt that feminicide embodies the most deadly logic of masculinity, that its perpetrators are misogynist and racist killers, the focus on working-class men deflects attention away from the multiple structures of violence in the lives of women" (Fregoso 2003, 14). Two powerful literary accounts that work to provide complex readings of the events include Alicia Gaspar de Alba's novel *Dessert Blood: The Juarez Murders*, and poet and human rights activist Marjorie Agosin's *Secrets in the Sand: The Young Women of Juarez.*
5. This is wonderfully illustrated through the book design for pivotal texts in Chicana literary and cultural criticism, particularly the cover images provided by multimedia artist Alma Lopez. For three examples of her work that illustrate her strategic engagements with the iconography of Chicana identity outlined in this chapter, see her cover images created for the following texts: "Our Lady" for Alberto Sandoval-Sanchez and Nancy-Saporta Sternbach, eds., *Puro Teatro: A Latina Anthology* (Tucson: University of Arizona Press, 2000); "Adelita" for Alberto

Sandoval-Sanchez and Nancy Saporta Sternbach, eds., *Stages of Life: Transcultural Performance and Identity in U.S. Latina Theater* (Tucson: University of Arizona Press, 2001); and a digital velvet image based on the cover paining "Cinco Esencias" for Alicia Gaspar de Alba, ed., *Velvet Barrios: Popular Culture and Chicana/o Sexualities* (New York: Palgrave Macmillan, 2003).

6. Tey Diana Rebolledo notes, "Roman Catholicism has long emphasized the importance of the Virgin Mary, and followers of the cult of *Mariansimo*, or Mariology, strive to emulate the Virgin's faith, self-abnegation, purity, care of her physical as well as spiritual child(ren), and passivity. This tradition emphasized by the church, has heavily influenced many Hispanas who look to the Virgin to intervene for them in their daily lives" (1995, 49–50). Mary Pat Brady describes the extended role of the Catholic church as follows: "From the sanctioning of land as holy, as a site of divine transcendence, to the removal of land from public access (cloistering, for example), to the ideological centering of churches in relationship to homes and other workplaces, Catholicism has indicated its awareness of and commitment to controlling the relationships between space and social power" (Brady 2002, 103).
7. Rebolledo explains, "For Chicano culture, the Virgin de Guadalupe represents characteristics considered positive for women: unselfish giving, intercession between earth and spirit, and the ideal qualities of motherhood. She is the higher being who can be appealed to on a very personal level" (1995, 53). Gloria Anzaldua further explains, "Today, *la Virgen de Guadalupe* is the single most potent religious, political and cultural image of the Chicano/*mexicano*. . . . Because *Guadalupe* took upon herself the psychological and physical devastation of the conquered and oppressed *indio* she is our spiritual, political and psychological symbol. . . . To Mexicans on both sides of the border, *Guadalupe* is the symbol of our rebellion against the rich, upper and middleclass; against their subjugation of the poor and the *indio*" (1987, 30). For a wide-ranging discussion of the role La Virgen de Guadalupe in Mexican and Chicano history, politics, religion, art, and literature, see Ana Castillo, ed., *Goddess of the Americas: Writings on the Virgin of Guadalupe* (New York: Riverhead Books, 1996). For focused readings about further treatments in Chicana literature, see also Mary Pat Brady, "Sandra Cisneros' Contrapuntial 'Geography of Scars'" in *Extinct Lands, Temporal Geographies*, 111–36 on the role of *Virgen* iconography in Cisneros's short story collection *Woman Hollering Creek*.
8. For a wonderfully detailed and critically complex discussion of the cultural centrality of La Malinche and la Virgen mythology and the transmission of culture, see Diana Taylor, "Memory as Cultural Practice: Mestizaje, Hybridity, Transculturation" in *The Archive and the Repertoire* (Durham, NC: Duke University Press, 2003), 79–109.
9. Alicia Arrizon details this myth as a cultural paradigm as follows: "La Malinche or Malintzin Tenepal was a young Tabascan woman given to Hernan Cortes by her tribe. She became his mistress, the mother of one of his children, and a translator. Many cultural critics and historians maintain that without her, the conquest of Mexico would have been difficult, perhaps even impossible. For Chicana

feminists, La Malinche is significant not only as an important historical subject, but also as a powerful symbol who represents the ethnic spilt between the indigenous people and the Spanish *conquistadores*" (1999, 81). Cherrie Moraga focuses on the ways the myth negatively influences Chicanas' sense of themselves sexually and politically: "The sexual legacy passed down to the mexicana/Chicana is the legacy of betrayal, pivoting around the historical/mythical female figure of Malintzin Tenepal. As a native woman and translator, strategic advisor and mistress to the Spanish conqueror of Mexico, Hernan Cortez, Malintzin is considered the mother of the mestizo people. But unlike La Virgen de Guadalupe, she is not revered as La Madre Sagrada, but rather slandered as La Chingada, meaning 'the fucked one,' or La Vendida, sell-out to the white race" (1983, 91). For a comprehensive historical discussion, see Cordelia Candelaria, "La Malinche, Feminist Prototype," in *Chicana Leadership: The Frontiers Reader*, ed. Yolanda Flores Niemann, et al. (Lincoln: University of Nebraska Press, 2002), 1–14.

10. Tey Diana Rebolledo further explains the connections between these mythic figures in the following excerpt: "The image of La Llorona, the weeping woman, brought together Indian and Spanish folklore legends. In both cultures there were prevalent images of women whose children had been murdered, or who themselves murdered or abandoned their children and could not rest thereafter. . . . La Llorona was a syncretic image connected both to the Spanish medieval notions of *animas en pena*, spirits in purgatory expiating their sins, and to the Medea myth. . . . In folklore, the images of La Llorona and La Malinche merge until in many areas they are transformed into a unitary figure" (1995, 62–63).
11. In her discussion of the role of Malinche mythology in representations of Latina gender and sexuality in performance, Alicia Arrizon writes, "The sexuality of Latinas has typically been defined with reference to male desire and colonial domination. The *sensuality* of Latinas is flaunted and exploited in popular media, but most of the time, their *sexuality* is subjected to internal and external cultural domination" (*1999*, 23). Significantly, in the story of La Virgen de Guadalupe's appearance to Juan Diego, she speaks to a man who then serves as a conduit to other men. The following documentation by folklorist John Bierhorst of Luis Lasso de la Vega's 1649 telling of the mythic story of the Virgin of Guadalupe clearly illustrates this point: "'My child,' said the lady, 'you must understand that there are many people who could be my messengers, but you are the one I have chosen, and through you my command will be carried out. Go back to the bishop and tell him again that the one who sent you is the virgin, Saint Mary, mother of the spirit of God'" (Bierhorst 1990, 121). Here one can read La Virgen de Guadalupe as part of a homosocial triangle charging the relationship of power between two men. As a virgin, she represents no threat to man since she has no physical demands. Her actual role is to confirm what Juan Diego wishes should be carried out. Ultimately, it is her position as a messenger from God speaking to men that defines her agency.
12. Luis Alfaro's solo performance play *Downtown*, in *O Solo Homo*, ed. David Roman and Holly Hughes (New York: Grove Press, 1998), 313–48; and Gil

Cuadros's cross genre collection of writing, *City of God* (San Francisco: City Lights Press, 1994) explore this theme well. Visual artist Alex Donis's silkscreen-on-litho poster titled "I Lied" powerfully attends to these points through this simply but forcefully directed phrase superimposed over a traditional image of the Virgin (reproduced in the section "Las varidadas encarnaciones de la Virgin," in *Contemporary Chicana and Chicano Art*, ed. Gary D. Keller et al., 2:116–35).

13. Yvonne Yarbro-Bejarano's reading of the play as follows shares these points of observation: "The play demonstrates how Chicana/o sexual and gender identity is constructed through the male ideal in the context of the family" (Yarbro-Bejarano 2001, 51).
14. Diana Taylor theorizes the way such female icons as La Malinche and La Virgen de Guadalupe represent at once limitation and possibility in the following quote: "Though seemingly irreconcilable, the figures form two sides of the same coin, incarnating the consciousness of struggle: you are either with us or against us, our savior or a traitor, the Virgin or Malinche. This double figure, in all cases, is positioned as the link (the intermediary) between the old and the new, the past, present, and future, the European and the Indigenous, the local and the hemispheric, the repertoire and the archive. Her body allows the "new" to come into the world, be it the new race, a new belief system, a new sense of national or ethnic identity" (Taylor 2003, 99).
15. Yarbro-Bejarano's reading continues, "Immersed in the politicization of her ethnicity as an activist Chicana, Leticia has become radicalized by both racial and gender experiences. Her character captures the contradiction of fighting for justice around issues of race within the movement, while only the men, who she refers to ironically as 'Raza gods' (78) have the power. This insight has enabled her to articulate the gender inequality reproduced in her own home, as in the earlier dialogue with Hortensia ('I have something between my legs'). Far from cutting herself off from her family and culture because she has allied herself with feminist values, Leticia's feminism emerges fundamentally out of her specific experience as a Chicana; she responds to white patriarchy as well as to Chicano machismo" (Yarbro-Bejarano 2001, 58).
16. Indeed, the subject of mothers and the maternal permeate Moraga's oeuvre. All of Moraga's work centers on the subjectivity of women, from her landmark work as a contributor and anthologist, to *This Bridge Called My Back* and *Cuentos: Stories by Latinas*, to her volume of poetry and essays, *The Last Generation*, to her writing on queer motherhood, *Waiting in the Wings*. Her first play, *Giving Up the Ghost*, focuses on women and historical, personal, and cultural trauma; her ensuing *Shadow of a Man* looks at how men and masculinity impact multigenerational familial relationships between women; and *Heroes and Saints*, the third of these works that many critics read together as a trilogy, continues the themes of her earlier plays through further focusing on women acting within the public sphere of community politics and cultural activism. Moraga's more recent *The Hungry Woman, A Mexican Medea* uses the Medea myth to explore issues also grounded in the mythology that informs Chicana identity and the engendering of nationalism, especially the myths of La Malinche and La Llorona.

17. Similarly, Eden Torres argues, "If we know ourselves well enough to read through our historical and personal memories, as well as our experiences, we may begin to understand what is being revealed and expressed (Torres 2003, 19).
18. In the following excerpt, Sandra Cisneros writes of her need to temporarily disavow her image in order to develop a strong sense of herself as a Chicana: "Virgencita de Guadalupe. For a long time I wouldn't let you in my house. I couldn't see you without seeing my ma each time my father came home drunk and yelling, blaming everything that ever went wrong in his life on her. I couldn't look at your folded hands without seeing my abuela mumbling, 'My son, my son, my son. . . . ' Couldn't look at you without blaming you for all the pain my mother and her mother and all our mother's mothers have put up with in the name of God. . . . I wasn't going to be my mother or my grandma. All that self-sacrifice, all that silent suffering. Hell no. Not here. Not me" (1996, 127).
19. Moraga and Anzaldua are coeditors of *This Bridge Called My Back: Writings by Radical Women of Color* (New York: Kitchen Table: Women of Color Press, 1981).
20. Art historians Shifra Goldman and Tomas Ybarra-Frausto observe the centrality of these symbols to visual artists of the Chicano movement, noting, "The Virgin de Guadalupe and the red, black, and white thunderbird flag appeared in nearly every protest and demonstration" (Goldman and Ybarra-Frausto in *CARA*, 85). Gloria Anzaldua provides a broader historical context for the employment of Virgen imagery during that cultural moment as follows: "During the Mexican Revolution, Emiliano Zapata and Miguel Hidalgo used her image to move el pueblo mexicano toward freedom. During the 1965 grape strike in Delano, California and in subsequent Chicano farmworkers' marches in Texas and other parts of the Southwest, her image on banners heralded and united the farmworkers. Pachucos (zoot suiters) tattoo her image on their bodies" (Anzaldua 1987, 29). More contemporary illustrations of the employment of la Virgen as speaking and listening to the culturally disenfranchised and dispossessed include Ester Hernandez's La *ofrenda* serigraph (reproduced as a cover image for *Chicana Lesbians: The Girls Our Mothers Warned Us About*) and the digital photography of Delilah Montoya that places the image in relationship to the history of colonialism expanded into the present prison industrial complex. See her cover image for *Aztlan: A Journal of Chicano Studies* 27, no. 1 (Spring 2002).
21. "Acto" is Luis Valdez's term designed to capture his stylized short prop plays. It plays on the terms "one act" and "activism."
22. This image is reproduced in Alicia Gaspar de Alba's *Chicano Art: Inside/Outside the Master's House* (1998, 30) and *Chicano Art: Resistance and Affirmation* (1991, 325).
23. Chela Sandoval uses the term "transdisciplinarity" to refer to the rich and varied register of critical maneuvering performed within Chicana and Chicano studies in her contributed comments to "Roundtable on the State of Chicano studies," Eric R. Avila, Karen Mary Davalos, Chela Sandoval, and Rafael Perez-Torres, in *Aztlan: A Journal of Chicano Studies* 27, no. 2 (Fall 2002):141–52.
24. Within Chicano culture, the image of the Virgin Mary has always been used to inspire and instruct. Chicano movement nationalists regularly positioned her as

an icon of maternal female leadership born from a culturally bound sense of spirituality and to visually signify a direct link to a historical past characterized by a passionate sense of revolution.

25. Moraga writes of the significance of this history, especially for women, that "some may find their American dream and forget their origins, but the majority of Mexico's descendents soon comprehend the political meaning of the disparity between their lives and those of the gringo. Certainly the Mexican women cannery workers of Watsonville who maintained a two-year victorious strike against Green Giant in the mid-eighties, and farm workers organized by Cesar Chavez's UFW in the late sixties and early seventies are testimony to the political militancy of the Mexican immigrant worker. More recently, there are the examples of the Mothers of East Los Angeles and the women of Kettleman City who have organized against the toxic contamination proposed for their communities. In the process, the Mexicana becomes a Chicana (or at least a Mechicana); that is, she becomes a citizen of this country, not by virtue of a green card, but by virtue of the collective voice she assumes in staking her claim to this land and its resources" (Moraga 1993, 155–56).
26. Key pieces from Lopez's series are reproduced in Gary Keller, Mary Erickson, Kaytie Johnson, and Joaquin Alvarado, eds., *Contemporary Chicana and Chicano Art: Artists, Works, Culture, and Education, vol. 2* (Tempe: Bilingual Press/Editorial Bilingue), 80–85. In that same volume, see also the special insert, "Las variadas encarnaciones de la Virgen" (116–35), which offers an overview of key works and illustrates the aesthetic translations of her image by various Chicana and Chicano artists. Lopez discusses the history behind her ongoing work with the image as follows: "I started working with the image in 1978 because she was the most popular female political image used by the United Farm Workers in demonstrations and in progressive immigrant support groups." Speaking about her controversial image *Guadalupe Walking* (1978), reproduced as a cover for the Mexican magazine *fem.*, Lopez explains her reading and rewriting of La Virgen de Guadalupe. She says, "Looking at the image closely, I discovered that her dress was so long that it gathered at her feet, so I trimmed the cloth to let her feet and legs move. I felt that I had removed her from bondage, from having been trapped in her clothing" (2002, 80).

References

Alarcon, Norma, Ana Castillo, and Cherrie Moraga, eds. 1993. *The sexuality of Latinas*. Berkeley: Third Woman Press.

Alarcon, Norma. 2002. Chicana feminist literature: A re-vision through Malintzin/or Malintzin putting flesh back on the object. In *This bridge called my back*, ed. Cherrie Moraga and Gloria Anzaldua, 202–11. 3rd ed. Berkeley: Third Woman Press.

Anzaldua, Gloria. 1987. *Borderlands/la frontera: The new mestiza*. San Francisco: Aunt Lute.

Arrizon, Alicia. 1999. *Latina performance: Traversing the stage*. Bloomington: University of Indiana Press.

Bierhorst, John. 1990. *The mythology of Mexico and Central America*. New York: William Morrow.

Brady, Mary Pat. 2002. *Extinct lands, temporal geographies: Chicana literature and the urgency of space*. Durham, NC: Duke University Press.

Broyles-Gonzalez, Yolanda. 1994. *El teatro campesino: Theater in the Chicano movement*. Austin: University of Texas Press.

Candelaria, Cordelia. 2002. La Malinche, feminist prototype. In *Chicana leadership: The frontiers reader*, ed. Yolanda Flores Niemann, Susan M. Armitage, Patricia Hart 1–14. Lincoln: University of Nebraska Press.

Castillo, Ana, ed. 1996. *Goddess of the Americas: Writings on the Virgen de Guadalupe*. New York: Riverhead Books.

Cisneros, Sandra. 1996. "Guadalupe the sex goddess." In *Goddess of the Americas: Writings on the Virgen de Guadalupe, ed.* Ana Castillo, 45–61. New York: Riverhead Books.

Colindres, Claudia. 1993. A letter to my mother. In *The sexuality of Latinas*, ed. Norma Alarcon, Ana Castillo, and Cherrie Moraga. Berkeley: Third Woman Press.

De la Torre, Adela, and Beatriz M. Pesquera, eds. *Building with our hands: New directions in Chicana studies*. Berkeley: University of California Press, 1993.

Gaspar de Alba, Alicia. 1998. *Chicano art inside/outside the master's house*. Austin: University of Texas Press.

Davalos, Karen Mary. 2001. *Exhibiting mestizaje: Mexican (American) museums in the diaspora*. Albuquerque: University of New Mexico Press.

Fregoso, Rosa Linda. 2003. *MeXicana encounters: The making of social identities on the borderlands*. Berkeley: University of California Press.

Garcia, Alma, ed. 1997.*Chicana feminist thought: The basic historical writings*. New York: Routledge.

Gomez-Pena, Guillermo. 1996. The two Guadalupes. In *Goddess of the Americas: Writings on the Virgen de Guadalupe, ed.* Ana Castillo, 178–83. New York: Riverhead Books.

Griswold del Castillo, Richard, Teresa McKenna, and Yvonne Yarbro Bejarano, eds. 1991. *Chicano art: Resistance and affirmation, 1965–1985*. Los Angeles: Wight Art Gallery.

Keller, Gary, Mary Erickson, Kaytie Johnson, and Joaquin Alvarado, eds. 2002. *Contemporary Chicana and Chicano art: Artists, works, culture, and education*. Vol. 2. Tempe: Bilingual Press/Editorial Bilingue.

Lopez, Tiffany Ana. 2003. Emotional contraband: Prison as metaphor and meaning in U.S. Latina drama. In *Captive audience: Prison and captivity in contemporary theater*, ed. Thomas Fahy, 25–40. New York: Routledge.

———. 2005. Critical witnessing in Latina/o and African American prison narratives. In *Prose and cons: Essays on prison literature in the United States*, ed. D. Quentin Miller, 62–77. Jefferson, MO: McFarland.

Mesa-Baines, Amalia. 1991. Quest for identity: Profile of two Chicana muralists based on interviews with Judith Baca and Patricia Rodrigues. In *Chicano art: Resistance and affirmation, ed.* Griswold del Castillo, Richard Griswold del Castillo, Teresa McKenna, and Yvonne Yarbro-Bejarano. Los Angeles: Wight Art Gallery.

Moraga, Cherrie. 1983. *Loving in the war years/lo que nunca paso por sus labios*. Boston: South End Press.

———. 1993. *The last generation*. Boston: South End Press.

———. 1994. *Heroes and saints and other plays*. Albuquerque: West End Press.

———. 1997. *Waiting in the wings: Portrait of a queer motherhood.* New York: Firebrand Books.

Nieto Gomez, Anna. 1997. La Chicana: Legacy of suffering and self-denial. In *Chicana feminist thought: The basic historical writings*, ed. Alma Garcia, 48–53. . New York: Routledge.

Rebolledo, Tey Diana. 1995. *Women singing in the snow: A cultural analysis of Chicana literature*. Tucson: University of Arizona Press.

Taylor, Diana. 2003. *The archive and the repertoire: Performing cultural memory in the Americas*. Durham, NC: Duke University Press.

Torres, Eden. 2003. *Chicana without apology: The new Chicana cultural studies*. New York: Routledge.

Trujillo, Carla, ed. 1998. *Living Chicana theory*. Berkeley: Third Woman Press.

———. 1991. *Chicana lesbians: The girls our mothers warned us about.* Berkeley: Third Woman Press.

Yarbro-Bejarano, Yvonne. 2001. *The wounded heart: Writing on Cherrie Moraga.* Austin: University of Texas Press.

PART 3

Global and Domestic Economies

CHAPTER 8

Culture, Dislocation, and Citizenship

Toby Miller

We are in a crisis of belonging, of who, what, when, and where. More and more people feel as though they *do not* belong, more and more people are *applying* to belong, and more and more people are not *counted* as belonging. It is a crisis of culture and population, of living together. This chapter addresses the crisis through three principal foci: the social significance of culture, the dislocation of populations, and the response of cultural citizenship. I establish that culture increasingly operates as a resource for nations, note why this is necessary given their increasing cultural mixing (particularly in the United States), and interrogate responses via cultural citizenship that seek to operationalize resources for living together.

Culture

The word "culture" derives from the Latin *colare*, which implies tending to and developing agriculture as subsistence. With the emergence of capitalism's division of labor, culture came both to embody instrumentalism and abjure it via the industrialization of farming on the one hand, and the cultivation of taste on the other. In keeping with this distinction, culture has usually been understood in two registers via the social sciences and the humanities—truth versus beauty. This was a heuristic distinction in the sixteenth century, but it became substantive over time. Eighteenth-century German, French, and Spanish dictionaries bear witness to a metaphorical shift into spiritual cultivation. The spread of literacy and printing saw customs and laws passed on, governed, and adjudicated through the written word as textualization supplemented and supplanted force as a guarantor of authority via such pointed satire as prints celebrating the repeal of the Stamp Act in colonial America. During the same period, consumer society developed, through horse racing, opera, art exhibits, masquerades, and balls. There is a simple demographic corollary. Britain, for example, had a population of 9,000,000 at the commencement of the nineteenth century, of whom 20 percent lived in towns. It was self-sufficient in agriculture. But with the Industrial Revolution, half the population became urban dwellers. Food was imported, and cultures developed textual forms that could be exchanged (Williams 1983, 38; Benhabib 2002, 2; de Pedro 1999, 61–62, 78n1; Briggs and Burke 2003, 10, 38, 60; Jones 2003).

Culture is now a marker of differences and similarities in taste and status within groups. In today's humanities, theater, film, television, radio, art, craft, writing, music, dance, and games are judged by criteria of quality and meaning, as practiced critically and historically. For their part, the social sciences focus on the languages, religions, customs, times, and spaces of different groups, as explored ethnographically or statistically. So whereas the humanities articulate differences through *symbolic* norms (for example, which class has the cultural capital to appreciate high culture, and which does not), the social sciences articulate differences through *social* norms (for example, which people cultivate agriculture in keeping with spirituality, and which do not) (Wallerstein 1989). This bifurcation also has a representational impact, whereby the "cultural component of the capitalist economy" is "its socio-psychological *superstructure*" (Schumpeter 1975, 121). The impact is indexed in cultural labor: the *poligrafi* (what would now be called "professional writers") of fifteenth-century Venice and the hacks of eighteenth-century London generated popular and influential conduct books, works of instruction on everyday life that marked the textualization of custom and the emergence of new occupational identities (Briggs and Burke 2003, 57).

This venerable switching point between customary and aesthetic cultures continues to fascinate: in the three decades leading up to 2000, the number of self-help books in the United States more than doubled, and between a third and a half of *Yanquis*[1] bought one, lending their credit to a $2.48 billion-a-year industry of tapes, DVDs, videos, books, and "seminars" on making oneself anew—a whole array of consumables in place of adequate social security. The U.S. population spends $700 million per year on self-help literature, and one fifth of the public has read crossover titles between evangelical Christianity and self-help, as per the *Left Behind* series. Each item promises fulfillment while delivering a never-ending project of work on the self (McGee 2005, 11–12; Baylor Institute for Studies of Religion and Department of Sociology 2006; "Centrifugal Forces" 2005).

The canons of judgment and analysis that once flowed from the humanities/social sciences distinction (and kept aesthetic tropes somewhat distinct from social norms) have collapsed in on each other: "Whoever speaks of culture speaks of administration as well, whether this is his [*sic*] intention or not" (Adorno 1996, 93). Art and custom have become resources for markets and nations—reactions to the crisis of belonging, and to economic necessity. Collective concerns with maintaining and developing a "cultural legacy" have been supplemented by commercial drives to "invent and create new forms of culture"—not as a side effect, but in place of agriculture and manufacturing (Venturelli n.d., 16). As a consequence, culture is more than textual signs or everyday practices. It also provides the legitimizing ground on which particular groups (e.g., African Americans, gays and lesbians, the hearing impaired, or evangelical Protestants) claim resources and seek inclusion in national narratives. And culture is crucial to both advanced and developing economies as a service, a textual export, and a source of dignity and mutual aid (Yúdice 2002, 40; 1990; Martín-Barbero 2003, 40).

This intermingling has implications for both aesthetic and social hierarchies. Culture comes to "regulate and structure . . . individual and collective lives" (Parekh 2000, 143) in competitive ways that harness art and collective meaning for governmental and commercial purposes. So the Spanish minister for culture can address Sao Paolo's 2004 World Cultural Forum with a message of cultural maintenance that is about both economic development and aesthetic and customary preservation. Culture is understood as a means to growth via "cultural citizenship," through a paradox—that universal (and marketable) value is placed on the specificity of different cultural backgrounds. Similarly, Taiwan's premier can broker an administrative reorganization of government as a mix of economic efficiency and "cultural citizenship" (quoted in "Foro Cultural" 2004; "Yu to Propose 5 Fresh Policy Goals Today" 2004).

This simultaneously instrumental and moral tendency is especially important in the United States, albeit in a rather different way, for the United States is virtually alone among wealthy countries, both in the widespread view of its citizens that their culture is superior to that of others and in the successful sale of that culture around the world (Pew Research Center for the People & the Press 2003; Miller *et al.* 2001, 2005). The United States has blended preeminence in the two cultural registers, exporting both popular prescriptions for entertainment (the humanities side) and economic prescriptions for labor (the social-sciences side). These have become signs and sources of the global crisis of belonging, even as their sender displays a willful ignorance of why the rest of the world may not always wish to follow its example despite buying its popular culture (Carreño 2001, 22). But the United States wrestles with its *own* cultures, too.

Immigrants are crucial to the nation's foundational *ethos* of consent because they represent alienation from their origin and endorsement of their destination. Bonnie Honig (1998) has shown that immigrants and their cultures have long been *the* limit case for loyalty, as per Ruth the Moabite in the Jewish Bible or Old Testament. Such figures are both perilous for the sovereign-state (where does their fealty lie?) and symbolically essential (as the only citizens who make a deliberate decision to swear allegiance to an otherwise mythic social contract). This makes achieving and sustaining national culture all the more fraught, for just as their memory of what has been lost is strong, so is their host's necessity to shore up "preferences" expressed for U.S. norms. Liberal philosophy long held that the integration of migrants would follow from the acquisition of citizenship and a nondiscriminatory, culture-blind application of the law once successive generations mastered the dominant language and entered the labor market as equals with the majority. But the patent failure to achieve this outcome saw governments recognizing cultural differences, intervening to counter discrimination in the private sector, and imposing quotas for minority hiring (Kymlicka 2000, 725).

This has led in turn to a reaction from neoliberalism and conservatism against such state participation, on economic and nationalist grounds. Multiculturalism, a movement founded in respect for difference, is accused of a "racial particularism" that threatens liberalism (Alexander 2001, 238) through the assiduous efforts of sinister-sounding "ethnocultural political entrepreneurs" who mobilize constituencies devoted to "sectional demands" (Barry 2001, 21). Journalist Peter Brimelow (1996) of the Center for American Unity says that U.S. Latinos comprise "a strange anti-nation," and the Center for Immigration Studies, a right-wing think tank, bemoans the advent of "post-Americans" who have "a casual relationship" with the United States rather than a love affair, typifying them as citizens "of nowhere in particular" (Krikorian 2004). (Count me in.) Kennedy staffer, pop historian, and pundit Arthur Schlesinger, Jr., (1991) diagnoses a "disuniting of America" through the revival of "ancient prejudices" by academic multiculturalists who imagine then concretize social divisions that barely existed beforehand. Reagan bureaucrat, pop ethicist, and serial gambler William J. Bennett (1992) calls for a "cultural war" that will reinforce "traditional" values. He opposes today's counterhistories that threaten previously dominant Whiggish narratives of a nation led by great men in thrall of the beacon of democracy. The outcome is a threat to the golden heritage of Jeffersonian democracy (when propertied men were voters, women were emotional and physical servants, African Americans were slaves, and native peoples fought to survive).

Dislocation

A global population crisis began in the 1960s and has continued since because of several factors: changes in the global division of labor, as manufacturing left the first world and subsistence agriculture was eroded in the third world; demographic growth through unprecedented public-health initiatives; increases in refugees following numerous conflicts among satellite states of the United States and the Soviet Union; transformations of these struggles into intra- and transnational violence when half the imperial couplet unraveled; the associated decline of state socialism and triumph of finance capital; vastly augmented human trafficking; the elevation of consumption as a site of social action and public policy; renegotiation of the 1940s–1970s compact across the West between capital, labor, and government, reversing that period's redistribution of wealth downward; deregulation of key sectors of the economy; the revival of Islam as a transnational religion and political project; and the development of civil-rights and social-movement discourses and institutions, extending cultural difference from tolerating the aberrant to querying the normal, and commodifying the result. The dilemmas that derive from these changes underpin political theorist John Gray's critique of "the West's ruling myth . . . that modernity is a single condition, everywhere the same and always benign," a veritable embrace of Enlightenment values (2003, 1). Modernity has just as much to do with global financial deregulation, organized crime, and religious violence as it does with democracy, uplift, and opportunity, and it has just as much to do with neoliberalism, religion, and authoritarianism as it does with freedom, science, and justice (Gray 2003, 1–2, 46).

Of the approximately 200 sovereign states in the world, over 160 are culturally heterogeneous, and they are comprised of 5,000 ethnic groups. Between 10 and 20 percent of the world's population currently belongs to a racial and linguistic minority in their country of residence, and 900 million people affiliate with groups that suffer systematic discrimination. Perhaps three-quarters of the world system sees politically active minorities, and there are more than 200 movements for self-determination in nearly 100 states (Thio 2002; Abu-Laban 2000, 510; Brown and Ganguly 2003, 1n1; Falk 2004, 11). Even the "British-Irish archipelago," once famed "as the veritable forge of the nation state, a template of modernity," has been subdivided by cultural difference as a consequence of both peaceful and violent action and a revisionist historiography that asks us to note the millennial migration of

Celts from the steppes; Roman colonization, invading Anglos, Saxons, Jutes, Frisians, and Normans; attacking Scandinavians; trading Indians, Chinese, Irish, Lombards, and Hansa; and refugee Europeans and Africans (Nairn 2003, 8).

There are now five key zones of immigration—North America, Europe, the Western Pacific, the Southern Cone, and the Persian Gulf—and five key categories of immigration: international refugees, internally displaced people, voluntary migrants, the enslaved, and the smuggled. The number of refugees and asylum seekers at the beginning of the twenty-first century was 21.5 million—3 times the figure 20 years earlier (United Nations Development Programme 2004, 6, 2; Massey 2003, 146; Cohen 1997). The International Organization for Migration estimates that global migration increased from 75 million to 150 million people between 1965 and 2000, and the United Nations says that 2 percent of all people spent 2001 outside their country of birth, more than at any other moment in history. Migration has doubled since the 1970s, and the European Union (EU) has seen arrivals from beyond its borders grow by 75 percent in the last quarter century (Castles and Miller 2003, 4; Annan 2003).

This mobility, whether voluntary or imposed, temporary or permanent, is accelerating. Along with new forms of communication, it enables unprecedented cultural displacement, renewal, and creation between and across origins and destinations. Most of these exchanges are structured in dominance: the majority of international investment and trade takes place within the first world, while the majority of immigration is from the third world to the first world (United Nations Development Programme 2004, 30; Schweder, Minow, and Markus 2002, 26; Pollard 2003, 70; Sutcliffe 2003, 42, 44).

In response to new migration, there are simultaneous tendencies toward open and closed borders. Opinion polling suggests that sizable majorities across the globe believe their national ways of life are threatened by global flows of people and things. In other words, their cultures are under threat. At the same time, they feel unable to control their individual destinies. In other words, their subjectivities are under threat. Majorities around the world oppose immigration, largely because of fear. No major recipient of migrants has ratified the United Nation's 2003 International Convention on the Protection of the Rights of All Migrant Workers and Members of their Families, even though these countries benefit economically and culturally from these arrivals (Pew Research Center for the People & the Press 2003, 2004; Annan 2003).

There have been many outbursts of regressive nationalism, whether via the belligerence of the United States, the anti-immigrant stance of Western Europe, or the crackdown on minorities in Eastern Europe, Asia, and the

Arab world (Halliday 2004). The populist outcome is often violent, resulting in, for example, race riots in thirty British cities in the 1980s, pogroms against Roma and migrant workers in Germany in the 1990s and Spain in 2000, the *intifadas*, migrant-worker and youth struggles in France in 1990 and 2005, and so on. Virtually any arrival can be racialized, though particularly negative feelings are reserved for expatriates from former colonies (Downing and Husband 2005, xi, 7). The two most important sites of migration from the third world to the first world—Turkey and Mexico—see state and vigilante violence alongside corporate embrace in host countries, while donor nations increasingly recognize the legitimacy of a hybrid approach to citizenship (Bauböck 2005, 9).

Throughout the generous and tortured, selfish and thoughtful, but above all, dialectical history of nativism and migration, the United States has desired foreign workers but excluded them from public benefits, admired them for their economic and cultural contributions but criticized their multiple affinities, and claimed them as signs of ethical superiority but questioned their utility. This dialectic continues, wavering constantly between amiable acceptance and collective condemnation, an ongoing oscillation between patrician policies of welcome and populist pieties of rejection (Coutin 2003).

The first great wave of immigration, at the turn of the twentieth century, left the United States 87 percent white or European American, a proportion that remained static through the 1950s. The twentieth century saw the U.S. population grow by 250 percent (the equivalent figures are under 60 percent for both France and Britain). In the past decade, the country's Asian and Pacific Islander population increased by 43 percent, and its Latino population by 38.8 percent. Between those two groups and African Americans and Native Americans, about 100 million U.S. residents can now define themselves as minorities. Latinos and Asians in the United States are proliferating at 10 times the rate of whites, such that today, the percentage of white Americans is down to 70 percent of the population. It is projected to be 53 percent in 2050. The foreign-born segment of the country is 34 million—representing double the proportion in 1970 and an increase by half the figure of foreign-born citizens in 1995—and immigration across the 1990s was up 37.7 percent compared to the previous decade. Almost half the people living in Los Angeles and Miami were born outside the country, and Latinos accounted for half the growth in the U.S. population between 2003 and 2004. Latino immigrants were also appearing in new sites, like Iowa and North Carolina. After a downturn following the economic and security failures of the new century, by 2004, numbers were on the rise again (United Nations Development Programme 2004, 99; "The Americano Dream" 2005;

Massey 2003, 143; *Hispanic Fact Pack* 2005; Passel and Suro 2005). As for the labor force, in 1960, 1 in 17 workers was from outside the United States, mostly from Europe. Today, the proportion is 1 in 6, the majority being from Latin America and Asia. And the trend is accelerating. Between 1996 and 2000, people born overseas comprised close to half the net increase in the labor force (Mosisa 2002, 3). Migrants are also disproportionately represented among the poor, with 1 in 5 being from Latin America, while foreigners in general receive 75 cents for every dollar paid to *Yanquis* by employers. Of course, these official figures do not disclose the full picture. It has been suggested that 9 million people live in the United States without immigration documents, and they are joined by 300,000 new arrivals annually. In addition, hybridity is increasingly the norm. In 1990, 1 in 23 U.S. marriages crossed race and ethnicity. In 2005, the figure was 1 in 15, an increase of 65 percent (Tienda 2002; Mosisa 2002, 9; Castles and Miller 2003, 5; Schweder, Minow, and Markus 2002, 27; El Nasser and Grant, 2005a, 2005b).

Across the nation, applications to become a citizen have increased in volume over the past decade in response to legislative, economic, and cultural shifts (Freeman *et al.*, 2002). And yet this is also a moment when *dispositifs* for understanding populations have become less and less accurate because many minorities mistrust the state and do not provide the data requested. This has cast the U.S. Census into a crisis over the last 15 years (Hannah 2001, 519). In addition, the increased number of people of Spanish-language descent has compromised the methods of racialization that the U.S. government and U.S. marketers, politicians, and social movements have nourished over the past 200 years. Neither the federal census, nor social-science orthodoxy, nor Latinos accept "Hispanic" as a race in the way that they and others accept—albeit ambivalently—Asian, black, Native American, white, Pacific Islander, or "mixed" heritage as races. In the 2000 Census, 42 percent of Latinos selected "some other race" as the category that best illustrated their social situation. This signifies the ambiguities of class and citizenship more than anything else, since those who identified as white were the wealthiest and had "immigration papers" (Tafoya 2004).

Cultural Citizenship

These complex politics form the backdrop to cultural citizenship as it has been understood within the West over the past fifteen years. Seven key formations have theorized the phenomenon, each with strong links to the public sphere. They are associated with cultural studies, sociology, anthropology, political theory, neoliberal philosophy, ethnic studies, law, history, and international relations. How well have they done the job, and what has been their public impact?

First, cultural-studies sociologist Tony Bennett and colleagues in the Anglo Australian cultural-policy studies movement focus on a guaranteed set of competencies that governments should give citizens via "both the provision of cultural facilities and the regulation of cultural industries" across all aspects of artistic capital (Chaney 2002, 168). In a way that reads rather condescendingly, but in fact seeks to engage in an uplift and dissemination that respect popular knowledges, Bennett borrows from the liberal *donnée* that the most effective form of government rules via free individuals who must be given the skills to live both autonomously and socially. His primary interlocutors are the cultural bureaucracies of Australia and the Council of Europe, and his admirers include progressives in search of influence beyond affective protest and critique ("Citizenship and Cultural Policy" 2000; Bennett 1998, 2001; Miller and Yúdice 2004). Skeptical of what he sees as ludic protest against the state and capital, Bennett nevertheless recognizes that social-movement identities must be acknowledged by the modern liberal state. This line buys into the economic opportunities delivered by globalization *and* the need for local heritage to both counter and participate in it.

Second, Chicano anthropologist Renato Rosaldo and colleagues in Californian, Texan, and New York Chicano, Tejano, ethnic, and Latino studies look to a guaranteed set of rights for U.S. minorities, claimed at the level of the vernacular or the everyday, in order to "establish a distinct social space" through a combination of self-incorporation into the United States and the maintenance and development of a separate heritage and identity (Flores and Benmayor 1997b, 1–2). Their primary interlocutors are Chicano and Latino social movements, and their admirers include the *Fresno Bee*, while many of their ideas were first promoted in the *New York Times* as part of debates about multiculturalism in universities (Rosaldo 1997; Flores and Benmayor 1997a; Rodriguez and Gonzales 1995; "A Campus Forum on Multiculturalism" 1990).

Rosaldo sees cultural citizenship as a "deliberate oxymoron." It bridges difference and sameness in calling for economic and political equality on the joint grounds of maintaining identity and exercising "full membership" in the wider community (1994, 402). He claims that the difficulty with encouraging minority groups in theUnited States to vote, and the low levels of naturalization for non-Asian minority immigrants (in the 1990s, 57.6 percent of Asian immigrants became U.S. citizens, versus 32.2 percent of Latinos [Aleinikoff 2000, 130]), can be addressed by promoting multiple affinities to "former" languages, places, or norms, *and* to adopted countries. This kind of thinking is enshrined in the Indian Constitution, which enforces a common criminal code but regulates civil law through minority cultures, a legacy from thousands of years during which the *Dharmashastra* governed via collective identities rather than individual entitlements (Parekh 2000, 191; Das 2002, 85; Beteille 1999). It also informs the United Nations Educational, Scientific, and Cultural Organization's (UNESCO) Institute for Education, which emphasizes collective as much as individual human rights, and regards cultural citizenship as a development from, and antidote to, assimilationist ideals (UNESCO Institute for Education 1999).

Third, the Canadian-based political theorist Will Kymlicka and a number of slightly heterodox Anglo American colleagues seek a *rapprochement* between majority white settlement, "immigrant multiculturalism" (newer voluntary migrants, who, according to Kymlicka, deserve few cultural rights) and "minority nationalism" (first peoples, the dispossessed, and the enslaved, who deserve many cultural rights) via the notion of culture as an aid to individual autonomy through engagement with collective as well as individual histories. The position is in keeping with Canada's history as the first commonwealth country to establish its own citizenship system and its status as an official practitioner of multiculturalism since 1971 (Jenson and Papillon, 2001). And it applies elsewhere. Kymlicka's primary interlocutors are states dealing with ethnic minorities, and his admirers include the *Wall Street Journal* and the United Nations Development Programme, where he served as a principal consultant for its 2004 venture into culture. The UN's chief expert on indigenous peoples, Rodolfo Stavenhagen, indexed this impact in his keynote address at the 2003 Congreso Internacional de Americanistas on moving from indigenous status to cultural citizenship (Kymlicka 1995, 2000; Zachary 2000; United Nations Development Programme 2004; "Chile-Indigenas" 2003).

When the Soviet Union broke up into close to twenty countries, Moscow was content to see twenty-five million ethnic Russians remain in what it refers to as "the near abroad" (Rich 2003). Its former republics had two choices in dealing with these sizable and often wealthy minorities: propound a retributive cultural nationalism that marginalized the Russian language and set religious, racial, and linguistic criteria for citizenship (which Estonia and Latvia did, relegating Russians from "setting the cultural agenda of the public sphere" to setting the agenda for "the private/communal" one); or adopt a pragmatic civic policy that offered entitlements based on territory, fealty, and labor (as was done in Ukraine and Kazakhstan) (Tiryakian 2003, 22; Laitin 1999, 314–17). The former are now trying to defuse the resultant conflicts via Russian-language schools and cultural groups—courtesy of a Kymlicka consultancy. At the same time, they seek to change their cultural image, abjuring the nomenclature "Baltic" and "post-Soviet" in favor of

"Scandinavian" and "pre-European Union." Needless to say, they are "encouraged" to incorporate Russian minorities by the prospect of accession to EU membership and money via adherence to the European Convention on Nationality (Zachary 2000; van Ham 2001, 4; Bauböck 2005, 2–3, 5; see also Feldman 2005).

Where Rosaldo and his colleagues seek to transform citizenship in the interests of those marginalized by the majority, Bennett, Kymlicka, and their respective supporters utilize it for a general purpose that takes account of minorities. For Rosaldo, U.S. culture is distinguished by Latino disenfranchisement. Cultural difference substantively trumps formal universalism, and it is not good enough to follow the standard arms-length approach of liberal philosophy whereby state institutions adopt a neutral stance on cultural maintenance. Rosaldo is critical of neoliberalism and liberal philosophy for their myths of the accultural sovereign individual, which in fact assume a shared language and culture as the basis of government. Liberal philosophy's "civic nationalism" involves an allegiance not merely to the state, but also to images of nationhood that stretch across public and private realms (Runnymede Trust Commission 2000, 19, 36). Kymlicka thinks along similar lines but endorses liberalism, provided that it allows real protection of minorities by government—as a matter of justice and self-interest. For Bennett, culture is a set of tools for living that derives its value from the achievement of specific purposes, rather than being expressive ends in themselves. He sees government as a project of constituting, not drawing upon, the liberal individual, and is agnostic about its sovereign-individual claims. Bennett and Kymlicka's cosmopolitan approaches remain rooted, for pragmatic reasons, in the nation, because it is assumed to provide a boundary of fealty that can appeal to the better sentiments of its inhabitants.

The fourth theoretical formation, vocalized by the philosopher Amélie Oksenberg Rorty, is a neoliberal capture of the first three positions. In this view, cultural maintenance and development should be by-products of universal access to education, a "primary condition of free and equal citizen participation in public life" (1995, 162). Rorty opposes public funding to sustain familial or religious cultural norms, calling instead for a curriculum that will generate flexible cosmopolitans who learn about their country and its "global neighbors" (1995, 164; also see Stevenson 2003). Rorty's argument is a culturalist restatement of human-capital *nostra* about individuals maximizing their utility through investment in skills, with links to Bennett's call for citizens to learn a set of cultural competences. She rejects cross-cultural awareness as an essential component of good citizenship and justice, but endorses it as good business sense (Runnymede Trust Commission 2000, 234). This is in line with the United Nations Development Programme, which argues that "culturally diverse societies" are necessary preliminaries to the eradication of poverty rather than a nice by-product or afterglow (2004, v).

In India, the Planning Commission, a key instrument of Nehruvian secularism and modernization in the early years of nationhood, was unfashionable by the 1990s. It gave way to such euphemisms for neoliberal projects as "empowerment" (Beteille 1999). The nation's Central Board of Film Certification promulgates the *Citizen's Charter*, which calls on the public to engage in a form of citizen censorship. The *charter* begins with the query, "Who will bell the cat?" avowing that "do it yourself!" is the best means of acting against movie theaters showing materials that audiences dislike. It lays out tasks that consumers should undertake when entering cinemas, such as looking for certification, categorization, deletions as per a state "cut list," and so on—all in the name of "the interests of your fellow citizens" (2004).

In Mexico, this neoliberal trend reached its apogee when President Vicente Fox repeatedly and notoriously challenged reporters querying the record of neoliberalism with: "¿Yo por qué? . . . ¿Qué no somos 100 millones de mexicanos?" (Why ask me? . . . Aren't there 100 million other Mexicans?) (quoted in Venegas 2003). The burden of his words—offered in such delightful company as business leeches like Carlos Slim—was that each person must assume responsibility for their material fortunes. The fact that not every one of those Mexicans has control over the country's money supply, tariff policy, trade, labor law, and exchange rate might have given him pause. Or not. Clearly, Rorty's instrumental approach may lead to cultural erasure, for all its cosmopolitanism. Such fellow travelers cast doubt not only on her work, but also on any cultural-citizenship formations that embrace neoliberalism *tout court*.

All these logics are engaged by the fifth key formation of cultural citizenship, the UK Runnymede Trust Commission's *report The Future of Multi-Ethnic Britain* (2000). Its chair was the political theorist and future member of the House of Lords Bhikhu Parekh, and its secondary public face in the UK media came from Parekh's fellow commissioner, Stuart Hall. The commission examined racial questions in national social and cultural institutions, education, policing, and welfare. The following reactions to their work give a sense of how deep cultural conflicts run within citizenship: "Sub-Marxist gibberish"; "out-of-touch nonsense"; "an insult to our history and intelligence"' ("'British' is Already Inclusive and Elastic" 2000). The authors were accused of "a lack of loyalty and affection for Britain" (Parekh 2001). The *Daily Mail* reacted by producing a "list of ten dead white heroes of the last millennium" (Seaford 2001, 108). William Hague, then the leader of the Conservative Party, derided the *report* as an index of the left's "tyranny of political correctness and . . . assault on British culture and history" (2000, 28), while *The*

Scotsman referred to it as "a grotesque libel against the people of this land and a venomous blueprint for the destruction of our country" (Warner 2000). Jack Straw, then the home secretary, rejected the linkage of Britishness to white racism (Back *et al.* 2002, 447).

This indicates how much can be at stake in these debates, beyond Bennett's technical specifications of cultural-policy interventions, Rosaldo's feel-good vernacular multiculturalism, Kymlicka's attempt to "get along" in newly free, newly chauvinistic postsocialist environments, or Rorty's faith in an inclusive curriculum animated by enlightened self-interest. That becomes clearer still in the sixth formation, which addresses the limits of neoliberalism. Amy Chua, a lawyer operating from a comparative ethnic studies perspective—and publishing with a U.S. trade house rather than an academic press—investigates in a global frame the intersection of neoliberalism, ethnic-minority economic oligarchies, and democracy: what happens when wealthy minorities confront popular backlashes against their economic power that gain expression in a majoritarian rejection of cultural difference. While the economy enriches "the market-dominant minority, democratization increases the political voice and power of the frustrated majority" (2003, 124). As Chua puts it, provocatively and with the clear regret of a fan of both capitalism and democracy, this is about the conundrum "that turns free market democracy into an engine of ethnic conflagration" (2003, 6).

Her work describes indigenous majorities protesting their weakness. Class, corruption, and race jumble together, as "market-dominant minorities, along with their foreign-investor partners, invariably come to control the crown jewels of the economy . . . oil in Russia and Venezuela, diamonds in South Africa, silver and tin in Bolivia, jade, teak, and rubies in Burma" (2003, 10). Free markets concentrate *wealth dis*proportionately, while democracies concentrate *politics pro*portionately. Political enfranchisement and its economic opposite are mediated through cultural difference, and the outcome is revolutionary. The horrors of Rwanda and the former Yugoslavia in the 1990s illustrate what happens when ethnonationalist populism draws on majority resentment to quash minority economic power. Empowering majorities can lead to violence against the wealthy based on cultural difference. Powerful minorities must protect their interests through benevolence (2003, 11–13, 16–17).

The seventh and most powerful formation derives from the historian and professional anti-Palestinian Bernard Lewis and cold war political scientist, Vietnam War architect, and English-only advocate Samuel Huntington. In the post-Soviet 1990s, these two men turned to culture for geopolitical explanations. Lewis (1990) coined the expression "clash of civilizations" to capture the difference, as he saw it, between the separation of church and state that had generated the successes of the United States versus their intercalculation in Islamic nations, which had produced those countries' subordinate status. Forget *Yanqui* support of authoritarian antidemocrats and *coups* that furthered oil exploitation—Islamic *ressentiment* is all about the United States insisting that Caesar get *his* due, and god *his*. Huntington appropriated the "clash of civilizations" to argue that future world-historical conflicts would not be "primarily ideological or primarily economic," but rather "cultural" (1993, 22). What this does, of course, is to dematerialize politics—and most specifically, excuse the policies and programs of the United States government and corporations as only broadly relevant to the loathing of that nation elsewhere.

In the United States, Huntington's Olympian grandiosity was lapped up by the *bourgeois* media, ever-ready to embrace "a cartoon-like world where Popeye and Bluto bash each other" (Said 2001). The "clash twins'" grotesque generalizations have gained immense attention over the past decade, notably since September 11, 2001. Journalists promote the notion of an apocalyptic struggle between good and evil, plundering Lewis and Huntington on the differences between Western and Islamic cultures. Across the daily press and weekly and monthly magazines of ruling opinion, extrastate violence is attributed to Islam in opposition to freedom and technology, never as the act of subordinated groups against dominant ones. The *New York Times* and *Newsweek* gave Huntington room to account for what had happened in terms of his "thesis," while others took up the logic as a call for empire, from the supposed New Left (*Dissent* magazine and other progressives who share this common *Yanqui* blind spot) to leading communitarians and even the comparatively sane neoliberals of the *Economist* newspaper. Arab leaders met to discuss the impact of the Lewis-Huntington conceit, Italian Prime Minister Silvio Berlusconi invoked it, and UNESCO's director general prefaced that benighted body's worthy declaration on cultural diversity with a specific rebuttal (Rusciano 2003; Said 2001; Matsuura 2001). And as the U.S. occupation of Iraq entered its third year, military commanders and senior noncommissioned officers were required to read Huntington, along with V. S. Naipaul and *Islam for Dummies* (Schmitt 2005).

Elsewhere, *El País*'s cartoonist Máximo traumatically constructed a dialogue alongside the tumbling World Trade Center as follows: "Choque de ideas, de culturas, de civilizaciones" (Clash of ideas, of cultures, of civilizations) drew the reply "Yo lo dejaría en choques de desesperados contra instalados" (I'd call it the clash of the desperate against the establishment) (quoted in García Canclini 2002, 16). The *Arab News* aptly typified the Lewis-Huntington thesis as "Armageddon dressed up as social science," while Israel's *Ha-aretz* regarded its "hegemonic hold" as "a major triumph" for Al-Qaeda (quoted in Rusciano 2003, 175).

Study after study has disproved Lewis and Huntington's wild assertions about growing ethnic struggle since the cold war and a unitary Islamic culture opposed to a unitary West. Such claims fatally neglect struggles over money, property, politics, and creed (Fox 2002; Norris and Inglehart 2003, 203; United Nations Development Programme 2004). The clash-of-civilizations thesis does not work if it is applied to Iran supporting Russia against Chechen rebels, India against Pakistan, or the U.S. attitude to the Iran-Iraq War. But why bother with world-historical details when you are offered "international relations with politics taken out" (Abrahamian 2003, 535)?

Huntington's later critiques of Spanish speakers in the United States (2004) led to support from the Center for Immigration Studies and a battery of influential pop-policy intellectuals. The chorines included cold warrior Zbigniew Brzezinski, old-school area-studies founder Lucian Pye, Nixon and Reagan servant James Q. Wilson (who was also an advocate of the "broken windows" theory in support of severe punishments for minor wrongdoings), and reactionary *Newsweek* journalist Fareed Zakaria. The agile cultural citizens at http://www.vdare.com, self-appointed keepers of the flame of a lost tribe of *Yanqui* whiteness, were busy endorsing Huntington as well (Krikorian 2004; Ajami *et al.* 2004; Brimelow 2005). The awkward fact that just 21 percent of third-generation Latinos identify with their countries of origin, and that most U.S.-born Latinos have much more conservative views on immigration than recent arrivals (*Hispanic Fact Pack* 2005, 50; Suro 2005, 2) must be left out for this nonsense to flourish—not to mention the fact that Huntington's beloved early settlers, whose *ethos* is supposedly central to the United States, were as wrapped up in burning witches, haranguing adulteresses, and wearing foppish clothing and wigs as they were concerned with spreading democracy (Lomnitz 2005). The argument is wrong morally, pragmatically, and empirically. But it *is* cultural.

Conclusion

The arid lands of Bennett and the humidispheres of Rosaldo, Kymlicka, Parekh, and Chua illustrate the improbability of wiping from history the differences between indigenes, dominant settlers, and minority migrants. Rorty contrives a human-capital merger of all the above. Lewis and Huntington offer an ideological justification for hollowing out material history and accounting for Western hegemony in cultural terms. It seems that Bennett's competences, Rosaldo's resistances, and Kymlicka, Parekh, and Chua's relativisms can be accommodated (albeit with their rhetorics softened at some points and hardened at others) in a neoliberal worldview whose limits are set via the hyperculturalism and closet nationalism of the "clash" theorists. All for the cultural in the most cultural of all possible worlds, with the capstone being an efficient and effective work force whose tolerant cosmopolitanism is brokered on a respect for difference that becomes a guarantor of individual advantage in a globally competitive labor market, along Judaeo-Christian lines.

Each of these approaches is dealing with heavily practical yet highly emotional, and profoundly populist yet avowedly technical, forms of thought. As such, they inevitably rub up against contradictions. Bennett must deal with the incommensurability of neoliberal and statist prescriptions. Rosaldo must make peace with the fact that government is frequently the court of appeal for vernacular protest. Kymlicka and Parekh must come to terms with the economic limits to liberal philosophy. Rorty must engage the obstinate collectivism and hybridity of culture and the fact that neoliberalism is no more metacultural than any other form of thought. Chua must acknowledge the constitutive inequality and brutality of capitalism. Lewis and Huntington must explain the reality of U.S. Middle Eastern policy and more precise histories than their grandiosities will allow. And all must do so in a context that Bill Clinton (2002) has correctly identified as an environment of global interdependence without global integration.

Cultural citizenship can work toward a more equitable world if it rejects the technicism, utopianism, liberalism, nationalism, and neoliberalism of business-as-usual cultural citizenship. In answer to the theoreticism and technocracy of neoliberalism, we can point to participatory and popular budgeting systems undertaken by leftist regional and urban governments in Kerala, India, Mexico City, and Porto Alegre, Brazil, over the past fifteen years, and Brazil's *sindicato cidadão* (citizens' trade union) (Chathukulam and John 2002; Heller 2001; Dagnino 2003, 7; Ziccardi 2003). We can also form strategic alliances with opponents of neoliberalism from within its complex web of self-deception, such as George Soros, who made his fortune on the financial markets but now sees that "the untrammeled intensification of *laissez-faire* capitalism and the spread of market values into all areas of life is endangering our open and democratic society" (1997).

My concern is that the cultural Left got what it wanted: culture at the center of politics and sociopolitical analysis. But it was not Queer Nation and Stuart Hall. It was creepy Christianity and Samuel Huntington. This outflanking has meant that culture can be utilized to trump progressive approaches and politics. We need to rearticulate it to the economy and to Politics (with an intentionally capitalized *P*), not to a misleading, antimaterialist sphere of ideation.

Note

1. I have used the Spanish word for Yankee, *Yanqui*, here to draw attention to the inherent problems with the term "American."

References

The americano dream. 2005. *Economist*, July 16, pp. 8–9.

Abrahamian, Ervand. 2003. The U.S. media, Huntington and September 11. *Third World Quarterly* 24 (3): 529–44.

Abu-Laban, Yasmeen. 2000. Reconstructing an inclusive citizenship for a new millennium: Globalization, migration and difference. *International Politics* 37 (4): 509–26.

Adorno, Theodor W. 1996. *The culture industry: Selected essays on mass culture*. Trans. Gordon Finlayson, Nicholas Walker, Anson G. Rabinach, Wes Blomster, and Thomas Y. Levin. Ed. J. M. Bernstein. London: Routledge.

Ajami, Fouad, Richard Betts, Gerge Borjas, Stephen Bosworth, Zbigniew Brzezinski, Eliot Cohen, Francis Fukuyama, et al. 2004. In defense of Huntington. *Foreign Policy (*November–December): 4.

Aleinikoff, T. Alexander. 2000. Between principles and politics: U.S. citizenship policy. In *From migrants to citizens: Membership in a changing world*, ed. T. Alexander Aleinikoff and Douglas Klusmeyer, 119–72. Washington, D.C.: Carnegie Endowment for International Peace.

Alexander, Jeffrey C. 2001. Theorizing the "modes of incorporation": Assimilation, hyphenation, and multiculturalism as varieties of civil participation. *Sociological Theory* 19 (3): 237–49.

Annan, Kofi. 2003. "Emma Lazarus lecture on international flows of humanity. November 21.

Back, Les, Michael Keith, Azra Khan, Kalbir Shukra, and John Solomos. 2002. New Labour's white heart: Politics, multiculturalism and the return of assimilation. *Political Quarterly* (November 21): 445–54.

Barry, Brian. 2001. *Culture and equality: An egalitarian critique of multiculturalism*. Cambridge: Polity.

Bauböck, Rainer. 2005. Citizenship policies: International, state, migrant and democratic perspectives. *Global Migration Perspectives* 19. Geneva: Global Commission on International Migration.

Baylor Institute for Studies of Religion and Department of Sociology, Baylor University. 2006. *American piety in the 21st century: New insights to the depth and complexity of religion in the U.S.*

Benhabib, Seyla. 2002. *The claims of culture: Equality and diversity in the global era*. Princeton, NJ: Princeton University Press.

Bennett, Tony. 1998. *Culture: A reformer's science*. London: Sage.

———. 2001. *Differing diversities: Transversal study on the theme of cultural policy and cultural diversity*. Strasbourg Cedex: Council of Europe Publishing.

Bennett, William J. 1992. *The devaluing of America: The fight for our culture and our children*. New York: Touchstone.

Beteille, Andre. 1999. Citizenship, state and civil society. *Economic and Political Weekly*, September 4.

Briggs, Asa, and Peter Burke. 2003. *A social history of the media: From Gutenberg to the Internet*. Cambridge: Polity.

Brimelow, Peter. 1996. *Alien nation: Common sense about America's immigration disaster*. New York: HarperPerennial.

———. 2005. "Why Vdare.com/the white doe?" *Vdare.Com*. http://vdare.com.
"British" is already inclusive and elastic. 2000. *Independent*, October 12, p. 3.
Brown, Michael E., and _umit Ganguly. 2003. Introd. to *Fighting words: Language policy and ethnic relations in Asia*, ed. Michael E. Brown and _umit Ganguly, 1–17. Cambridge, MA: Massachusetts Institute of Technology Press.
A campus forum on multiculturalism. 1990. *New York Times*, December 9, p. 5.
Carreño, José. 2001. El día en que los estadounidenses desperataron de un sueño. In *11 de septiembre de 2001*, ed. Frida Modak, 20–23. Buenos Aires: Grupo Editorial Lumen.
Castles, Stephen, and Mark J. Miller. 2003. *The age of migration*. 3rd ed. New York: Guilford Press.
Central Board of Film Certification. 2004. *Citizen's Charter*.
Chaney, David. 2002. Cosmopolitan art and cultural citizenship. *Theory, Culture & Society* 19 (1–2): 157–74.
Chathukulam, Jos, and M. S. John. 2002. Five years of participatory planning in Kerala: Rhetoric and reality. *Economic and Political Weekly* (December 7).
Centrifugal forces. 2005. *Economist*, July 16, pp. 4–7.
Chile-indigenas: Relator de la ONU se reunira con indigenas chilenos. 2003. *Spanish Newswire Services*, July 18.
Chua, Amy. 2003. *World on fire: How exporting free market democracy breeds ethnic hatred and global instability*. New York: Doubleday.
Citizenship and cultural policy. 2000. *American Behavioral Scientist* 43, no. 9.
Clinton, Bill. 2002. The path to peace. *Salon.com*, September 10. http://salon.com.
Cohen, Robin. 1997. *Global diasporas: An introduction*. Seattle: University of Washington Press.
Coutin, Susan Bibler. 2003. Cultural logics of belonging and movement: Transnationalism, naturalization, and U.S. immigration politics. *American Ethnologist* 30 (4): 508–26.
Dagnino, Evelina. 2003. Citizenship in Latin America: An introduction. *Latin American Perspectives* 30 (2): 3–17.
Das, Veena. 2002. *Critical events: An anthropological perspective on contemporary India*. New Delhi: Oxford University Press.
de Pedro, Jesús Prieto. 1999. Democracy and cultural difference in the Spanish constitution of 1978. In *Democracy and ethnography: Constructing identities in multicultural liberal states*, ed. Carol J. Greenhouse and Roshanak Kheshti, 61–80. Albany: State University of New York Press.
Downing, John, and Charles Husband. 2005. *Representing "race": Racisms, ethnicities and media*. London: Sage.
El Nasser, Haya, and Lorrie Grant. 2005a. Immigration causes age, race split. *USA Today*, June 9, p. 1A.
———. 2005b. Diversity tints new kind of generation gap. *USA Today*, June 9, p. 4A.
Falk, Richard A. 2004. *The declining world order: America's imperial geopolitics*. New York: Routledge.
Feldman, Gregory. 2005. Culture, state, and security in Europe: The case of citizenship and integration policy in Estonia. *American Ethnologist* 32 (4): 676–94.

Flores, William V., and Rina Benmayor, eds. 1997a. *Latino cultural citizenship: Claiming identity, space, and politics*. Boston: Beacon Press.

———. 1997b. Constructing cultural citizenship. In *Latino cultural citizenship: Claiming identity, space, and politics*, ed. William V. Flores and Rina Benmayor, 1–23. Boston: Beacon Press.

Foro cultural: Ministra espanola dice que la cultura es pilar para el desarollo. 2004. *Spanish Newswire Services*, June 30.

Fox, Jonathan. 2002. Ethnic minorities and the clash of civilizations: A quantitative analysis of Huntington's thesis. *British Journal of Political Science* 32 (3): 415–35.

Freeman, Gary P., Luis F. B. Plascencia, Susan González Baker, and Manuel Orozco. 2002. Explaining the surge in citizenship applications in the 1990s: Lawful permanent residents in Texas. *Social Science Quarterly* 83 (4): 1013–25.

García Canclini, Néstor. 2002. *Latinoamericanos buscando lugar en este siglo*. Buenos Aires: Paidós.

Gray, John. 2003. *Al Qaeda and what it means to be modern*. London: Faber and Faber.

Hague, William. 2000. Why I am sick of the anti-British disease. *Daily Telegraph*, October 13, p. 28.

Halliday, Fred. 2004. The crisis of universalism: America and radical Islam after 9/11. *openDemocracy*, September 16. http://www.opendemocracynet.

Hannah, Matthew G. 2001. Sampling and the politics of representation in U.S. census 2000. *Environment and Planning D: Society and Space* 19 (5): 515–34.

Heller, Patrick. 2001. Moving the state: The politics of democratic decentralization in Kerala, South Africa, and Porto Alegre. *Politics & Society* 29 (1): 131–63.

Hispanic Fact Pack. 2005. *Advertising Age* with Association of Hispanic Advertising Agencies.

Hispanic and Asian populations expand. 2000. *New York Times*, August 30, p. A16.

Honig, Bonnie. 1998. Immigrant America? How foreignness "solves" democracy's problems. *Social Text* 56:1–27.

Huntington, Samuel P. 1993. The clash of civilizations? *Foreign Affairs* 72 (3): 22–28.

———. 2004. *¿Quiénes somos? Los desafíos a la identidad nacional estadounidense*. Trans. Albino Santos Mosquera. México: Paidós.

Jenson, Jane, and Martin Papillon. 2001. *The changing boundaries of citizenship: A review and a research agenda*. Canadian Policy Research Networks.

Jones, Richard. 2003. The new look—and taste—of British Cuisine. *Virginia Quarterly Review* 79 (2).

Krikorian, Mark. 2004. Post-Americans. *National Review Online*, June 22. http://www.nationalreview.com.

Kymlicka, Will. 1995. *Multicultural citizenship: A liberal theory of minority rights*. Oxford: Oxford University Press.

———. 2000. A North American view. *Journal of Ethnic and Migration Studies* 26 (4): 723–31.

Laitin, David D. 1999. The cultural elements of ethnically mixed states: Nationality re-formation in the Soviet successor states. In *State/culture: State-formation after the cultural turn*, ed. George Steinmetz, 291–320. Ithaca, NY: Cornell University Press.

Lewis, Bernard. 1990. The roots of Muslim rage: Why so many Muslims deeply resent the west, and why their bitterness will not be so easily mollified. *Atlantic Monthly* (September): 47–58.

Lomnitz, Claudio. 2005. American soup. *Boston Review*, March 10.

Martín-Barbero, Jesús. 2003. Proyectos de modernidad en América Latina. *Metapolítica* 29:35–51.

Maryniak, Irena. 2003. The new slave trade. *Index on Censorship* 32 (3): 87.

Massey, Douglas S. 2003. The United States in the world community: *The limits of national sovereignty*. In *The fractious nation? Unity and division in American life*, ed. Jonathan Rieder and Stephen Steinlight, 143–54. Berkeley: University of California Press.

Matsuura, Koichiro. 2001. La riqueza cultural del mundo reside en su diversidad dialogante. *Déclaración Universal de la UNESCO Sobre la Diversidad Cultural*. UNESCO.

McGee, Micki. 2005. *Self-help, inc.: Makeover culture in American life*. New York: Oxford University Press.

Miller, Toby, Nitin Govil, John McMurria, Richard Maxwell, and Ting Wang. 2005. *Global Hollywood 2*. London: British Film Institute.

Miller, Toby, Geoffrey Lawrence, Jim McKay, and David Rowe. 2001. *Globalization and sport: Playing the world*. London: Sage.

Miller, Toby, and George Yúdice. 2004. *Política cultural*. Trans. Gabriela Ventureira. Barcelona: Editorial Gedisa.

Mosisa, Abraham T. 2002. The role of foreign-born workers in the U.S. economy. *Monthly Labor Review* (May): 3–14.

Nairn, Tom. 2003. Democracy & power: American power & the world. *openDemocracy*, January 9, 16, and 23; February 4 and 20. http://www.opendemocracynet.

Norris, Pippa, and Ronald Inglehart. 2003. Public opinion among Muslims and the west. In *Framing terrorism: The news media, the government, and the public*, ed. Pippa Norris, Montague Kern, and Marion Just, 203–28. New York: Routledge.

Parekh, Bhikhu. 2000. *Rethinking multiculturalism: Cultural diversity and political theory*. Basingstoke: Palgrave.

———. 2001. Reporting on a report. Keynote address to the Political Studies Association of the United Kingdom.

Passel, Jeffrey S., and Roberto Suro. 2005. *Rise, peak, and decline: Trends in U.S. immigration 1992–2004*. Pew Hispanic Center.

Pew Research Center for the People & the Press. 2003. *Views of a changing world June 2003*.

Pew Research Center for the People & the Press. 2004. *A global generation gap: Adapting to a new world*.

Pollard, Jason. 2003. Common entrance exams. *Index on Censorship* 32 (2): 70–81.

Putnam, Robert D. 2000. *Bowling alone: The collapse and revival of American community*. New York: Simon and Schuster.

Rich, Vera. 2003. The price of return. *Index on Censorship* 32 (3): 82–86.

Rodriguez, Roberto, and Patrisia Gonzales. 1995. Cultural idea for citizenship is catching on. *Fresno Bee*, May 15, p. B5.

Rorty, Amélie Oksenberg. 1995. Rights: Educational, not cultural. *Social Research* 62 (1): 161–70.

Rosaldo, Renato. 1994. Cultural citizenship and educational democracy. *Cultural Anthropology* 9 (3): 402–11.

———. 1997. Cultural citizenship, inequality, and multiculturalism. In *Latino cultural citizenship: Claiming identity, space, and politics*, ed. William V. Flores and Rina Benmayor, 27–38. Boston: Beacon Press.

Runnymede Trust Commission. 2000. *The future of multi-ethnic Britain*. London: Profile.

Rusciano, Frank Louis. 2003. Framing world opinion in the elite press. In *Framing terrorism: The news media, the government, and the public*, ed. Pippa Norris, Montague Kern, and Marion Just, 159–79. New York: Routledge.

Said, Edward. 2001. We all swim together. *New Statesman*, October 15, p. 20.

Schlesinger, Arthur, Jr. 1991. *The disuniting of America*. Knoxville: Whittle Direct Books.

Schmitt, Eric. 2005. New U.S. commander sees shift in military role in Iraq. *New York Times*, January 16, p. 10.

Schumpeter, Joseph A. 1975. *Capitalism, socialism and democracy*. New York: HarperPerennial.

Schweder, Richard A., Martha Minow, and Hazel Rose Markus. 2002. Introd. to *Engaging cultural differences: The multicultural Challenge in Liberal Democracies*, ed. Richard A. Schweder, Martha Minow, and Hazel Rose Markus, 1–13. New York: Russell Sage Foundation.

Seaford, Helen. 2001. The future of multi-ethnic Britain: An opportunity missed. *Political Quarterly* 72 (1): 107–12.

Soros, George. 1997. The capitalist threat. *Atlantic Monthly*, February.

Stevenson, Nick. 2003. Cultural citizenship in the "cultural" society: A cosmopolitan approach. *Citizenship Studies* 7 (3): 331–48.

Suro, Roberto. 2005. *Attitudes toward immigrants and immigration policy: Surveys among U.S. Latinos and in Mexico*. Pew Hispanic Center.

Sutcliffe, Bob. 2003. Wealth of experience. *Index on Censorship* 32 (2): 42–51.

Tafoya, Sonya. 2004. *Shades of belonging*. Pew Hispanic Center.

Thio, Li-Ann. 2002. Battling Balkanization: Regional approaches toward minority protection beyond Europe. *Harvard International Law Journal* 43:409–68.

Tienda, Marta. 2002. Demography and the social contract. *Demography* 39 (4): 587–616.

Tiryakian, Edward A. 2003. Assessing multiculturalism theoretically: *E pluribus unum, sic et non. International Journal on Multicultural Societies* 5 (1): 20–39.

UNESCO Institute for Education. 1999. *Cultural citizenship in the 21st century: Adult learning and indigenous peoples*.

United Nations Development Programme. 2004. *Human development report 2004: Cultural liberty in today's diverse world*.

van Ham, Peter. 2001. The rise of the brand state: The postmodern politics of image and reputation. *Foreign Affairs* 80 (5): 2–6.

Venegas, Juan Manuel. 2003. ¿Yo por qué?, insiste Fox; ¿qué no somos 100 millones de mexicanos? *La Jornada*, Politica 3, August 2.

Venturelli, Shalini. n.d. *From the information economy to the creative economy: Moving culture to the center of international public policy*. Washington, D.C.: Center for Arts and Culture.

Wallerstein, Immanuel. 1989. Culture as the ideological battleground of the modern world-system. *Hitotsubashi Journal of Social Studies* 21 (1): 5–22.

Warner, Gerald. 2000. British identity threatened by phony race relations industry. *Scotsman*, October 15, p. 20.

Williams, Raymond. 1983. *Keywords: A vocabulary of culture and society*. Rev. ed. New York: Oxford University Press.

Yu to propose 5 fresh policy goals today. 2004. *Taiwan News*, September 17.

Yúdice, George. 1990. For a practical aesthetics. *Social Text* 25–26:129–45.

———. 2002. *El recurso de la cultura: Usos de la cultura en la era global*. Barcelona: Editorial Gedisa.

Zachary, G. Pascal. 2000. A philosopher in red sneakers gains influence as a global guru. *Wall Street Journal*, March 28, pp. B1, B4.

Ziccardi, Alicia, ed. 2003. *Planeación participativa en el espacio global: Cinco programas parciales de desarollo urbano en el distrito federal*. Mexico: Universidad Nacional Autónoma de México.

CHAPTER 9

Toward a Theorization of the U.S. "Prison Regime"

White Supremacy, Bodily Immobilization, and the "Society Structured in Dominance"

Dylan Rodriguez

Introduction: Regimes of Immobilization

Sometimes forgotten in the current epoch of "globalized" and hypermobile technologies of power are the *regimes of bodily immobilization* that counterpose social formation and global civil society with the production of new mass-based carceral forms, (undeclared) war zones, and what might be called unfree worlds. I contend that the particular production of U.S. global power in which we are all differently encircled, located/dislocated, and implicated at the current moment works and weaves through the institutionality, peculiar coercive technology, and socially ordering and disarticulating logic of the U.S. prison regime. That is, I am convinced that the visceral and persistently abstracted logic of bodily domination that crystallizes in the regime of the American prison is fundamental to the articulation of U.S. state-mediated and state-sanctioned methods of legitimated "local" (state) violence at sites across the planetary horizon. Addressing this particular moment and geography of mass-based, rigorously institutionalized, and altogether normalized human capture, this chapter is structured around two theoretical concerns.

First, in elaborating a conception of the post-1970s U.S. "prison regime,"[1] I am examining a historical and political condition that has been materially and figuratively dislocated or has *disappeared* to the underside of the U.S.

social formation and, as such, structured outside the legitimate or acceptable "political" domains of civil society (including and beyond its resident activists, professional intellectuals, and most social movements). Further, the layered, intersectional technologies of imprisonment (across scales of individualizing and mass-based techniques of bodily immobilization) have come to form the premises of a *global* antisocial formation that has become fundamental to the very intelligibility of "America"—as an ideological and cultural gravity of identity and identification, signifier of material dominion and occupation, and as a racially gendered mobilization of militarized policing and juridical force. In this sense, "The Prison" (as both a geographic and discursive production)[2] is conceptually and institutionally constitutive of contemporary "empire," the earthly social ordering that is simultaneously emblematized and mobilized by the United States.

Here, I am offering a historical definition of the United States prison regime that emerges from a genealogy of its structuring technologies of racial violence. Critically departing from the work of Orlando Patterson and Michel Foucault, I distinguish both the scale and scope of the prison regime as a specific mobilization of (state) power that relies on a particular reified institutional form ("The Prison") while generating a technology of domination that constitutively exceeds the narrow boundaries of that very same juridical-carceral structure. A critical genealogy of the U.S. prison regime is necessary, I argue, because it simultaneously *contextualizes* and *sites* the emergence of imprisonment as an *essential* element of the American social and racial formation. While others have begun to delineate the "globalization" of these mutually constitutive technologies of domination—for example, into the conspicuously "extradomestic" sites of Guantanamo Bay and Abu Ghraib[3]—I am closely examining the *genesis and prototyping* of this expansive carceral formation at the localized sites of the "domestic."

Second, I re-examine and revise Stuart Hall's durable and relevant theorization of racism as a primary modality of social formation, that is, as a central power axis of the "society structured in dominance."[4] Centering a definition of white supremacy that borrows from and extends Hall's and radical political theorist Ruth Wilson Gilmore's complementary conceptions of racism, I offer a working framework for theorizing the prison regime as the *apparatus of production* for a newly conceived, and socially determinant, white supremacist social ordering. I argue that affording such primacy to the prison's technologies of domination is both theoretically appropriate and utterly necessary, to the extent that the United States historically—and currently—has inscribed its social, political, and cultural coherence through the durable, white supremacist *institutionality* of variable mass-scale technologies of racialized immobilization and bodily disintegration.

A final note of contextualization is that the formation of the prison industrial complex has spurred a new critical idiom that generally speaks to the racialized disparities, brutalities, economic wastefulness, and overall moral corruption and corruptibility of the structures in place. Numerous conferences, academic and journalistic articles, book-length studies, memoirs, public policy initiatives, and investigative reports, along with ongoing efforts to reform jurisprudence and policing, have fostered an incipient counterstate discourse. Casting light on the state's increasing production of discriminatory, "racist," "classist," and (less frequently) "sexist" forms of criminalization and punishment, this liberal-to-progressive discourse pivots on a rhetorical emphasis on the state's *excessive* (and, at times, illegal or unconstitutional) displays of civic power. Usually accompanying this emphasis on the state's excesses is some version of political and institutional reform agenda grounded in notions of fairness, (civil) "rights," and civic responsibility (on behalf of both the state and the citizenry).[5]

Often taken for granted in this emergent debate—and thus excluded from the realm of critical discussion—is an implicit belief structure, in fact a lightly revised patriotism, that imagines the possibility of an even-handed, enlightened, and "good" policing-criminalization nexus. At the heart of this political logic is a refusal to confront the *essential white supremacist violence* of juridical retribution, state repression, and official regimes of aggressive physical-psychological torture and ritualized (collective) bodily invasion. By extension, the implicit willingness of many academics and activists to participate in the "reform" and reproduction of that violence remains a fundamental problem for more radical critics of jurisprudence, prisons, and that nexus of relationships composing the prison industrial complex.

There is a particular historical urgency in the current struggle for new vernaculars that *disarticulate* the multilayered, taken-for-granted state practices of punishment, repression, and retribution from common notions of justice, peace, and the good society. Arguably, it is this difficult and dangerous task of disarticulation, specifically the disruption and displacement of a powerful, socially determinant "law and order" common sense,[6] that remains the most undertheorized dimension of contemporary anti- and counterprison activism and research. This essay gestures toward the productive disruption of this harmful stasis, and thus concludes with a brief meditation on the current relevance of Frantz Fanon's critical theory of colonialism and liberationist struggle.

Conceptualizing the "Prison Regime"

My use of the term "prison regime" differentiates both the *scale* and *object(s)* of analysis from the more typical macroscale institutional categories of "the prison," "the prison system," and, most recently, "the prison industrial complex." The conceptual scope of this term similarly exceeds the analytical scope of prison management, prison policy, and "the prison (or prisoner's) experience," categories that most often take textual form through discrete case studies, institutional reform initiatives, prison and prisoner ethnographies, and individualized biographical and autobiographical narratives. Rather, my working conception of the prison regime invokes a "meso" (middle, or mediating) dimension of processes, structures, and vernaculars that compose the state's modalities of self-articulation and "rule" *across* these macro and micro scales. It is within this meso range of dynamic, fluctuating articulations of power that the prison is inscribed as both a *localization* and constitutive logic of the state's production of juridical, spatial, and militarized dominion.

I consider the range and parameters of the prison regime to encompass both the conventional definition of "dominion" as a discrete territory controlled by a ruling order or state, as well as its etymological relation to the Latin word *dominium*, a conception of power that posits "absolute dominion in tangible things."[7] The specificity of imprisonment as a regime of power is its *chattel logic*, or structure of abject and nonhuman objectification: to the extent that the prisoner or "inmate" is conceived as the fungible property of the state (as mentioned in the Introduction of this chapter, the Thirteenth Amendment designates the "convict's" juridical eligibility for "involuntary servitude," or enslavement), the captive is both the state's abstracted legal property, obligation, and intimate bodily possession. Orlando Patterson's explication of the roots of slavery as follows offers a useful framework through which to comprehend the root structure of this carceral-punitive regime: "The Romans invented the legal fiction of dominium or absolute ownership, a fiction that highlights their practical genius. . . . By emphasizing the categories of persona (owner) and res (thing) and by rigidly distinguishing between corporeal and incorporeal things, the Romans created a new legal paradigm. . . . An object could only be a tangible thing. *More important . . . property was no longer a relation between persons but a relation between persons and things*. And this fiction fitted perfectly its purpose, to define one of the most rapidly expanding sources of wealth, namely slaves."[8]Patterson's historical explication of slavery here facilitates a genealogy of the prison that situates its emergence as a direct derivative of the American particular and genocidal white supremacist variation on the centuries-old practice of human slavery. While the U.S. prison may be broadly conceptualized as a dynamic arrangement, or changing and strategic coalescence of power, political interest, and structural coherence, its "postemancipation" form has pivoted—*fundamentally*—on its capacity to strategically operationalize the putative "legal fiction" of (white supremacist) *dominium*. This strategic mandate has become especially crucial to the reconstruction of the prison regime in its post-1970s "law and order" incarnation.

"The prison," as a durably reified American juridical structure and indispensable pillar in the (white) imagination of societal well-being (or "law and order"), is consistently a work in progress, in fact the geographic and discursive site of a seemingly endless political-military labor that variously establishes, rearticulates, and reforms the material content and putative social meaning of state-proctored human capture. A genealogy of the prison regime is, in part, an organic history of this labor that works from the premise that the prison is neither a natural nor inevitable feature of the social landscape: *its dominion must be constantly defined and redefined, defended, and justified.*

A critical or radical genealogy of the prison regime—as opposed to a traditional history or sociology of the prison as a discrete institution—thus foregrounds the processes and struggles through which the coherence of this categorical arrangement—the grounding of the prison's dominion—is restored through and from varieties of historical crisis. We must, in other words, pay fundamental theoretical attention to the historical inconsistencies, structured anxieties, political contradictions, and constitutive crises that characterize the sociohistorical *production* of the prison and its accompaniments.[9] Essential to the political drama of this production is the structuring tension between the following two essential productions of the regime itself:

1. The prison regime's constitutive technology of violence: the sanctioning and exercise of dominium (absolute ownership and "inner power") over its human captives, a total power that does not require formal political approval or ethical consent from the ostensible polity
2. The overarching political project of portraying the prison as an (abstracted) object of state "authority": the discursive construction of the prison as a respectable and commanding institution that securely inhabits the realm of an everyday common sense and enjoys a popular consent around the apparatus of its rule.

The structuring tension between the regime's technology of violence (which is impervious to the vicissitudes of "consent") and self-constructing discourse (which produces and galvanizes popular consent) amplifies the centrality of the prison regime to the state's *pedagogical* project of rendering itself intelligible to its presumed audiences, including and beyond its formal polity. The prison regime has become an indispensable element of American statecraft, simultaneously a cornerstone of its militarized (local and global) ascendancy and spectacle of its extracted (or coerced) authority over targeted publics. The specificity of the prison regime as a production of state power is its rigorous and extravagant marshalling of technologies of violence, domination, and subjection otherwise reserved for deployment in sites of declared (extradomestic) war or martial law.

This reconceptualization of the prison regime resonates with Michel Foucault's seminal discussion of the displacement of unitary sovereign powers in modern and postmodern social formations. Foucault is famously concerned with the production of regimes of power through situated apparatuses and institutions (e.g., the asylum, the clinic, the prison, the military) that in turn circulate power socially through various embodiments, including symbolic orderings, "sciences," military and paramilitary technologies, and strategically sited and situated human bodies. In a lecture dated January 14, 1976, Foucault contends,

> Our object is not to analyze rule-governed and legitimate forms of power which have a single center, or to look at what their general mechanisms or its overall effects might be. *Our object is, on the contrary, to understand power by looking at its extremities, at its outer limits at the points where it becomes capillary*; in other words, to understand power in its most regional forms and institutions, and especially at the points where this power transgresses the rules of right that organize and delineate it, oversteps those rules and is invested in institutions, is embodied in techniques and acquires the material means to intervene, sometimes in violent ways.[10] [emphasis added]

Foucault's "capillary power" designates the manner in which power circulates, materializing through the form and movement of its outermost (extreme) points of expression. The prison, precisely such a capillary site for the production and movement of power, exerts a dominion that reaches significantly beyond its localized setting. This is to argue that the post-1970s emergence of a reformed and reconceived prison regime has become central to constituting the political logic as well as the material reproduction of the U.S. social formation.

It is worth addressing Foucault's conceptualization a bit further, noting that capillaries, in the medical definition, are "the tiny blood vessels that connect the arterioles (the smallest divisions of the arteries) and the venules (the smallest divisions of the veins)." These blood vessels, like the prison, form crucial sites of passage for the transfer of the (social) body's life-sustaining nutrients as well as for the spread of (alleged social) disease, infection, and impurity. They are evidence of a functioning order, a living organism. "Although minute, the capillaries are a site where much action takes place in the circulatory system."[11] Apropos of this medical definition, an essential (warfare) technology of the prison regime is its circulation of violence through its legitimated practitioners—the bodies of designated agents (guards, doctors, wardens, prison educators) and guardians of the dominion—and simultaneous performance and materialization *on* the bodies of an immobilized captive population. This is to extrapolate Foucault's conception of capillary power beyond its metaphorical deployment, and to suggest its relevance as a literal designation for the materiality of the prison regime's modalities of violence on the imprisoned subject's *bodily* capillaries, that is her or his flesh and blood.

I am reconceptualizing the prison as a putative "centering" and consolidation of power that, in practice, necessarily exceeds and violates its official directives and juridical norms. This regime functions through excesses and violations, at times uncodified or nominally "illegal," though generally occurring within generously interpreted rubrics of institutional policy and protocol. As an arrangement of power that harnesses and rearranges its constitutive logics of human domination and disintegration, this regime constitutively belies and abrogates its "rule-governed" and "legitimate" discursive-institutional inscription as the prison. Incidentally, this remapping of the state and its regime of carceral violence disrupts extant liberal and progressive "human rights" critiques of imprisonment and policing practices, which largely reify such varieties of proctored bodily punishment as *pathologies* of the state, often framed in the language of "brutality" and "torture."

The contemporary U.S. prison regime is the complex formation of civil society's punitive underside, a presence that, rather then defining (a normatively white and white supremacist) civilization's "outside" or opposite in the simplest binary terms (lawfulness versus criminality, or civility versus savagery), instead poses an available set of signs, discourses, and sites for the production of coherence in the U.S. social order. Prison and civil society, while defined as inversions of one another, are not mutually exclusive domains of experience and existence (the status of parole, a release from imprisonment conditional on the perpetuation of the state's immediate and unmediated access to the parolee's body, may best illustrate this relation)—rather, they are overlapping and mutually constitutive historical productions, constantly reproduced by a material vernacular of crisis, and institutionalized through the conjoined realms of the juridical, the military, and the cultural.

To situate the prison's strategically sited technologies of violence and human subjection *as a normal and "everyday" regime of punishment* is to firmly locate these alleged excesses of the state within the larger sociohistorical fabric in which they are enmeshed, and of which they are constitutive. The state's contemporary modality of power and enunciation—its statecraft—works through the constant exceeding of its announced material boundaries and juridical limits. Brutality, torture, and excess should be understood as an essential element of American statecraft, not as its corruption or deviation. This is to suggest that the prison, as a state articulation of rigidly centered and conservatively ordered institutional power, does not actually exist, and that it is best conceptualized as a rigorously reproduced mythology of sober and narrowly deployed state power.[12] This mythology effectively rationalizes and renarrates a domestic (or systemically internal) site of aggressively one-sided, racially gendered warfare. Within the operative political technologies of the prison regime, war is business as usual, and the myth of the prison is its resident public relations campaign.

White Supremacy, the Prison Regime, and the Prison Industrial Complex

This conceptualization of the prison regime provokes an extensive theorization of state and state-sanctioned bodily violence as the central and productive technology of a "society structured in dominance." Stuart Hall's oft-quoted elaboration of racism as a central sociocultural production—and dynamic, politically structuring component—of modern social formations bespeaks the specificity of racist and racial ideologies as they are produced and "made operative" in different historical moments. His essay "Race, Articulation, and Societies Structured in Dominance"[13] rigorously examines the "ideological articulation" between racism and class relations, popular culture, and other modes of social thought and "popular consciousness." Hall is worth quoting at length, for the purposes of situating his theorization within this discussion of the U.S. carceral formation as follows:

> In each case, in specific social formations, racism as an ideological configuration has been reconstituted by the dominant class relations, and thoroughly reworked. If it has performed the function of that cementing ideology which secures a whole social formation under a dominant class, its pertinent differences from other such hegemonic ideologies require to be registered in detail. Here, racism is particularly powerful and its imprint on popular consciousness especially deep, because in such racial characteristics as colour, ethnic origin, geographical position, etc., racism discovers what other ideologies have to construct: an apparently "natural" and universal basis in nature itself. Yet, despite this apparent grounding in biological givens, outside history racism, when it appears, has an effect on other ideological formations within the same society, and its development promotes a transformation of the whole ideological field in which it becomes operative.[14]

I am interesting in putting a finer point on Hall's conception of racism's multiple (and transformative) articulations within social formation. Most importantly, I wish to consider imprisonment, punishment, and policing as the *categorical practices* through which hegemonic, overlapping conceptions of "freedom" and "peace"—themselves structured in dominance—cohere the

U.S. "society." A close examination of these regimes of social ordering—prisons, the law, (domestic and undeclared) warfare, and policing—contextualizes a historicized definition of white supremacy, which is essential to the theoretical framework that I am suggesting here.

White supremacist regimes organic (if not unique) to the United States—from racial chattel slavery and frontier genocide to recent and current modes of land displacement and (domestic and undeclared) warfare—are sociologically entangled with the state's changing paradigms, strategies, and technologies of human incarceration and punishment. The historical nature of this entanglement is widely acknowledged, although explanations of the structuring relations of force vary widely and conflict deeply.[15] For our theoretical purposes, white supremacy may be understood as a logic of social organization that produces regimented, institutionalized, and militarized conceptions of hierarchical "human" difference. There are three essential components to this theoretical framework.

First, as a historical discourse of power, white supremacy is premised on the conception and enforcement of the universalized white (European and Euro-American) "human" vis-à-vis the rigorous production, penal discipline, and frequent social, political, and biological neutralization or extermination of the (nonwhite) sub- or nonhuman. While such hierarchical differences are overwhelmingly constituted through discourses of "race," they are also made through references to and productions of "ethnicity," "nationality," "religion," "biology," and other discursive regimes. It is, however, the fundamental and durable opposition between the white universal human and the peculiar nonwhite sub-, semi-, or nonhuman that reproduces white supremacy as a force of social order.[16]

Second, in order to understand white supremacy as a complex technology of human domination, one needs to look no further than to Gilmore's conception of "racism" as the primary weaponry of white supremacy. Her conceptualization departs from hackneyed definitions of racism (as well as "racial discrimination," "racial inequality," and "race relations") that obscure historical relations of power and domination, and instead magnifies the centrality of race to the programmatic and hierarchical organization of life and death as follows: "Racism is the state-sanctioned and/or extra-legal production and exploitation of group-differentiated vulnerabilities to premature death, in distinct yet densely interconnected political geographies."[17] As a logic of social organization, white supremacy is scaffolded by technologies of killing that sediment in Gilmore's definition of racism, recalling histories of militarized mass-based liquidation, as well as normalized and institutionalized forms of racial population control and targeted decimation, including coerced inaccessibility to shelter, nutrition, and health care.

Third, white supremacy must be understood as inextricably gendered; its modalities of articulation and violence are specific to constructions and expropriations of the male and female "biological" and projections of masculine and feminine sexuality and social existence.[18] Critical race theorist Dorothy Roberts, in her study of U.S. judicial aggression against black women's reproductive freedoms, writes,

> Black procreation helped to sustain slavery, giving slave masters an economic incentive to govern Black women's reproductive lives. Slave women's childbearing replenished the enslaved labor force: Black women bore children who belonged to the slaveowner from the moment of their conception. This feature of slavery made control of reproduction a central aspect of whites' subjugation of African people in America. It marked Black women from the beginning as objects whose decisions about reproduction should be subject to social regulation rather than their own will. . . .
>
> All of these violations were sanctioned by law. Racism created for white slaveowners the possibility of unrestrained reproductive control. The social order established by powerful white men was founded on two inseparable ingredients: the dehumanization of Africans on the basis of race, and the control of women's sexuality and reproduction.[19]

Native American scholar and radical antiviolence activist Andrea Smith resonates with Roberts in her contention that

> communities of color become pollution from which the state must constantly purify itself. Women of color become particularly dangerous to the world order as they have the ability to reproduce the next generations of communities of color. . . .
>
> Colonizers such as Andrew Jackson recommended that troops systematically kill Indian women and children after massacres in order to complete extermination. . . .
>
> Consequently, Native women and women of color *deserve no bodily integrity* . . . or, as Chicago-based reproductive rights activist Sharon Powell describes it, women of color are "better dead than pregnant."[20] [emphasis added]

White supremacy, in this historical and theoretical context, may be conceptualized as a socially ordering logic rather than an "extremist" or otherwise marginal political ideology. By way of illustration, this is to consider the American social formation as the template for the Ku Klux Klan (a proudly "White Christian" organization), and to comprehend the complex role of "mainstream" American civil society (in conjunction with its precedent colonial, frontier, and plantation forms) as simultaneously the Klan's periodic political antagonist and historical partner in violence.[21]

To consider white supremacy as American social formation facilitates a discussion of the modalities through which this material racial logic constitutes and overdetermines the social, political, economic, and cultural structures that (a) institutionally compose the contemporary hegemony and (b) discursively form the common sense that is organic to its ordering. For the purposes of this text, I conceptualize white supremacy through its fundamental contrapuntality, the inscription of a fundamental relation between freedom and unfreedom, life and death, historically derived from the socially constitutive American production of white life and mobility through black, brown, and indigenous death and immobilization. The contemporary prison regime is, in this context, simultaneously the materialization of U.S. civil society's presumptive white corporate identity (inclusive of its post–civil rights "multicultural" articulations) and the production of a social logic essential to the current social order—a fabrication and criminalization of disorder for the sake of extracting and dramatizing order, compliance, and authority.

Thus, while Hall references racism as the ideological glue of a given hegemony, I am arguing that in the current era of mass imprisonment, white supremacist unfreedom—specifically, carceral technologies of human immobilization and bodily disintegration—provides the institutional form, cultural discourse, and ethical basis of social coherence, safety, and civic peace. It is therefore the normal functioning of the prison that bears interrogation, as opposed to its "brutal," "unconstitutional," "racist," "homophobic," or "sexist" excesses, corruptions, and institutional imperfections. The work of imprisoned radical intellectuals traces the contours and continuities of American civil society as a dynamic locality of white freedom, domesticating and proliferating the twinned constitutive logics of white bodily mobility and ascendant white historical and political subjectivity ("freedom") across scales of varying magnitude—from the grandiose racial property and white existential claims of the United States' political and juridical foundations, to the ongoing construction of the white American *telos*, and corresponding material narration of the white nationalist B*ildungsroman*.

As the U.S. prison, jail, INS or Homeland Security detainee, and incarcerated youth population approaches and surpasses the 2.5 million mark (as of this writing), the quantitative evidence only refracts the prison's qualitative transformation.[22] Activist-scholar and former political prisoner Angela Y. Davis has written and spoken extensively of the structures of "invisibility" accompanying the formation of state and corporate alliances through the development of a mass imprisonment regime. Echoing Davis, political prisoner Jalil Muntaqim argues that the elaboration and circulation of a racially coded punitive state discourse assumes a material life of its own, as the constant dramatization of criminality, personal endangerment, and vengeance interpellates civil society's subjects.[23] He writes, "By shaping the collective consciousness and attitudes, the politicians are then able to pass into law draconian sanctions. Sanctions that appease the will of the people demanding a safe society . . . ultimately serve the interest of restructuring the industrial-military complex, by forging an infrastructure for the proliferation of prison building. . . . It anesthetizes the collective consciousness towards the desired end of permitting hundreds of thousands, if not millions more people to be incarcerated *at no moral or psychic detriment to those who constitute the majority of Americans*."[24]Muntaqim reminds us that the political and economic impetus behind this historical formation has generated a popular ethos of repression that renders criminalized populations and incarcerated people the collective objects of a normalized state violence. The most insidious aspect of this violence is that it is not simply a repressive response to social upheaval, collective disobedience, or criminal activity, that is, the (neo)liberal state is not simply coercive, but is also productive of and symbiotic with the logic and culture of what Gilmore aptly names "industrialized punishment."[25]

Carceral state violence is thus the figurative and material nexus of multiple logics of domination and hegemony in the post-1960s era: it is a white supremacist formation that is simultaneously (though always unevenly) constituted by a vectoring of power trajectories that entwines the often reified analytical categories of "race," "gender," "class," "sexuality," "age," and bodily and mental "(dis)ability." To the extent that the state has come to rely on the pageantry of the sociopolitical crisis for its various productions of social coherence, it has also reconstructed the political and cultural fabric of policing, punishment, and incarceration. The following section discusses the manner in which a new and necessary exterior to civil society, premised on the rehabilitation and security of civil society's common white supremacist normativity, has transformed the prison into a constitutive center of the existing hegemony. This new constitutive center reinscribes social formation by consolidating the emergent carceral formation as a new site of structured antisociality and civic death.

Conclusion: "The Abolition of One Zone"

To appropriate Frantz Fanon's meditation in a different time and place, a war of social truths rages beneath the normalized violence of any such condition of domination as that encompassed by the U.S. prison regime and the living apocalypse it engenders. It is the Manichean relation between colonized and colonizer, "native" and "settler," or here, free and unfree, that conditions the subaltern truths of both imminent and manifest insurgencies. Speaking to the anticolonialist nationalism of the Algerian revolution, Fanon writes,

> The problem of truth ought also to be considered. In every age, among the people truth is the property of the national cause. No absolute verity, no discourse on the purity of the soul, can shake this position. The native replies to the living lie of the colonial situation by an equal falsehood. His [*sic*] dealings with his fellow-nationals are open; they are strained and incomprehensible with regard to the settlers. Truth is that which hurries on the break-up of the colonialist regime; it is that which promotes the emergence of the nation; it is all that protects the natives, and ruins the foreigners. In this colonialist context there is no truthful behavior: and the good is quite simply that which is evil for "them."[26]

Truth, for Fanon, is precisely that which generates and multiplies the historical possibility of disruptive, subversive movement against colonial oppression. The evident rhetoric of oppositionality, of the subaltern "good" that necessarily materializes "evil" in the eyes of domination, offers a stunning departure from the language of negotiation, dialogue, progress, moderation, and peace that has become hegemonic in discourses of social change and social justice, in and outside the United States. The native's "equal falsehood" is, in fact, a necessary and ethical response to a regime that renders a hegemonic truth through the regulated death and deterioration of the native's body and society. Perhaps most importantly, the political language of opposition is premised on its open-endedness and contingency, a particular refusal to soothe the anxiety generated in the attempt to displace a condition of violent peace for the sake of something else, a world beyond agendas, platforms, and practical proposals. There are no guarantees, or arrogant expectations, of an ultimate state of liberation waiting on the other side of the politically immediate struggle against the settler colony.

Civil society's structure of freedom—however endangered and flimsily nominal—is defined and reproduced through the mass incarceration of the unfree "natives," the immediate "beings hemmed in,"[27] and specifically structured against the lineage of black slave ontology and the orbiting, approximating forms of enslavement and imprisonment that it yields. Thus, working within the logic of Fanon's terms, it is crucial to absorb that nonimprisoned ("free") people are largely constituted by "(white and multicultural) settlers" and an assimilated "native petit bourgeoisie," who at times disavow their political allegiance to the prison regime, yet who by their very existence—as the nominally free—define and fortify its domain. Fanon, addressing the Algerian "native intellectual" class—the colonized petit bourgeoisie whose political loyalties are cast in doubt during the movement of decolonization—posits a historically situated transformation of "truth," that is, its embodiment in the native and against the settler (and, perhaps, against the native petit bourgeoisie as well).

Writing at the very genesis of the contemporary prison regime in 1971, an anonymous poet in Soledad State Prison (California) prophetically lays bare the structural antagonism of the relation between the free and the unfree in "A Sunny Soledad Afternoon" as follows:

> come then, citizens, into the
> penal pits and claim us. come
> claim the tortured sons suffering
> toilet paper destiny. come and
> share our rue soup, zoological
> violences, and our common goals
> to nowhere but gone . . .
> come see skeletons
> tripping off the ends of monotone
> tongues and come hear the clatter
> of bones shattering on fragile
> stone floors. come view the solid
> wall horizon echoing empty-eyed
> stare until despair drinks dry
> the will to look.[28]

The overriding bitterness of the piece is deeply principled, the hostility toward the status of the "citizen" an expression of the political stakes at hand in the reading, interpretation, and circulation of the imprisoned poet's work by a nominally free audience (the text in which the poem was published, *Words from the House of the Dead*, is essentially a mimeographed compilation of writing and visual art smuggled from Soledad prison). This invitation to partake in a mind-numbing despair, to become intimate with living death, confronts the free person—particularly the self-identified progressive or radical activist—with the irreconcilable contradiction of embracing a freedom, or even waging a liberation struggle, that does not encompass an abolition of the poet's "sunny" Soledad. Henceforth springs the historical and political burden borne on (and often refused by) contemporary free world activists, most especially self-identified radicals, revolutionaries, and liberationists, whose condition of existence (that is, their relative social, political, and bodily mobility) entails the constant immobilization of their imprisoned analogues.

Notes

1. A fuller elaboration of some of the central components of this chapter appears in the author's recently published book, *Forced Passages: Imprisoned Radical Intellectuals and the U.S. Prison Regime* (Minneapolis: University of Minnesota Press, 2006).

2. Ruth Wilson Gilmore (University of Southern California) has been the most notable and nuanced voice on the formation of the U.S. prison apparatus as a political geography that is, at the same time, enabled and materially constructed by a particular discursive structure that links the crises of racism and globalization to state-ordained, mass-based punishment. While I most thoroughly absorbed her ideas on the conceptual-material relation between geography and discourse in the context of a fall 1999 seminar in the Department of Geography at the University of California, Berkeley, her scholarly publications (noted in the bibliography) have formed a readily accessible foundation from which I could develop other ideas in this chapter.
3. By way of a recent example of such a working delineation, see Leah Caldwell, "Iraqi Dungeons and Torture Chambers Under New, American Trained Management," *Prison Legal News* 15, no. 9 (September 2004): 1. See also Julia Sudbury, "Transatlantic Visions: Resisting the Globalization of Mass Incarceration," *Social Justice* 27, no. 3 (2000): 133–49.
4. Stuart Hall, "Race, Articulation, and Societies Structured in Dominance," in *Black British Cultural Studies: A Reader*, ed. Houston A. Baker Jr., Manthia Diawara, and Ruth H. Lindeborg (Chicago: University of Chicago Press, 1996), 56.
5. While examples of this discursive strain abound, some of the more prominent texts include Barry Scheck, Peter Neufeld, and Jim Dwyer, *Actual Innocence: Five Days to Execution, and Other Dispatches from the Wrongly Convicted* (New York: Doubleday, 2000); Mark Mauer, *Race to Incarcerate* (New York: New Press, 1999); John Irwin and James Austin, *It's About Time: America's Imprisonment Binge*, 3rd ed. (Belmont, CA: Wadsworth Publishing, 2001); and Joel Dyer, *The Perpetual Prisoner Machine: How America Profits from Crime* (Boulder, CO: Westview, 2001). While it is beyond my intent to conduct a sufficient review of these books here, they do clearly evidence the thrust of the progressive prison reformist argument as illustrated in my brief summation. As I will argue later in the chapter, racism and white supremacy are *socially determinant* features of American social formation—that is, they are inseparable from the very reproduction of the United States and cannot be "reformed" to the extent that they are primary technologies of social ordering. These texts conceive racism and racial "disparity" as reformable aspects of American policing, corrections, and jurisprudence, and thus fail to comprehend that the prison is *essentially* a structure of racial domination. I argue this point more thoroughly in *Forced Passages: Imprisoned Radical Intellectuals and the Formation of the U.S. Prison Regime* (Minneapolis: University of Minnesota Press, 2006).
6. My use of the term "common sense" derives from Antonio Gramsci's conception of the assumptions, truths, and general faiths that predominate in a given social formation or hegemony. See Antonio Gramsci, *Selections from the Prison Notebooks* (New York: International Publishers, 1971).
7. Orlando Patterson, *Slavery and Social Death: A Comparative Study* (Cambridge, MA: Harvard University Press, 1982), 31.
8. Orlando Patterson, *Slavery and Social Death: A Comparative Study* (Cambridge, MA: Harvard University Press, 1982), 31; emphasis added.

9. My use of genealogy here resonates with Foucault's assertion that "one has to dispense with the constituent subject, to get rid of the subject itself, that's to say, to arrive at an analysis which can account for the constitution of the subject within a historical framework. And this is what I would call genealogy, that is, a form of history which can account for the constitution of knowledges, discourses, domains of objects, etc., without having to make reference to a subject which is either transcendental in relation to the field of events or runs its empty sameness throughout the course of history." Michel Foucault, "Truth and Power" [interview], in *Power/Knowledge: Selected Interviews and Other Writings, 1972–1977*, ed. Colin Gordon (New York: Pantheon, 1980), 122.
10. Michel Foucault, "14 January 1976," in *"Society Must Be Defended": Lectures at the Collége de France, 1975–1976* New York: Picador, 2003), 27–28; originally published in French in 1997.
11. "Capillary," MedTerms Online Medical Dictionary, http://www.medterms.com.
12. Foucault writes, "I don't want to say that the State isn't important; what I want to say is that relations of power, and hence the analysis that must be made of them, necessarily extend beyond the limits of the State. . . . The State can only operate on the basis of other, already existing power relations. The State is superstructural in relation to a whole series of power networks that invest the body, sexuality, the family, kinship, knowledge, technology and so forth." Foucault, "Truth and Power," 122.
13. Hall, "Race, Articulation," in Baker Jr., Diawara, and Lindeborg, *Black British Cultural Studies*, 56.
14. Ibid.
15. See, for example, Angela Y. Davis, "From the Prison of Slavery to the Slavery of Prison: Frederick Douglass and the Convict Lease System," in *The Angela Y. Davis Reader*, ed. Joy A. James (Malden, MA: Blackwell, 1998); Alex Lichtenstein, *Twice the Work of Free Labor* (New York: Verso, 1996); Lawrence Friedman, *Crime and Punishment in American History* (New York: Basic Books, 1993); and Paul Keve, *Prisons and the American Conscience* (Carbondale: Southern Illinois University Press, 1991).
16. For an intellectual history of racism and racial ideology, see Winthrop Jordan, *White over Black: American Attitudes toward the Negro, 1550–1812* (Baltimore: Penguin, 1968); George Frederickson, *Racism: A Short History* (Princeton, NJ: Princeton University Press, 2002); George Frederickson, *The Black Image in the White Mind: The Debate on Afro-American Character and Destiny, 1817–1914* (New York: Harper and Row, 1971); and David Theo Goldberg, *Racist Culture* (Cambridge, MA: Blackwell, 1993).
17. Ruth Wilson Gilmore, "Race and Globalization," in *Geographies of Global Change: Remapping the World*, ed. R. J. Johnston, Peter J. Taylor, and Michael Watts (New York: Blackwell, 2002), 261.
18. In addition to the following passages from Roberts and Smith, see generally Anannya Bhattacharjee, "Private Fists and Public Force," in *Policing the National Body: Race, Gender, and Criminalization, ed.* Anannya Bhattacharjee and Jael Silliman, 1–54 (Cambridge: South End Press, 2002); and Judith A. M. Scully,

"Killing the Black Community," in *Policing the National Body: Race, Gender, and Criminalization*, ed. Anannya Bhattacharjee and Jael Silliman, 55–80 (Cambridge: South End Press, 2002). For a sociological examination of the crucial role of white women in contemporary white supremacist movements and organizations, see Kathleen M. Blee, *Inside Organized Racism: Women in the Hate Movement* (Berkeley: University of California Press, 2002).

19. Dorothy Roberts, *Killing the Black Body: Race, Reproduction, and the Meaning of Liberty* (New York: Vintage Books, 1999), 22–23.
20. Andrea Smith, "Better Dead than Pregnant: The Colonization of Native Women's Reproductive Health," *Policing the National Body: Race, Gender, and Criminalization*, ed. Anannya Bhattacharjee and Jael Silliman, 123–46 (Cambridge: South End Press, 2002), 123–24.
21. The Klan's primary website, at http://www.kkk.bz, conspicuously displays passages from the Bible alongside gratuitous images of the Capitol building, American eagles, and the U.S. flag. It is, quite literally, a classic American nationalist organization. Other white supremacist organizations, including patriot groups, neo-Nazis, and white militias, evince a similar commitment to the flourishing of a particular vision of American exceptionalism that draws from its core political and cultural legacies, including republicanism, "white rights" and "Christian values."
22. The figure 2.5 million includes imprisoned populations that are almost always excluded from common carceral body counts, including but not limited to children, undocumented peoples, and people detained under the exceptionalist auspices of the post-2001 U.S. "War on Terror." The most frequently quoted figures are from the United States Bureau of Justice Statistics. See, for example, Paige M. Harrison and Jennifer C. Karberg, "Prison and Jail Inmates at Midyear 2003" Washington, D.C., U.S. Department of Justice, NCJ 203947, May 2004). According to the Bureau of Justice Statistics (BJS), as of June 2003, there were 2,078,570 prisoners held in federal or state prisons and local jails.

    In addition, the U.S. Department of Justice's Office of Juvenile Justice and Delinquency Prevention writes in its 2002 annual report that there were 108,931 children incarcerated as of 1999 (*OJJDP Annual Report 2002*, NCJ 202038, p. 59). It is almost certain that the current population of imprisoned children exceeds this figure, especially since a growing number of youth under the age of 18 are being sent to adult jails and prisons (statistics on incarcerated populations typically have a 1-2 year lag, due to the time expended in collecting and calculating data). Finally, the Department of Homeland Security, which bureaucratically absorbed the older Immigration and Naturalization Service (INS), reports that in 2002, there were 188,547 non-citizens held in INS prisons on an average day (memorandum from Acting Inspector General Clark Kent Ervin, "Major Management Challenges Facing the Department of Homeland Security," March 2003).
23. Jalil Muntaqim (a.k.a. Anthony Jalil Bottom) first affiliated with the Black Panther Party when he was eighteen years old, after being recruited by elementary school friends who had since become Panthers. On August 28, 1971, he was captured, along with Albert Nuh Washington, in a midnight shoot-out with San

Francisco police. It has been alleged that Muntaqim and Washington attempted to assassinate a police sergeant in retaliation for the August 21, 1971, assassination of George Jackson, who during the time of his imprisonment had become an internationally recognized black liberationist thinker and antifascist, antiracist prison organizer (in part through the publication of his two books: *Soledad Brother* (Chicago: Lawrence Hill Books, 1994), originally published 1970; and *Blood in My Eye* (Baltimore: Black Classic Press, 1990), originally published 1972. Subsequently, Muntaqim, Washington, and Herman Bell—who came to be known as the "New York Three"—were charged with a host of revolutionary underground activities, including the assassination of New York City police officers for which they were given life sentences. Muntaqim has actively worked with a wide variety of activist and educational campaigns and organizations since his imprisonment, including his founding call for the Jericho Amnesty march in 1998 (which eventually catalyzed the formation of the Jericho Amnesty Movement) and the National Prisoners Campaign to Petition the United Nations in 1976. See Committee to End the Marion Lockdown, *Can't Jail the Spirit*, 5th ed. (Chicago: Committee to End the Marion Lockdown, 2002), 136–40. Also see Solidarity, "The New York Three: History and Case Background" (Montreal: Solidarity, February 2002), an informational essay published by Solidarity in February 2002. The essay may be obtained through Solidarity by mailing 2035 Boulevard, St. Laurent, Montreal, Quebec, Canada, H2X 2T3, or on the Internet at http://www.kersplebedeb.com/mystuff/profiles/ny3A.pdf. Jalil Muntaqim may be contacted at: Anthony Jalil Bottom, # 77A4283, Auburn Correctional Facility, 135 State Street, Auburn, NY, 13024.

24. Jalil Muntaqim (a.k.a. Anthony Jalil Bottom), "The Cold War of the 90's," *Prison News Service*, no. 52 (September–October 1995): 1–2; emphasis added.
25. See Ruth Wilson Gilmore, *Golden Gulag: Prisons, Surplus, Crisis, and Opposition in Globalizing California* (Berkeley: University of California Press, 2007).
26. Frantz Fanon, *The Wretched of the Earth*, trans. Constance Farrington (New York: Grove Weidenfeld, 1968), 50, originally published 1963.
27. Ibid., 52.
28. Anonymous, "A Sunny Soledad Afternoon," in *Words from the House of the Dead, ed. Joseph* Bruchac and William Witherup (Greenfield Center, NY: Greenfield Review Press, 1971).

Bibliography

Anonymous. "A Sunny Soledad Afternoon." In *Words from the House of the Dead*, edited by Joseph Bruchac and William Witherup Greenfield Center, NY: Greenfield Review Press, 1971.

Bhattacharjee, Anannya. "Private Fists and Public Force." In *Policing the National Body: Race, Gender, and Criminalization*, edited by Anannya Bhattacharjee and Jael Silliman. Cambridge: South End Press, 2002.

Blee, Kathleen M. *Inside Organized Racism: Women in the Hate Movement*. Berkeley: University of California Press, 2002.

Caldwell, Leah. "Iraqi Dungeons and Torture Chambers Under New, American Trained Management." *Prison Legal News* 15, no. 9 15, no. 9 (September 2004): 1.

Committee to End the Marion Lockdown. *Can't Jail the Spirit*. 5th ed. Chicago: Committee to End the Marion Lockdown, 2002.

Davis, Angela Y. *The Angela Y. Davis Reader*. Edited by Joy James. Malden, MA: Blackwell, 1998.

Dyer, Joel. *The Perpetual Prisoner Machine: How America Profits from Crime*. Boulder, CO: Westview, 2001.

Ervin, Clark Kent. "Major Management Challenges Facing the Department of Homeland Security." Memorandum to the Department of Homeland Security. March 2003.

Fanon, Frantz. *The Wretched of the Earth*. Translated by Constance Farrington. New York: Grove Weidenfeld, 1968. Originally published 1963.

Foucault, Michel. *Power/Knowledge: Selected Interviews and Other Writings, 1972–1977*. Edited by Colin Gordon. New York: Pantheon Books, 1980.

———. *"Society Must Be Defended": Lectures at the Collége de France, 1975–1976*. New York: Picador, 2003. Originally published 1997.

Frederickson, George. *The Black Image in the White Mind: The Debate on Afro-American Character and Destiny, 1817–1914*. New York: Harper and Row, 1971.

———. *Racism: A Short History*. Princeton, NJ: Princeton University Press, 2002.

Friedman, Lawrence. *Crime and Punishment in American History*. New York: Basic Books, 1993.

Gilmore, Ruth Wilson. "Race and Globalization." In *Geographies of Global Change: Remapping the World*, edited by R. J. Johnston, Peter J. Taylor, and Michael Watts. New York: Blackwell, 2002.

Goldberg, David Theo. *Racist Culture*. Cambridge, MA: Blackwell, 1993.

Hall, Stuart. "Race, Articulation and Societies Structures in Dominance." In *Black British Cultural Studies: A Reader*, edited by Houston A. Baker Jr., Manthia Diawara, and Ruth H. Lindeborg. Chicago: University of Chicago Press, 1996.

Harrison, Paige M., and Jennifer C. Karberg. "Prison and Jail Inmates at Midyear 2003." Washington, D.C.: U.S. Department of Justice, NCJ 203947, May 2004.

Irwin, John, and James Austin. *It's About Time: America's Imprisonment Binge*. 3rd ed. Belmont, CA: Wadsworth, 2001.

Jordan, Winthrop. *White over Black: American Attitudes toward the Negro, 1550–1812*. Baltimore: Penguin, 1968.

Keve, Paul. *Prisons and the American Conscience*. Carbondale: Southern Illinois University Press, 1991.

Lichtenstein, Alex. *Twice the Work of Free Labor*. New York: Verso, 1996.

Mauer, Mark. *Race to Incarcerate*. New York: New Press, 1999.

Muntaqim, Jalil. "The Cold War of the 90s." *Prison News Service*, no. 52 (September–October 1995): http://www.prisonactivist.org/pubs/jalil-cold-war-90s.html..

Office of Juvenile Justice and Delinquency Prevention (U.S. Department of Justice). *OJJDP Annual Report 2002*. U.S. Department of Justice, Office of Juvenile Justice and Delinquency Prevention, NCJ 202038, July 2004.

Patterson, Orlando. *Slavery and Social Death: A Comparative Study*. Cambridge, MA: Harvard University Press, 1982.

Roberts, Dorothy. *Killing the Black Body: Race, Reproduction, and the Meaning of Liberty*. New York: Vintage Books, 1999.

Rodríguez, Dylan. *Forced Passages: Imprisoned Radical Intellectuals and the U.S. Prison Regime*. Minneapolis: University of Minnesota Press, 2006.

Scheck, Barry, Peter Neufeld, and Jim Dwyer. *Actual Innocence: Five Days to Execution, and Other Dispatches from the Wrongly Convicted*. New York: Doubleday, 2000.

Scully, Judith A. M. "Killing the Black Community." In *Policing the National Body: Race, Gender, and Criminalization*, edited by Anannya Bhattacharjee and Jael Silliman. Cambridge: South End Press, 2002.

Smith, Andrea. "Better Dead than Pregnant: The Colonization of Native Women's Reproductive Health." In *Policing the National Body: Race, Gender, and Criminalization*, edited by Anannya Bhattacharjee and Jael Silliman. Cambridge: South End Press, 2002.

Solidarity. "The New York Three: History and Case Background." Montreal: Solidarity, February 2002.

Sudbury, Julia. "Transatlantic Visions: Resisting the Globalization of Mass Incarceration." *Social Justice* 27, no. 3 (2000): 133–49.

CHAPTER 10

The Mechanics of Empowerment
Migrant Farmworker Advocacy

Margaret Gray

Introduction[1]

There are increasing numbers of undocumented Latinos living in every part of the country. In some places, like the rural northeast, they are living well beyond the bounds of sheltering Latino communities. As workers forced to take the lowest-paying jobs, they lack political, economic, and social power to press claims with their employers directly, through public pressure, or through established political channels. As profit from their labor has increased, so have advocacy efforts to combat their exploitation. An emergent sector of community-based advocacy organizations called worker centers, operating outside the National Labor Relations Board structure, has sought to improve conditions for these undocumented immigrants and other low-wage workers. Worker centers tend to cater to low-wage, immigrant workers who are excluded, for one reason or another, from the purview of the union organizer.

In New York, the Workplace Project, serving Latino immigrants, successfully influenced the New York State Legislature to pass the strongest unpaid wages act in the country in 1997. In Las Vegas, the Dolores Huerta Center for Worker Rights, which serves the undocumented, pushed for the repeal of a law requiring criminal background checks on gambling industry employees. In Alexandria, Virginia, the Tenants' and Workers' Support Committee lobbied for a local living wage ordinance with the help of its client base, African Americans, Latinos, and immigrants. In 2005, working with Latino, Haitian, and Mayan Indian immigrants, the Coalition of Immokalee Workers in Florida won an agreement with fast food giant Yum! Brands (which owns the Taco Bell, Kentucky Fried Chicken, Pizza Hut, Long John Silvers, and A&W brands) to raise farmworker wages a penny per pound on tomatoes—an estimated 75 percent increase—and to monitor payment of the wages (Nieves 2005). In New York, the Justice for Farmworkers Coalition, targeting mostly Latino immigrants, has successfully pushed for the passage of 3 pro-farmworker laws, including a minimum wage law, which lead to a 68 percent increase over 8 years.

This chapter is a case study of this last example—New York farmworkers and their advocates. I show how advocacy organizations have striven to represent the interests of noncitizen, low-wage workers and how the results suggest a future direction for the worker center advocacy model. Advocates and their organizations appear necessary to promote the improvement of farmworkers' living and working conditions. In the final analysis, I argue that their efforts offer only certain types of important gains. They help to incorporate hitherto excluded individuals into the political system, situate workers' issues on politicians' and the public's agenda, and secure much-needed policy reforms. The next step is to transform the larger structural factors that fundamentally limit worker power. The main obstacle to further empowering workers is that advocates almost always end up emphasizing their own power resources rather than those of workers. This critique needs to be understood within the scope of the constraints operating on both advocates and workers. It is an incredible feat when advocacy efforts achieve gains on behalf of noncitizen, low-wage workers. And, at this point, a further examination of advocacy strategies is needed if we are to improve the possibilities for low-wage workers to be better positioned to represent their own interests. I conclude that advocacy organizations need to rework their strategies to stimulate the self-organization of workers.

My investigation falls into four sections. To provide context and the basis for my argument, I offer a brief description of advocacy, followed by an argument of the shortcomings of the mechanics of empowerment that the worker-center model offers. Second, to understand the farmworkers represented by the advocates, I present a brief snapshot of farmworkers' situations, which shows the constraints on their ability to use their power to represent themselves. I then move to an investigation of the New York case as an example of the worker-center advocacy model focusing on legislative advocacy. Finally, I offer an analysis of the current state of this advocacy model by exploring the differences between advocate power and worker power.[2]

Methodology

The data from this paper is derived from field studies of two groups: New York Hudson Valley farmworkers and New York farmworker advocates. My study is primarily qualitative, chiefly relying on interviews with members of those two groups. I conducted one hundred and thirteen one-hour, structured, open-ended interviews with farmworkers in New York's Hudson Valley, with the help of student interns. All interviews took place in workers' homes in labor camps located directly on the farms where they worked in the fall of 2002. To study New York farmworker advocates, I engaged in participant observation at dozens of meetings between 2001 and 2003. I conducted eleven semi-structured, open-ended interviews with farmworker advocates. Moreover, I spent a week "working" with the Centro Independiente de Trabajadores Agrícolas/Independent Farmworker Center (CITA) in the summer of 2003. In addition, I interviewed growers (farmworker employers) and other actors. Unless otherwise noted, quotes and statistics are from this author's own research.

Social Change and Advocacy

The type of advocacy addressed here is social change advocacy as practiced through nonprofit organizations. It is vital to keep in mind that such advocacy organizations serve the populations that are the *most* underrepresented in the U.S. political system, such as the poor, the homeless, minorities, the undocumented, and children. In general, nonprofit advocates target elite institutions and opinion shapers, not only in politics but also in society and culture at large. Advocates attempt to correct injustices through civic engagement (although they do not shy from controversy); their efforts may be understood as reform movements. Scholars differ on whether nonprofit advocates fit into a conceptual model of interest groups or social movements (Costain 1992; Hill 2000; Jenkins 1979; Wilson 2001). There is agreement, however, that nonprofit advocates pursue claims through mainstream political avenues of institutional change and civic engagement and not through the rule breaking that social movement scholars Frances Fox Piven and Richard Cloward discuss as necessary for social change (Cloward and Piven 1998).

Since the 1960s, nonprofit advocacy has been marked by a shift away from radical action. While the 1960s was a period of great social unrest in the United States, it also gave rise to a current of optimistic populism that saw the eventual decline of militant protest and the growth of organizational political activism (Reisch and Andrews 2001). The trend toward mainstream political engagement is demonstrated in the worker center advocacy model. Their successes, for the most part, have not been the result of broad social movements, spontaneous or threatening protests, or boycotts, but rather have emerged from acceptable political claim making—legislative visits, media campaigns, ally building, and signature gathering.[3] In contrast to workers leveraging their economic power, workers and advocates are devising nontraditional approaches to traditional politics and incorporating social movement strategies. These avenues have been pursued not only by advocates but also by advocates in alliance with workers, many of whom are undocumented.

The mission statements and public relations materials of advocacy organizations using a worker-center model highlight a trend away from professional advocacy, in which paid advocates define the goals and dictate strategies, toward worker organizing. Such organizing includes empowering members to be decision makers and leaders, building democratic organizational structures with members in leadership positions (including seats on boards of directors), and encouraging collective action by the members. One maxim that circulates among proponents of this model sums up the philosophy behind it as follows: "If you have come to help me, you are wasting your time, but if you have come because your liberation is bound up with mine, let's work together" (Watson 1992). In an article published in *WorkingUSA*, attorney and former worker-center organizer Steve Jenkins challenges the idea that the incorporation of the workers means this is not traditional advocacy. He argues that as long as elite institutions (the courts, media, and legislatures) are the sole target of campaigns and the goals are dependent on *persuading* elites as opposed to *coercing* them, we are unlikely to see the much-needed structural change that translates into worker power. This is consistent with Frances Fox Piven and Richard Cloward's arguments about the need for disruption to foster social change as opposed to strategies that work through formal political channels (Piven and Cloward 1979).

Worker centers attempt to establish a power base among the oppressed group and to set up democratic organizational structures so that professional advocates are not in the primary decision-making positions. The goal is to implement strategies that directly respond to the needs of those being organized. However, Jenkins's main assessment of these efforts is that when marginalized groups have so little power, it is not likely that, even when organized by worker centers, they will have much influence over those they target. This is because they are not being organized to recognize and use their own power, but rather to see themselves as representatives of the advocacy efforts. When advocates miss this point, they can overstate the value of empowerment and organizing and also misrepresent the balance of power between workers and advocates. In essence, then, he maintains, advocacy campaigns rely on workers to represent their plight, but it is not these workers who sway elite decision makers or their employers on the decisions that will improve their work conditions. In what follows, I will consider how Jenkins's arguments apply to the case of farmworker advocacy in New York.

New York Farmworkers and the Need for Advocates

It is only in the last two decades that Latino immigrants, mostly undocumented, have become the majority of the New York agricultural labor force (Pfeffer and Parra 2004). In the 1980s, after four decades of New York farms hiring predominantly Southern black workers for seasonal labor, a historic shift to Latino workers gained momentum. (In contrast, most large agricultural states have hired Mexicans as a significant portion of the agricultural workforce for the better part of the last century.) The majority of today's New York Latino farmworkers are undocumented Mexicans, largely from rural areas, lacking job skills, and largely unaware of labor laws. Historically, U.S. farmworkers have been extremely powerless, with their economic, social, and political opportunities restricted through both laws and informal practices for the purposes of maintaining a quiescent, labor pool (Majka and Majka 1982). The contemporary factors that exacerbate the weak position of New York farmworkers are their legal status and transnationalism, which produce three circumstances: fear of deportation and job loss due to workers' lack of legal permanent resident or citizenship status, aspirations to return to and permanently reside in their home countries, and rationalization of their situations through a habitual comparison of their situations to those of their friends and family members at home rather than with those of U.S. workers. These factors are constraints on workers' power to voice complaints, on their ability to improve their working and living conditions, and on their capacity to collectively organize.

The workers I interviewed lived and worked in a climate of fear, which inhibited their ability to complain and redress grievances. Accordingly, they perceived that the best way to protect their jobs—which provide vital income for their families—was to put aside personal concerns about their well-being and comply with their employers' demands. These workers were struggling to overcome poverty and fulfill short-term goals. Securing the following week's paycheck overrode long-term goals such as trying to improve their own workplace conditions. This was particularly true for workers who intended to leave farm work (66 percent of those I interviewed). When workers spoke to me about their fears, immigration officials or *la migra* was the most common concern.

Expressing his fear that immigration officials would take him away, fifty-one-year-old Alejandro from Mexico told me, "We are treated like unknown people. We are not fugitives. We come here to do farm work because we do not have jobs at home."[4] Javier, a twenty-five-year-old from Mexico City explained that he would rather be working with cars, but that his fear of the police prevented him from pursuing that work. Marcos, a forty-five-year-old from Mexico, had already been caught by immigration when crossing the border, and was fearful of authority figures and the police. In regard to his boss, Marcos said, "They treat us like nothing, they only want their work." At home he was paid in food, only enough to eat. He said, "We are poor. We struggle. We risk our lives to come here to work." He hoped to earn enough in New York to build a home in Mexico. Whether their fear stems from racism, their legal status, or knowledge of the boss's backlash against workers, it is palpable. Charles, a forty-something Jamaican guest worker who had been working in the United States since 1980, explained how he and his coworkers dealt with problems on the job. He told me, "Sometimes we don't. We are taught to be quiet."

Workers' behavior and decisions are guided by their plans to return to and permanently reside in their home countries, usually after a period of several years. (Guest workers' contracts require them to return home every year.) When asked directly, 75 percent of workers reported that their future plans included returning to their home countries to live there. While leaving the United States may or may not come to fruition, the *intention* to return home dampens workers' desires to improve their situations in the United States. As a result, they are generally willing to make tremendous sacrifices rather than risk being fired or deported. The main motive behind workers' willingness to sacrifice is perhaps most apparent in the fact that the majority of workers leave their wives and children behind to work in the United States. Despite the disproportionate number of men I interviewed (91 percent), a high percentage (68 percent) stated that they were married. An even higher percentage (71 percent) reported having children. These statistics illustrate the phenomenon of men migrating alone, without partners or families, in search of agricultural work so they may send money back home to their families (remittances). Many workers reported on the loneliness this caused. One worker I met had not yet seen his one-year-old son and would not do so for two more years. As most parents would understand, workers' parting from their children is not the result of a free choice, but rather a sign of their desperation and poverty, as well as their commitments to providing for their families. A frank answer from one respondent showed that the desire to return home dampened workers' interest in and capacity to change their situations in the United States. He told me he was not interested in being part of a union, "because we don't live here."

The workers I interviewed—many of whom were recent arrivals in the United States—habitually compared their situations to those at home, where few jobs existed and where a day's pay was less than an hour's wage in a low-paying U.S. job. This comparison stems from their perceptions of their situations in relation to their reference groups at home. A reference group offers an individual a perspective or worldview, to which one judges oneself through comparison (Shibutani 1955). Those I interviewed were mostly from rural areas and had, on average, a sixth grade education. Their political voice in their home countries was severely limited. The income from their U.S. jobs provided well for families at home. Workers had built houses and dug wells, installed electricity and plumbing, and contributed to community-building projects from their farmworker wages. As a result, these workers were, to some extent, appreciative of their opportunities to earn poverty-level wages. They were unlikely to fully comprehend, especially if they were newcomers, that they were more vulnerable to, and were more often the actual victims of, workplace abuse than U.S. citizens and green card holders.

Workers' identification with their reference groups ran deep since close kin ties in the United States also served to reinforce the expectations and standards of the home country. Three-quarters of all workers worked in the Hudson Valley with family or community members from their home countries. If we exclude guest workers, this number rises to 89 percent. Of those I interviewed, 60 percent worked with family and 42 percent with community members. One worker told me, "Almost my whole town is here." The kinship ties that helped workers find jobs in the United States also provided workers with a community of their peers. However, close-knit kin ties, while offering some semblance of a social network, in some ways reinforced isolation by separating workers from the wider communities in which they lived.

These transnational workers often saw considerable personal benefits to be derived from their labors and therefore easily found a way to justify their work environments—their average self-reported annual income was $8,078. This included Hudson Valley farm work plus other income (36 percent reported other income). Eager to earn wages and unable to relate to the exploitation of workers in the United States (exploitation is worse at home), these workers had little motivation to change their situations and may have felt confined to accept their working and living conditions. This acceptance was articulated to me many times. For example, in regard to pay, one worker told me, "I know it is not possible to be paid more." Another respondent told me, "We're not paid well; we can't ask for more." Because of workers' lack of organic collective action, advocates appear to be one of their few avenues for seeking to redress their grievances and improve their working and living conditions.

The Worker-Center Model and Legislative Campaigns

Janice Fine, in her pioneering scholarship on worker centers, has described what makes the worker-center advocacy model unique and has analyzed their efforts by isolating two types of activities (Fine 2003, 2005; Fine and

Werberg 2003). The first is *economic action organizing*, which targets private actors, and the second is *public policy organizing and advocacy*, which targets the government. Economic action addresses grievances and deals with workers' daily problems, with employers and landlords, for example. Policy advocacy includes working toward stronger enforcement of government regulations and stricter compliance on the part of employers, as well as promoting new legislation to improve working conditions. Policy also includes promoting immigration reform in favor of low-wage workers. According to Fine, worker-center advocacy organizations have been more successful in policy advocacy than economic action and, within policy advocacy, have achieved the most in regard to influencing local and state governments to pass legislation in support of low-wage workers. Fine argues that by taking the policy route, worker centers are promoting a long view of change as opposed to pushing for the immediate results that come with attending to workers' daily needs.

New York's coordinated advocacy efforts for farmworkers, which have gained speed since the early 1990s, fit well into the worker-center model. In New York, advocates have responded with righteous fervor to farmworkers' lack of political power, vulnerability to exploitation, cases of substandard living and working conditions, and lack of labor rights. In New York, as in most states, farmworkers (including citizens) are excluded from collective bargaining protections, the right to overtime, and the right to a day of rest, among other labor law exclusions. The most common grievances of farmworkers include non- or underpayment of wages, poor housing, and lack of respect, but New York has also seen documented cases of illegal firings, sexual harassment, human trafficking, forced labor, and workers being shot at in the fields while they were working.[5]

All these efforts have given momentum to the Justice for Farmworkers Coalition (JFW), a statewide group of organizations and individuals formed in the mid-1990s (Moya 2000). It is common for worker centers to work in coalition with other organizations. JFW's strategies include a legislative campaign, legal cases, negotiations with employers, public education, leadership development, grievance resolution through government agencies, compliance campaigns, raising class consciousness, and building solidarity. While all these strategies might be approached in a militant spirit, that is not the style of worker centers. They use the following tactics to reach their goals: peaceful public demonstrations, editorial writing, press conferences, picketing, marches, providing services, lobbying, and social events. As a result, this model relies on legal and legitimate channels to improve workers' living and working conditions. For example, advocates help workers visit legislators and other officials to express their concerns. Many of these workers are undocumented and therefore have little political power—they offer legislators neither votes nor campaign contributions. Yet legislators seem to be responding, perhaps because they calculate that they can court votes from other low-wage voters (and especially Latinos) by showing that they care about their issues. Worker centers also establish links with voters and ask them to represent by proxy the concerns of the undocumented.

The Centro Independiente de Trabajadores Agrícolas/Independent Farmworker Center (CITA) and other JFW members incorporate leadership training into their programming. It may be casual, as in the case of a workshop contrasting global and local economies, or it may be more formal, as in a course spread over several months. Often the aim is to introduce low-wage workers into the decision-making system of local and state politics and also to the broader political and economic structures that influence their lives. Many leadership trainings directly address constituents' lack of political power by developing workers' skills to petition elite institutions and by convincing them of their potential to overcome the constraints on their power. CITA, like most worker centers, also attempts to build membership, although most worker centers do not charge dues, as unions do, and have difficulty securing members. Moreover, CITA, like other worker centers, offers social opportunities such as soccer nights or leagues, seasonal parties, and listings of houses of worship that offer services in different languages. Approaching the work through leadership training and social and cultural services is intended to help workers overcome some of their political and social vulnerabilities and to involve them in the organization.

JFW's Legislative Campaign

JFW takes credit for the passage of three pro-farmworker laws. These are a 1996 law requiring employers to provide drinking water for all farmworkers (a previous law did not require drinking water to be provided if the employer had four or fewer employees); a 1998 law requiring portable toilets and handwashing facilities in the fields, or transportation to sanitation facilities, for all farmworkers (previously the law only covered workers if they numbered eleven or more); and a 1999 minimum-wage law that raised farmworkers' minimum wage and tied it to the state's minimum wage, an increase, at the time, of 21 percent. This became even more significant in light of the 2004 state minimum-wage increase of 39 percent over three years (New York State Department of Labor 2005, 3). By 2007, farmworkers' minimum wage will have risen 68 percent over eight years, from $4.25 to $7.15. Advocates have touted these successes as grand victories and used them to mobilize supporters.

Farmworkers are involved on many levels of JFW. For example, JFW expects farmworkers to dictate the overall direction of the legislative campaign—as articulated through CITA, which has the most direct contact with farmworkers and holds farmworker assemblies. In contrast, implementation of the legislative strategy has been handled almost exclusively by the advocates. In response, media attention on the campaign has spotlighted the advocates as much as the farmworkers. It is not uncommon for workers to take a backseat in the implementation of legislative campaigns. In similar circumstances nationwide, workers and their organizations have encouraged allies and advocates to use their resources to further workers' aims in the policy arena. The legislative campaign has not only led to the passage of pro-farmworker laws, but it also has been a vehicle for educating the public and legislators about working and living conditions for farmworkers.

The legislative campaign is a strategy that advocates and allies could engage in with relative ease compared to a farmworker organizing effort. The tactics of the legislative campaign included the distribution of press releases, position papers, and fact sheets on farmworkers in New York; making available public speakers (including workers); launching a media campaign; and issuing calls for supporters to get involved in a variety of ways. Supporters were asked to write, call, and visit their state legislators, and JFW offered materials and instructions for such contact, such as text suggestions for letters. JFW distributed a resolution for individuals and organizations to sign in support of farmworkers receiving the same rights as other workers, and it also provided talking points about the proposed laws, including point-counterpoint statements that responded to critics. Other tactics included JFW members meeting with the editorial boards of newspapers to ask for their support. Through these efforts, advocates established strong media connections, educated the public on farmworker conditions, and aroused public sympathy for the farmworkers' cause. For example, in 1999, the *New York Daily News* ran a fourteen-part editorial series titled "New York's Harvest of Shame" about conditions for farmworkers. This series has been credited with helping to influence the minimum-wage law for farmworkers, and the paper's editorial board won a George Polk Award for editorial writing.

Integral to the campaign has been the annual, festive Farmworker Advocacy Day (FAD), first held in 1995. This public event in the state's capital, including a rally with speakers, provides an opportunity for farmworkers and advocates to gain public attention, meet with state legislators, and make a case for farmworker equality under New York state law. More recently, JFW has organized annual ten-day long "marches for justice," reminiscent of the 1964 civil rights movement's Freedom March from Selma to Montgomery, which inspired farmworker marches in the late 1960s, led by Cesar Chavez.

Supporters are asked to join the march and FAD rally, as well as additional events such as vigils, dinners, and fiestas. These strategies reflect the individual and organizational capacities of farmworker advocates; they develop practical strategies relying on available resources.

The Pros and Cons of Advocacy

There is no simple way of evaluating the advances of the worker-center advocacy model. It is striking that issues of poor, low-wage, and mostly undocumented farmworkers should have achieved some representation and an allocated place on the state legislature's agenda. In her study of worker centers, Fine argues that the mere existence and sustainability of organizations like CITA that work for low-wage immigrants is a weighty accomplishment. She writes, "Those who would stand in judgment of community unions must acknowledge that they have had considerable success in altering the terms of debate, bringing the voices of low wage workers into politics, developing leaders and changing public policy. They have done this even in the face of scarce resources and almost no regional or national infrastructure. And they don't seem to be going away. . . . Just because they have yet to succeed at broader labor market intervention does not mean that they never will" (Fine 2003, 310–11). New York farmworker advocates have been offering workers opportunities to have their voices heard. In the absence of strong organic worker action, we can certainly claim that advocates have done farmworkers a great service, since their issues were not being addressed in any systematic way before the advocates' helped organize the campaigns.

Moreover, there has been backlash on the part of growers against advocates; this showed that growers felt threatened and has lent weight to the idea that advocates have been successful. Even as growers perceive advocates as a threat, it may be their potential that is threatening and not what has been achieved so far. Yet, from another perspective, what advocates have wrought can easily seem minimal. They have not garnered significant economic gains for workers, organized large numbers of them, nor altered the larger structural factors that limit worker power. Their legislative efforts have resulted in new laws, but these laws have not changed the overall conditions of farmworkers' labor. Moreover, altering the law is one thing, while ensuring that laws are implemented is another.

This evaluation, however, is more complicated than simply deciding whether the glass is half full or half empty. For one thing, it seems that it may be premature to evaluate the consequences of these efforts. Clearly, farmworkers are in urgent need of representation. Since the lack of legal collective bargaining protections and farmworkers' position in the labor market do not make them attractive candidates for unionization, certainly the efforts of CITA and JFW offer something that no one else is providing. Advocates are convinced that their gains are incremental, and that further successes will continue to build toward greater change. If this is not true, however, I would not then reason that the advocates' efforts were useless and not worth pursuing further. A full evaluation of what they have achieved requires an evaluation of their strategies and their future prospects.

It is fair to say that, thus far, advocates' gains have largely been political and not economic. This fits with Fine's aforementioned analysis (Fine 2005). There are two main reasons for this. First, farmworkers (and many other low-wage, contingent workers) have a limited ability to use their labor power to challenge the conditions of their employment through employee-employer negotiations. Second, advocates cannot replace workers' labor power. Rather, they offer their own form of power, which is primarily useful in petitioning elite institutions such as legislators, courts, the media, and funders as opposed to employers. As a result, the gains achieved are largely political. As might be obvious, while the political gains have had some influence, they have not accomplished what workers' self-organization might: workers harnessing their own power to leverage more immediate pay raises and improved working conditions as negotiated directly with the person responsible for providing them, the employer.

One of the main lines of reasoning for pursuing a legislative agenda, in the case of New York farmworker advocates, is that until farmworkers have the legal rights and protections of other workers, they will face significant obstacles in remedying their own situations. For example, while in most industries it is illegal to fire a worker for trying to collectively bargain, this is not true in agriculture (except for in a few states such as California). Advocates, who aim for the inclusion of farmworkers in New York's collective bargaining protections, contend that such a law would change the power relations of farm work and allow for a truer representation of workers. These advocates are not the only ones to advance this position. In his research on U.S. farmworkers, Marc Linder writes that, based on the historical record, farmworkers cannot limit their activities to negotiations with employers, but rather must push politically for growers to be forced to negotiate with them and with unions (Linder 1992, 301–2).

Advocates imagine that the inclusion of farmworkers in the state's labor laws will greatly enhance the abilities of organizations and even unions to mobilize workers, and for farmworkers to self-organize; this seems obvious. However, Linder contends that farmworkers' power is so limited that they often struggle just to have their existing rights recognized. He points to the number of legal cases that deal with workers trying to get paid what they earned. This returns us to a point Jenkins makes. He argues that organizing vulnerable groups often occurs without regard to whether that organized group could wield power (Jenkins 2002, 58). It is within this context that advocates face a conundrum: should they continue to pursue workers' issues through elite avenues that will lead to political gains, or might the political agenda be putting the cart before the horse by generating legal changes that workers are not able to take advantage of?

In the case of New York farmworker advocacy, JFW has a three-pronged strategy that includes not only the legislative campaign, but also legal casework and worker organizing. However, the last strategy has not been progressing as well as the other two. There are multiple reasons for the disparity in achievement between these strategies. Some of the reasons are local, pertaining to this specific case study, while others are more general. A full investigation into those would be of great interest, but is beyond the scope of this chapter. However, the deficit in worker organizing is an issue for most worker centers and organizations like them. To some extent, farmworker organizing in New York has fallen into the pattern that Jenkins describes as workers acting as advocates to represent themselves for the campaigns, even when workers are voicing their own concerns. Workers' symbolic role in campaigns is very effective, yet it needs to complement the worker organizing that concretely develops worker power through negotiations with employers with the goal of securing contracts.

CITA and other JFW members all agree that it is the latter type of worker organizing that is integral to changing conditions for New York farmworkers. All understand that the legal cases and legislative campaigns cannot offer what true organizing can. However, CITA is the only organization with the mission to organize workers, and its work has been progressing slowly since it officially opened its doors in 1991. In the meantime, the legislative campaign has become increasingly sophisticated. At present, there seems to be an imbalance between the legislative campaign, which relies on advocate power, and the organizing campaign, which compels worker power, and this is something that JFW members recognize. Consequently, the most relevant question that advocates can ask is: what is the best use of advocates' resources?

Advocates must strike a difficult balance between what they can achieve for farmworkers and what workers can achieve for themselves. As one of my respondents told me, the movement "has to move at the pace of the slowest members involved—the workers." Advocates can achieve certain types of success more quickly and easily than farmworkers can, such as policy change. Yet, just because this is where advocates are able to use their power, does that make it the best way to use their power? This is a key question now facing New York farmworker advocates. What is required is a significant shift in advocates' thinking and strategizing. One of the first steps in this direction is for advocates to realize that the major obstacle at present is not that workers do not have political or electoral power, but rather that advocates do not have labor power.

The power that the advocates offer cannot compensate for workers' inability to exercise their labor power. In an essay about community organizing, Piven and Cloward argue that community organizations cannot compare to unions. They cannot exercise worker strike power, and communities lack the industrial setting that allowed workers to establish the social structure that would serve as a foundation for union activity. Furthermore, unlike unions, community organizations cannot effectively act to discipline a workforce (Cloward and Piven 1998, 169). So, too, advocates, including those at CITA, do not have legal authority or protection if they attempt to represent workers in negotiations with their employers (except in legal cases). As a result, advocates are unable to target employers directly and instead have developed strategies targeting other sources of power, such as the New York State Legislature. If advocates believe they are compensating for workers' lack of political power, they are falling into the trap that Jenkins describes.

My research suggests that the legislative campaign has gained a life and a tempo of its own that is not complemented by success in worker organizing. But if advocates are to let the organizing campaign catch up, then they will have to give up wielding their own power, which means slowing down the legislative campaign and directing resources toward organizing. After more than a decade of organizing volunteers, funders, and supporting organizations to influence legislators and the public to respond to farmworkers' needs, how can they slow down the momentum? And how would they explain a downshift to their supporters? Integral to this process is the following articulation of their advocacy work as told to me by one of the main JFW advocates: "Farmworkers need people to stand with them." This is an important point to keep in mind. At present, the reverse seems true: advocates and allies need farmworkers to stand with them. When the balance of those involved leans too far toward the advocates, the gains will inevitably be limited.

Advocates are Necessary—But for What?

Advocates have been necessary to promote the recognition of New York farmworkers' grievances. Farmworkers have few resources at their disposal. But advocate power, as I have outlined earlier in this chapter, is also circumscribed within those limitations. Jenkins posits that advocates should focus on communicating workers' situations to elites in the hope of persuading them to support justice causes (Jenkins 2002, 61). Yet, this route is a reform model, aimed at righting wrongs and limiting illegal activities. Exposing workers' plights can lead to significant victories (Jenkins 2002, 62). However, these victories are of a certain type that do not create overarching change for workers, but rather usually offer small improvements for limited groups of workers.

While they identify these shortcomings of the advocacy model, Piven and Cloward also acknowledge its significance in keeping the idea of resistance alive (Cloward and Piven 1998, 189). Piven and Cloward take their critique further than Jenkins to describe what might create more substantial change in the lives of members of marginalized groups. Normal politics is not the answer; disruption is required. This may come in the form of altering production at a worksite, civil disruption, or, in the case of a voting population, causing an electoral shift. They do take care to point out, however, that such disruption is only possible at certain moments in history and that disruption risks repression (Cloward and Piven 1998). For farmworkers, this does not appear to be one of those moments. Rather, the exploitation of low-wage immigrant workers occurs under what Fine describes as the "perfect storm" of factors, including a lack of labor protection, a lack of regulation of newer labor market structures, and an immigration policy that promotes an underclass of workers (Fine 2005, 23).

I am not proposing that all advocates' efforts should be shifted to organizing workers to confront employers. However, I am proposing that the balance of efforts may need to be shifted as advocates' efforts increase. While public education campaigns, legislative lobbying, media efforts, and growing a community of allies are all valuable strategies, I suggest that there is a point when advocacy efforts are not complementing organizing efforts, but rather replacing them. Advocates need workers not just to represent their own plights, but also to fight for justice themselves. This is not a matter of legitimacy, although advocates without the participation of marginalized groups are certainly weaker. The larger issue is about recognizing that reform efforts are possible through normal politics. Reform is necessary and advocates can play an important role in fostering it. Yet, as long as advocacy organizations espouse radical change, as opposed to reform only, workers must attempt to address their grievances directly with employers.

This was most apparent during the end of the 2005 New York State Legislative session. Advocates had well-meaning legislative allies on board who were ready to push forward a "day of rest" bill that JFW nonetheless thought was very weak. The JFW advocates turned around and put their efforts into preventing the passage of the bill. This decision to preempt what they perceived was a merely symbolic gain illustrates another truth of advocacy power: the further removed efforts are from the employer-employee relationship, the more likely it is that workers' interests will be compromised.

This is the nature of politics, particularly for the disenfranchised. It is when workers negotiate with their employers directly that the least amount of compromise can be made and workers can press their most authentic claims in a direct manner. The challenge, therefore, is for advocates to reevaluate the mechanics of empowerment in light of their goals. For workers' situations to fundamentally alter, advocates will need to slowly shift away from what they can most easily accomplish and offer workers more opportunities to exercise what little power they can, with the knowledge that the advocates will be right behind them.

Notes

1. The author of this chapter is a member of the Justice for Farmworkers Coalition and a former board member of Rural and Migrant Ministry. She would like to extend her gratitude to the Twenty-first Century ILGWU Heritage Fund for funding her research on Hudson Valley farmworkers.
2. This chapter has been influenced by, and dovetails with, the work of Steve Jenkins and Janice Fine.
3. The example of the Coalition of Immokalee Workers is an exception; their success was due to a successful, nationwide boycott of Taco Bell on the part of many groups with the power to mobilize consumers' economic power.
4. I use pseudonyms in place of farmworkers' real names.
5. See testimony and the statement from the New York State Senate-Assembly Puerto Rican/Hispanic Task Force (1995). See also Moya 2000. The Web site of Farmworker Legal Services (FLSNY) has descriptions of cases pending and completed that describe a variety of alleged labor violations. See http://www.flsny.org.

References

Cloward, Richard A., and Frances Fox Piven. 1998. Disruptive dissensus: People and power in the industrial age. In *Reflections on community organization: Enduring themes and critical issues*, ed. J. Rothman. Itasca, IL: F. E. Peacock.

Costain, Anne N. 1992. Social movements as interest groups: The case of the women's movement. In *The politics of interests: Interest groups transformed*, ed. M. P. Petracca. Boulder: Westview Press.

Farmworker Legal Services of New York. 2007. *Organizational Web site.* http://www.flsny.org.

Fine, Janice. 2003. Community unions in Baltimore and Long Island: Beyond the politics of particularism. PhD diss., Department of Political Science, Massachusetts Institute of Technology.

———. 2005. *Worker centers: Organizing communities at the edge of a dream; executive summary*. Washington, D.C.: Economic Policy Institute.

Fine, Janice, and Jon Werberg. 2003. *Worker centers map, national study on workers centers*. Washington, D.C.: Economic Policy Institute and the Neighborhood Funders Group.

Hill, Frances R. 2000. *Nonprofit organizations' advocacy activities: Association, participation and representation*. Washington, D.C.: Urban Institute Press.

Jenkins, J. Craig. 1979. What is to be done: Movement or organization? *Contemporary Sociology* 8:222–28.

Jenkins, Steve. 2002. Organizing, advocacy, and member power: A critical refection. WorkingUSA 6 (2): 56–89.

Linder, Marc. 1992. *Migrant workers and minimum wages: Regulating the exploitation of agricultural labor in the United States*. Boulder, CO: Westview Press.

Majka, Linda C., and Theo J. Majka. 1982. *Farm workers, agribusiness, and the state*. Philadelphia: Temple University Press.

Moya, Minerva. 2000. FAD: A history of Farmworker Advocacy Day. *The voice of farmworkers: A journal to commemorate Farmworker Advocacy Day 2000, Albany, New York*, 21–23.

New York State Department of Labor. 2005. Minimum wage order for farm workers. Part 190 of title 12 of the official compilation of codes, rules and regulations. Based on labor law changes effective January 1, 2005. Promulgated by the Commissioner of Labor Pursuant to Article 19-A of the New York State Labor Law. Albany, NY. Available at http://www.labor.state.ny.us/formsdocs/wp/PART190s.pdf.

New York State Senate-Assembly Puerto Rican/Hispanic Task Force. 1995. Separate & unequal: New York's farmworkers. Albany: New York State Senate-Assembly Puerto Rican/Hispanic Task Force, Joint Temporary Task Force on Farmworker Issues.

Nieves, Eveyn. 2005. Accord with tomato pickers ends boycott of Taco Bell. *Washington Post*, March 9, p. A6.

Pfeffer, Max J., and Pilar A. Parra. 2004. *Immigrants and the community*. Ithaca, NY: Cornell University Press.

Piven, Frances Fox, and Richard A. Cloward. 1979. *Poor people's movements: Why they succeed, how they fail*. 1st ed. New York: Pantheon Books.

Reisch, Michael, and Janice Andrews. 2001. *The road not taken: A history of radical social work in the U.S.* Philadelphia: Brunner-Routledge.

Shibutani, Tamotsu. 1955. Reference groups as perspectives. *American Journal of Sociology* 60 (6): 562–69.

Watson, Lila. 1992. Untitled. In *Health for Women*. Brisbane: Department of Health, 3:1. Quoted in Damien Riggs, "Benevolence and the Management of Stake: On Being 'Good White People,'" in *Philament: An Online Journal of the Arts and Culture*, no. 4 (August 2004), available at http://www.arts.usyd.edu.au/publications/philament/issue4_Critique_Riggs.htm.

Wilson, Graham K. 2001. The dual motives of interest group studies. Paper read at European Consortium for Political Research Conference, September, University of Kent, Canterbury.

CHAPTER 11

Orientalism and the New Global:
The Example of India

Anjan Chakrabarti, Stephen Cullenberg, and Anup Dhar[1]

Nowadays we are often told that the third world is dead. This underlies another proposition that, with the third world as the Other disappearing, the Orientalist framework is no longer relevant. We consider the pronounced death of the third world and the implied irrelevance of the Orientalist framework as theoretically weak, premature, and politically counterproductive. With the new global order emerging, the third world gets displaced as its external Other into a new plane. We trace the economic history of India and deconstruct the mainstream Indian development paradigm to reveal this emerging contour of Orientalism. Specifically we attempt to read the economic history of India and its transition through different moments of Orientalism, moments that are distinct but each nevertheless help one space—the West, North, or New Global Order—define itself and protract its superiority by producing an external Other.

Following the adoption of the New Economic Policy (NEP) in the early 1990s, the ongoing Indian transition toward a new society has been forwarded in terms of a big bang progressive move to a free market economy that will encourage a high level of capitalist growth. This transition will also see the merger of the Indian economy into the global order and thus free another way to rewrite India's transition from a self-sufficient economy toward an open competitive economy. We are thus told that India's transition to a capitalist market economy can only be relevant and effective in the context of a global transition. India's destiny is to be part of the global economy that in turn is indexed by the unquestioned superiority of (global) capitalism. In other words, these representations of India's transition cannot but accept the superiority of the model of global transition taking capitalism as the telos of world civilization. In such a discourse of transition, capitalism or global capitalism is never forwarded as a question to be confronted, but rather its superior existence is assumed as given.

More recently, many have started questioning the basis of running the story of India's transition along this line. Anjan Chakrabarti and Stephen Cullenberg (2001, 2003) elaborate why the representation of the Indian unilateral big bang transition to capitalism is faulty. They use a class-focused approach to disaggregate the Indian economy to numerous forms of economic practices, not all of them capitalist. This means that India's transition in terms of the transition of its economy and the associated noneconomic processes remain extremely complex, making nonsense the reduction of this complexity to simply one essential form of practice—capitalism. Similar arguments, from slightly different angles, have been made by J. K. Gibson-Graham (1996) and Kalyan Sanyal (2001).

On the other hand, David Ruccio, Stephen Resnick and Richard Wolff (1990), Michael Hardt and Antonio Negri (2000), Resnick and Wolff (2001), Chakrabarti and Anup Dhar (2002) and Chakrabarti (2003) have argued that the new global order underwrites a scenario of global capitalist hegemony that functions through the overdetermined interstices of economic, cultural, and political processes. Paraphrasing their basic argument, we can aver that while India goes out to embrace the globe, the globe in turn is fast imploding into India and sucking the Indian society into its global webs of relations that, these authors argue, telescope the instance of global capitalist hegemony.

There are then two impulses. The economy, including the Indian economy, is comprised of numerous capitalist and noncapitalist practices while the transition of the Indian economy into a part of the new global order brings into contention—within India—the instance of global capitalist hegemony, which encapsulates the overdetermined webs of power relations through which global capital attempts to manage, control, and subjugate noncapital and its forms of life into its regime of truth. Thus, the economy remains complexly constituted by capitalist and noncapitalist forms of social practices, but the knowledge over the economic and the discursive practices that the knowledge produces procreates the global capitalist hegemony. (Global) capitalism is therefore a fantasy appearing as an all-encompassing closed system. Because (global) capitalism is incomplete, impossible, and lacking in closure, it must be held together by overdetermined webs of power relations in the intersecting space of the economic, cultural, and political in order to enable the fantasy to continue.

The class-focused approach thus provides an alternative way of producing the truth—another regime of truth—and this language has rich possibilities in disarticulating and displacing putative representations of the economy into hitherto new ones. Here, in this chapter, we explore one such possibility in analyzing the transition of the Indian economy, especially in the current era of globalization. We use the class focus representation to highlight the point that the Indian transition since the time of British India has also been the journey of Orientalism. While the forms of Orientalism have changed, the framework through which the transition of the Indian economy has been looked at has remained Orientalist. This treatment follows closely in the footsteps of the pioneering works of Partha Chatterjee (1986), and particularly Ajit Chaudhury (1994), Chaudhury, Anup Das and Chaudhury (2000) and Chakrabarti and Cullenberg (2003).

We are especially concerned with the current phase of the transition of the Indian economy initiated after the adoption of the New Economic Policies, which, as we mentioned earlier, attempts to force a transition of the Indian economy into a free market global economy. We ask: is the problem of Orientalism then finally over as the division between the West or North and East or South gets blurred through the emerging convergence of many of their axes of society into a new global order that represents a free market economy with global capitalist hegemony? We answer: no. Orientalism is still thriving. We only need to see it differently since, with the emerging evolution of the new global order, the figuration and place of Orientalism has changed. The Orientalist framework is no longer between the West and East or the North and South, but instead between the new global order and an excluded space we call the third world.

In contrast to the usual mainstream development representations, we then present an alternative class representation of India's transition as, among other things, also taking place within the Orientalist framework. While much discussion on Orientalism has taken place over culture and politics, there are, to our knowledge, hardly any that deal with the place of Orientalism through the text of the economy, and none that has tried to deal with the same in the context of India's ongoing transition following NEP into the emerging global order.[2]

This foreclosure of the economy from the discussion of Orientalism is surprising and disturbing if we witness, as we shall show, the changing place and figuration of Orientalism from its historic site of culture and politics to the economy. Orientalism, of course, by definition, remains a cultural phenomena, but its effect remains overdetermined by elements of power, that is, the political, and is now profoundly economic in character. In short, the text of Orientalism has greatly, although not exclusively, shifted to the plane of the economic even though it remains a complex product of cultural, political, and economic processes as it makes its grip over the economy. In this regard, we emphasize that our focus on class as an alternative representation of the economy is not due to any narcissistic attachment to it, but rather because our point could only be made through a class discourse of the economy. Our unique reading will not only help shift the focus of Orientalism to the economy and help problematize the economy, but we believe that such a reading will additionally open up counterhegemonic possibilities in dealing with India's transition that have hitherto avoided the attention of radical thinkers. While we will not delve into questions of counterhegemony, we will certainly ask the readers to remain sensitive to the possible openings of such topics in the course of the discussion.

Let us begin with a quick discussion of the class-focused approach, for that remains the model—the organizing principle—of producing a different language through which an alternative (politically enabling) description of the economy can be inaugurated and an alternative discourse on India's transition can be fashioned. We will then relay the history of the Indian transition in terms of the Orientalist framework. Finally, we will produce what we call the new development paradigm, attached inalienably to the production of the new global order that only displaces the problem of Orientalism to a different plane. The discussion there will focus on producing the third world in this era of new global order.

Class, Global Capital, and Its Hegemony

Our description of society, including that of India, is based on a decentered class conception of the economy and society. Such a decentered approach follows the seminal approach of Resnick and Wolff (1987). Resnick and Wolff's approach has seen fundamental extensions in Satya Gabriel (1990), Cullenberg (1992), Gibson-Graham (1996), Chaudhury and Chakrabarti (2000), Chakrabarti and Cullenberg (2001, 2003), and Resnick and Wolff (2003) regarding the question of class, economy, society, and its transition and development. This Marxian attempt is greatly an effort to mend and recover the language of class as an alternative exposition of truth.

Resnick and Wolff deploy *class* as an entry point, standpoint, and perspective working point within the *overdetermined* web of relations to create a new Marxian discourse on society and change. Building on Louis Althusser's notion of overdetermination and defining it as a mutual constitutivity of processes that informs the logic of the social, Resnick and Wolff—who pioneered the concept of reading class as an adjective (that is, as a process)—highlight two fundamental moments within the economy. The first is the distinction between necessary labor and surplus labor. The former captures the amount of labor performed to reproduce the existence of the laborer (and her family), and surplus labor is defined as labor performed over and above necessary labor. Class, and this is the second fundamental moment, refers to processes relating to the performance, appropriation, distribution, and receipt of surplus labor. Class processes are specific to an enterprise—be they in the private, state, or household sectors. Within an enterprise, class processes can be grouped into fundamental class, as constituting of the performance and appropriation of surplus labor, and into subsumed class, making up the distribution and receipt of surplus labor. The central category of Marxian exploitation emerges from the notion of a fundamental class process; exploitation is defined as the surplus labor not appropriated by the performers of that surplus labor, otherwise appropriation is nonexploitative. Fundamental classes can be exploitative as well as nonexploitative and can be mapped into capitalist, communist, communistic, self or ancient, slave, and feudal forms. For example, the feudal fundamental class process refers to the exploitative appropriation of surplus labor.

Exploitation is the contentious category in Marxist theory since it raises the ethical question: do we accept the theft of labor and of a society dominated by a trope of the theft? Marxist theory is unique for its ethical position against exploitation. Moreover, each such fundamental class process cannot exist on its own and instead is constituted—literally brought into existence—not only by the subsumed class processes but also by other nonclass processes. While there are other means of articulating the notion of enterprise (through the goal of profit maximization, for example), Marxists provide a unique description of enterprise or class structure as being constituted by fundamental and subsumed class processes, and nonclass processes geared toward the reproduction of the class processes. These nonclass processes encompass the economic (rather than class), cultural, political, and natural processes. Explanation is thus class- or economy-focused, but not class- or economy-specific. The putative presence of a self-constituted, independent, and autonomous economy is an impossibility if we read the economy in class terms. The economy is forever drawing on the noneconomy for its oxygen (and vice versa).

Political practices in such a Marxist theory are class practices or class-related practices sometimes called class struggle. The three fundamental political issues that crop up around Marxism are the following: to fight for changes in the fundamental class processes with the goal to end class exploitation in society, to fight for changes in subsumed class processes in order to transform the conditions of existence that underlie a fundamental class process (see Resnick and Wolff 1987), and to struggle for changes in those nonclass processes that transform the conditions of existence for various class processes—fundamental and subsumed. Marxists take the ethical position of struggling for those class and nonclass processes that procreate nonexploitative practices.

In such a Marxist theory, the society is a complex institutional configuration of innumerable numbers of heterogeneous and multilayered class processes. At any point in time, all these distinct class processes could potentially coexist together within a society. A specific *configuration* of class structure is defined as the social totality. Drawn from a specific, that is, partial class perspective, social totality is decentered (it cannot be defined in terms of a specific form of class such as capitalist) and disaggregated (numerous types and forms of class processes intersecting, compensating, and reinforcing one another), being pulled and pushed into different directions by the contradictory effects that constitute it. Moreover, since processes are in an overdeterminist state of change due to, among others, numerous class struggles occurring in different axes of society, these bring in contradictory effects, causing a transition of the class configuration and, subsequently, deepening further the decentering and heterogeneity of society.

This Marxian approach then forces an encounter of unique economic practices within a decentered and heterogeneous social terrain. At the level of such practices that significantly determines the formation of the political subject and the constitution of the political space, we encounter not simply capitalist practices but also noncapitalist practices (see Resnick and Wolff 1987; Resnick and Wolff 2003; Gibson-Graham 1996, 2003; Gibson-Graham, Resnick, and Wolff 2000; Gibson-Graham, Resnick, and Wolff 2001; Chakrabarti 1996, 2001; Chakrabarti and Cullenberg 2001; Chakrabarti and Cullenberg 2003). One thus cannot reduce the economy to the singular substance of accumulation or forces of production or profit maximization that serve as the imputed motif of capitalist classes as in standard orthodoxy. Such motifs, as and when they are emphasized, reflect an almost divine-like gravitational pull of the economy to capitalism that is contested in Marxism. Indeed, the claim of an all-encompassing storm of capitalist juggernaut stutters and falters in the face of noncapitalist existences that continue to procreate and spawn within the rich web of any complexly overdetermined society.

The politics of the social play an important role in deciding which types of class processes would dominate in a specific time and space, which in turn significantly determines the historical evolution of society. Take the case of capitalism, which, historically, has lived with intense contradictions between its private and state forms. Resnick and Wolff (2003) have elaborated on how the struggle over the forms of society in the Soviet Union turned from one between the communist enterprises and the capitalist enterprises in its early stage into one taking place between state capitalism and private capitalism. They describe the history of how private capitalism came to dominate the Soviet society at the expense of its private counterpart and other forms of class processes, and its consequence for the way the Soviet society evolved. The collapse of the Soviet Union and, with it, the planning system, has significantly dented the legitimacy of state capitalist class processes, and coupled with the discourse of globalization celebrating the logic of the market and commodity economy, the balance has clearly shifted in favor of private capitalist class processes. All over the world, class processes pertaining to state capitalist enterprises are being severely undermined, resulting in a slow but steady parcelling out of these enterprises into private hands. And since these state enterprises are large, privatization is in effect leading to a transfer of these into the "global" capitalist class processes, where the meaning of the global in the context of the capitalist class process will now be elaborated.

What is global capital? Resnick and Wolff (2001) ask us to rethink the existence of global enterprise from a class standpoint. A global enterprise in India (IN), for example, would have the following class equation[3] to consider:

$$\Sigma\text{: SViIN} + \Sigma\text{: SSCRiIN} + \Sigma\text{: NCRiIN} = \Sigma\text{: SSCPINk} + \Sigma\text{: XINk} + \Sigma\text{:YINk} \quad \text{(a)}$$

where SV = Surplus Value produced and appropriated by the enterprise;

Σ: SSCR = Subsumed class revenue;
Σ: NCR = Nonclass revenue;
Σ: SSCP = Sum of subsumed class payments;
Σ: X = Sum of payments made to secure SSCR;
Σ: Y = Sum of payments made to secure NCR.

The two sides of the equation refer to revenues that flow from variegated processes—class and nonclass—to which the enterprise or class structure is articulated. The left-hand side of (a) represents the revenue side of the enterprise, while the right-hand side represents its expenditure required to reproduce the conditions of existence of the components in the revenue side. Σ:∞SSCP reflects subsumed class payments made by the enterprise to ensure the flow of SV. Σ: SSCR captures the subsumed class revenues of the enterprise, that is, any revenue it generates from its occupation of subsumed class positions with respect to other firms. It might include returns such as dividends, ground rents, merchant fees, and so on. The reproduction of these subsumed revenue class positions, in turn, requires expenditure or payments for those social positions that will ensure the reproduction of Σ: SSCR. Such payments are gathered around Σ: X. Similarly, Σ: NCR stands for all nonclass revenues earned by the enterprise, such as the return on loans advanced to productive labourers. Σ: Y stands for the expenditure or payments required to reproduce the conditions of existence of Σ: NCR.

An enterprise or class structure is a complex site of these multiple sources of class revenues, nonclass revenues, and expenditures. In order to bring out the global dimension of an enterprise, the subscript *i* is used in the left-hand side to index the various global locations from where the revenues are drawn, and the superscript *k* in the right-hand side is used to capture the global locations of expenditure. In other words, the sites where the flows of revenue and expenditure occur are splintered across the globe, and the enterprise draws its meaning from this very decentered albeit global existence. Processes of fundamental classes, subsumed classes, and nonclasses that globally connect into capitalist enterprise are the *circuits of global capital*, and the totality of the stocks and flows embodying the circuits of global capital is what we define as *global capital*. When, say, a noncapitalist enterprise gets connected with a capitalist enterprise at any level, we say that it has locked into the circuits of global capital and, by default, into global capital. This is not to say that, in doing so, noncapitalist enterprises become capitalist but, simply, that these hook themselves into the circuits of global capital.

It is commonplace knowledge that such decentered global enterprises are almost exclusively privately capitalist, where we understand their global capitalistic feature as a privately exploitative class process in the context of commodity production that includes, among others, labor power as a commodity.[4] Marx calls surplus labor, in the context of commodity production, surplus value. Subsequently, the master (or nodal) signifiers of global capitalist enterprise—or of global capital—are commodity and surplus value that structure the other floating signifiers (efficiency, competition, individualism, and so on).

So we ask: how does global capital acquire its hegemonic character? There are three moments of hegemony that need emphasis. We begin with the first. Chakrabarti and Dhar (2002) and Chakrabarti (2003) extend the theories of Resnick and Wolff (2001) and Hardt and Negri (2000) to argue that capital (the product of capitalist exploitative enterprise) acquires its global character through disarticulation (production, appropriation, distribution, and exchange no longer happening in one site) and hence disaggregation (the activities of global capital—production, distribution, and circulation—happen in different regions of the world). The circuits of global enterprises (production, distribution, and the exchange of goods and services embodying the capitalist performance, appropriation, distribution, and receipt of surplus labor) are no longer related specifically to the West and North (say, Hindustan Lever headquartered in the West), but rather, they may be and they are very much part and parcel of the Eastern and Southern economies as well (say, Ranbaxy headquartered in India). Capital becomes globally imperial with its circuits of production, distribution, and receipt of surplus labor and its conditions of existence moving as if directionless into the distant corners of the globe. Its reach knows and respects no boundaries, and that is how global capital becomes the economic life-form of the new global order, which is constituted by multilayered and variegated processes—political, natural, and cultural.

It is crucial to understand that the imperial scope of global capital is not independent of the cultural and political space. These spaces, which were once tuned to national interests, including national capital, must now be reconfigured to suit and facilitate the entry of global capital. This reconfiguration further encompasses the entire gamut of the social terrain—a reconfiguration of the legal and state apparatus, dominant notions of entrepreneurship and consumerism, judgment of performance (through market-judged efficiency, for example), customs and mores, tastes, space, family, and so on. Global capital thus exists within the overdetermined webs of economic, cultural, and political processes that are within social life itself; it exists within social life, helping produce and regulate the different moments and turns of social life. Global capital in turn becomes spongy, being pulled and pushed through the contradictory influences of the economic, political, and cultural processes. The recurring transformation of social life forces a continual mutation, displacement, and renewal of the circuits of global capital. This symbiotic relation between the circuits of global capital and social life is what makes global capital so different from other historic forms that capital may have previously acquired.

The second moment of hegemony is through the discourse of globalization that produces the knowledge that gives sanctity to those discursive practices that sanctify global capital, along with its metonymic signifiers, and helps create the architecture constituting institutions that attempt to control and regulate the production of social life. What possible forms will the circuits of global capital take, and who will have the right to enter and exit the circuits? How are possible crises within social life going to be defined, located, and dealt with? The global architecture struggles over these questions. The third moment of hegemony refers to how global capital is able to manage, control, and subdue the noncapitalist class practices such that these appear as simply global capital's metaphoric surplus that is, as its extension, thereby disarming any counterhegemonic political impulse that one could possibly generate from such practices. The three moments of hegemony (which will regularly crop up in the course of the discussion below) compensate, intersect, and reinforce one another, and in doing so, articulate a global regime of power that produces, protects, and sanctifies the dominance of global capital. We call this the regime of the new global order.

This scenario depicts a movement toward a universal-like unified new global order in which the old binary between West and East or North and South becomes problematic. With the globe imploding into the one in this depiction, the South is getting integrated into the axes of the North. The North is no longer a distant space or imaginary; rather, it is right there inside the South, making nonsense its very naming as "South." If the North-South division gets blurred, then does the Other and, with it, the Orientalist frame disappear? Is there an outside space that is bereft of the social life that we talked about and that can neither be produced nor regulated by the regimes of power driving the internal principles of global capital? Does the regime of global power then need to make another hegemonic move that will be uniquely targeted toward controlling and subduing the excluded Other?

We want to begin the process of answering these questions by tracing the brief economic history of India and the changing context and place of Orientalism in that journey. That will help us in understanding the current transition of the Indian society following the adoption of NEP, and it will take us right into the heart of our problematic: the current crisis of the category of third world and of the Orientalist framework itself in the formulation of the emerging development paradigm of India.

India's Development Journey: An Encounter with Orientalism

Since its colonization by the British, India's development journey has been an integral part of the Orientalist thematic. Typically, the Orientalist model, following the initial postcolonial turn given by Edward Said, was made of the West, its internal Others (the Slavs, for example), and its external Other—the three moments comprising the first, second, and third worlds. We are here dealing with the encounter of the West with its external Other—the encounter of the first world with the third world. India remained the West's construction of its external Other, a construction through which the West was able to define itself as such and project its superiority. This construction helped represent Indians as native, tribal, simple-minded, and idyllic villagers, ignorant and unhealthy people, and members of a communal society with no history (or change), ruled by despots.

The Other, in turn, was shown as having a bad side and good side—bad Other and the good Other. Typically, the West identified and collapsed the so-called complex Other (that it constructed) to its bad side and then attempted to rewrite the history of the Other through its intervention. There were then two aspects to the Orientalist model pertinent to a country like India: firstly, and generally, the West defined an external Other in order to protract its name and superiority to itself as well as to the rest of the world; and secondly, it collapsed its own construction of the complex Other into the bad Other, which served as a justification of its intervention within the terrain of the Other. The Other cannot save itself from its bad Other; this can only be done by an outside force—the West. One can read this theme of a civilizing mission as constituting the basis of the British intervention in India. In fact, in a way, this theme is the most potent motif that underlies the Orientalist framework and foreign interventions into the domain of the Other even today. Chaudhury (1994) and Chaudhury, Das, and Chakrabarti (2000) describe in detail how the British Empire was able to mix its own principles with those of the Other to displace, homogenize, and colonize the Other.

The Orientalist model continued, albeit differently after India gained independence from the British in 1947. One of the magic wands that now was supposed to bridge the gap between the West and East became development. Development became the new mantra of India's societal transition to the West, constituting a complex series of discursive practices that attempted to coalesce India's diverse society and multiple Others into a system of dispersion that procreated a regime of truth—the truth of Western superiority. This truth was now to be India's destiny: Western capitalism. It must be noted that while independent India was heavily influenced by the Soviet Union, it never really adopted the Soviet model. The model closest to describing India's development paradigm was the Lewis model, which tries to describe the mechanics of the transition of a third world country like India toward a modern capitalist society (Chakravarty 1987)

It is important to understand that the postindependent form of Orientalism is very different from that existing before independence. We can describe it as a new phase of Orientalism in India. The exercise of Orientalism can no longer be openly directed or practiced by foreigners (say, Britishers or Americans), but must instead be produced from within—from within the domain of the prevalent Other. These development practices are internally procreated by domestic subjects substituting for the external rulers: this defines the historical turn in the Orientalist model of postindependent India. Discourse of development encapsulates the Orientalist model because it again, albeit in a different form, produces the binary reflecting the superiority of the West—good West versus bad East, industrial West versus agricultural East, modern West versus traditional East, educated West versus uneducated East, secular West versus religious East, democratic West versus despotic East, rational West versus obstinate East, and so on. Even with its so-called independence, history must repeat itself: the East must be salvaged from itself through the development journey that telescopes the superiority of the West over the East.

However, since development practices are now internally produced, the problem of reconciling the good Other and the bad Other within the East becomes more complex. It is against this background that one must read the conflict between Jawaharlal Nehru (the first prime minister and a very formidable one) and Mahatma Gandhi (the father of the nation), a conflict that effectively amounted to a struggle between the good Other (Nehru standing for Western style progress) and the bad Other (Gandhi standing for the obstinate East). This conflict really was not only about how the Other would evolve independently of the West but also about how to position oneself in terms of the West, that is, in terms of the Orientalist model. Orientalism, despite the apparent absence of any physical colonizer, remained the organizing principle of the postindependence political struggle within India. The complexity and severity of the conflict can be gauged from the following quotes by Gandhi and Nehru (the first two quotes are from Gandhi, and the last quote is by Nehru):

> I am always reminded of one thing which the well-known British economist Adam Smith has said in his famous treatise *The Wealth of Nations*. In it he has described some economic laws as universal and absolute. Then he has described certain situations which may be an obstacle to the operation of these laws. These disturbing factors are the human nature, the human temperament or altruism inherent in it. Now the economics of *khadi* is just the opposite of it. Benevolence which is inherent in human nature is the very foundation of the economics of *khadi*. What Adam Smith has described as pure economic activity based merely on the calculations of profit and loss is a selfish attitude and it is an obstacle to the development of *khadi*; and it is the function of a champion of *khadi* to counteract this tendency (Gandhi 1958, 59:205–6).[5]
>
> My own view is that evils are inherent in industrialization, and no amount of socialization can eradicate them (Gandhi 1958, 63:241).
>
> We are trying to catch up, as far as we can, with the Industrial Revolution that occurred long ago in Western countries (Nehru 1954, 93).

Opposing his guru Mahatma Gandhi, Jawaharlal Nehru was determined to industrialize India and transform it into a modern Western-like society, which he took as a superior form of society.

According to Nehru, the transition from a backward agricultural society to a modern industrial one was the only possible road for India to progress. The biggest obstacle to such a transition was identified in the dearth of material capital. Because of the paucity of material capital, industrialization came to be identified with an unending, inexorable process of capital accumulation.

Industrialization through capital accumulation became the substance of the postindependent Indian development paradigm. Moreover, in line with Nehru's wishes, India's industrialization process was propelled by the state sector, since it was argued that the private sector did not have the resources to create the basic infrastructure and means of production needed for industrialization. The idea was not to kill the private sector, but rather to facilitate its growth (through its expansion in the consumer goods sector) by providing the private sector with the necessary capital that it lacked.

The idea of a strong state propelling the logic of industrialization through capital accumulation created its own momentum and translated by the 1980s into a virtual monopoly of the state over the capital goods sector, giving the state control over what might be called the commanding heights of the economy. The private enterprises that were mainly concentrated in the consumer goods sector depended upon the state enterprises for survival because most of their indispensable inputs come from the state sector. The quantitative involvement of the state in the Indian economy was backed up by qualitative involvement, which was critical for the reproduction of its private enterprises. This qualitative involvement came about through a complicated licensing system that made it mandatory for private enterprises to seek licenses for establishing new units and for expanding the capacity of the existing units, control over imports through licensing, restrictions on exports, administrative control over exchange rates, a large sum of transfers to the agricultural sector and other sectors like health and education, high income and corporate taxes, as well as control over the banking and the insurance system. This was backed by an import substitution policy that virtually debarred foreign competition, protected Indian industries—state and private—and took India into the path of a self-sufficient, something akin to an autarkic, economy.

Yet, since independence, the path of capitalist development in India via industrialization has not been easy and without compromises. Due to political considerations already mentioned, the Gandhian tradition of *khadi*, which is a different and diametrically opposite set of economic policies as compared to ones directed at growth through industrialization, had to be accounted for in the Indian development paradigm. And, because the Gandhian philosophy is so crucially based on the economic philosophy of *khadi*, the Indian economic policies had to combine the growth-oriented "maximization" policies and the Gandhian job-oriented "benevolent," nonprofit policies. This accommodation stretched to the agricultural sector that was fundamentally left untouched after independence and that was comprised of numerous so-called traditional, noncapitalist enterprises. The compromise with the so-called traditional, backward agricultural forces can be lumped with Gandhi's because, from the point of view of the modernists, these are comprised of elements that are driven by a no-profit, nonaccumulation standpoint and as such constitute the bad Other.

Despite accommodating Gandhi, there was no doubt in the elite circle, which includes the academic elite, that progress via the logic of industrialization through capital accumulation was the key to (capitalist) growth and the eradication of poverty and unemployment. It was also believed that progress and rationality would win, that the good Other would integrate itself into the West, and that the bad Other would wither away by getting eaten up in the long run by the ever-expanding industrial sector and its complementary visage of modernity. Consequently, industrialization through capital accumulation was accorded a privileged position as compared to the Gandhian policy of *khadi*, which nevertheless, along with the noncapitalist forces in agriculture, had to be accommodated, for the time being, in formulating economic decisions. The problem for the Indian developmental state, then, comes down to the performance of a dual act of legitimizing the logic of industrialization through capital accumulation and accommodating the Gandhian tradition of *khadi* (the anticapitalist set of economic policies), two fundamentally contradictory positions. This complex way of looking at the development of capitalism in India is what differentiated India's development paradigm from the rest.

As per this policy, over time, the Gandhian tradition of *khadi* got integrated in the informal sector (or small scale sector), which has since then acquired enormous space in India. The informal sector has played a critical role in the Indian economy and has acquired a significant position as a reservoir of employment. As of 1998–1999, the total number of enterprises within the informal sector in India was 31.21 *lakhs*, its value of production amounted to Rs 5,27,515 *crores* which is roughly 40 percent of the value added in the manufacturing sector, contributing to 35 percent of the total exports in 1998–1999, and by 1999–2000, this sector employed around 17,850 million people (Government of India, Ministry of Finance 2000; Government of India, Ministry of Finance 2001).

This phase of India's development policy continued from 1950 to roughly 1990. In between, however, and greatly as a result of the development discourse, both the East and West changed considerably. Firstly, the East has seen some amount of industrialization and thus took the turn toward what is called underdevelopment (a capitalist sector with a huge noncapitalist sector). The good Other has been translated into and included as at least an internal Other of the West. This assimilation that overlapped the economic, cultural, and political spheres ultimately led to the transition of the East into what is now called the South. Secondly, the West, too, underwent a transition. To begin with, the European influence merged and to a large extent was replaced by the American and Soviet dominance (both of which, though, were not to remain), and a large segment of the East (Japan, South Korea, and so on) had become industrialized (or progressive in the typical Western imaginary of development). This in turn started the movement toward what has come to be known as the North. Thus, we find that the West and East have reconfigured into the North and the South. Our focus remains on the Orientalist frame and the search for the third world (the Other that remains excluded from the West or North). We will use the terms West and North as well as East and South interchangeably, keeping well in mind the impulse of the binary embedded in the Orientalist frame.

It is against such a backdrop that a new phase of Indian history began. While the rumblings of reforming the Indian economy could be heard in the mid-1980s, the real seismic change began in 1991–1992. In 1991–1992 India, launched a reform package popularly known as the New Economic Policy (NEP) that has initiated a massive transition of the Indian society. Mainstream discourse projects India's transition in terms of the criteria of efficiency and market-based pricing mechanisms purported to enact a double switch: a switch from government control of the economy to a "free" market capitalist economy, and a complementary switch from an import substitution regime to an export promotion one (Jalan 1991; Bhagwati and Srinivasan 1993; Bhagwati 1993; Joshi and Little 1996; Ahluwalia and Little 1998; Sachs, Varshney, and Bajpai 1999). Such changes were required, it was argued, to take India from its low growth into the high-growth path by deepening and expanding the industrialization process.

The government rationale for the NEP was a combination of what has been referred to as a response to a macroeconomic and microeconomic crisis situation. The macroeconomic crisis is seen in turn as being both internally (through the fiscal deficit) and somewhat externally (due to the balance of payments crunch) produced, while the microeconomic crisis signifies serious efficiency and incentive failures. According to the government, the two sets of problems are linked since, as Jagdish Bhagwati and T. N. Srinivasan, the two strong supporters of the government's economic reform, put it, "The macroeconomic problems . . . had been accentuated by, if not largely been a result of, the microeconomic inefficiencies" (Bhagwati and Srinivasan 1993, ii). The NEP is directed to redressing these sets of macroeconomic and microeconomic or structural problems, even though the essence of the macroeconomic problems is clearly traced to microeconomic distortions. That is why the thrust of the reform has been on transforming the micro-level sites of production and distribution of goods and services.

Since much of the efficiency and incentive failure was identified with the government's control of the economy, the target of the liberalization program is to decrease the state's share in the overall economy and free the power of resource allocation to the market, thereby making competition and the standpoint of profit maximization the dominant theme of organizing the economy. The government has, in the long run, taken the road to cut down its expenditures, especially its transfer payments, by dramatically reducing subsidies, closing down or selling part of the state industries to private (capitalist) sectors, and closing or cutting down many service operations; by making a shift toward a more market-determined exchange rate and open-door trade policies; instituting a new set of industrial, agricultural, and banking policies that pay more attention to principles of competition, profitability, efficiency and outward- (export-) oriented growth, and calls for less involvement of the government in economic decisions, especially those related to output and pricing. Policies designed to effect these changes are still unfolding, both at the planning and functional level, but there is no doubt as to the direction of these changes. The change in the government's role were no less dramatic. The NEP, which by changing the meaning of development is, among other things, geared toward challenging the prevailing meaning of government by radically altering its role from having an active and all-encompassing involvement in the economic sphere to promoting a particular economic environment that fosters capitalist growth with efficiency.

These changes unfolding in India are unabashedly neoliberal in spirit. These changes point to a newly emerging dominant paradigm of development that seems to be currently serving as the new magic wand of progress. There are two critical moments that we want to highlight with regard to India's changing development paradigm that makes this phase of its history distinct from the earlier one.

The first is the de-emphasis of the hitherto held anchor signifier of accumulation. While capitalist growth through industrialization still remains the key to development under NEP, quietly, it seems, the overpowering position of the anchor signifier of accumulation and subsequently the growth logic of industrialization through capital accumulation has been abandoned. Instead, the shift in NEP is now geared toward achieving capitalist growth through market and commodity expansion (which in turn guarantees efficiency and competition) and from the standpoint of profit maximization. This de-emphasis of accumulation and shifting emphasis toward market expansion and the standpoint of profit maximization coincided with the World Bank's changing view about the anchoring power of accumulation. Earlier, the World Bank had a similarly held positive view of capitalist growth via the logic of industrialization through capital accumulation, although it remained skeptical of the self-sufficiency logic grounded on the imports substitution policy that governments like India followed. By early 1990s, the World Bank self-criticized its earlier held "rosy optimism of aid-financed, government-led, accumulationist strategies of development" that "was a goal of policy to increase saving and investment and thus the rapid accumulation of capital (1991, 33).

The World Bank realized that such growth does not trickle down and in fact causes massive dislocation. Moreover, such a capital accumulation–based approach requires the nation-state to have command or overall control over the economy, especially over resource allocation. With the clear delinking of the economy from the control of the nation-state—especially with regard to the allocation of resources, which is now slowly but surely passing from state control to market control—as one of the fundamental tenets of neoliberal reform package, such an accumulation-based strategy of development appears anachronistic and thus obsolete. In fact, the World Bank's current development goal is now two-pronged and does not include the empowering anchor role of accumulation in the developmental logic. It is to "put in place growth-enhancing, market oriented policies (stable macroeconomic environment, effective law and order, trade liberalization, and so on) and ensure the provision of important public services that cannot be well and equitably supplied by private markets (infrastructure services and education, for instance)" (2000, 89). India's shift in de-emphasising accumulation as the principal anchor of development thus merges with the shift in the World Bank, reflecting a convergence of their emerging development paradigm. But then such a convergence is not surprising if we understand both the World Bank and India as trying to place their current development paradigm in line with the newly materializing global order.

This takes us to the second momentous shift of India's development paradigm as constituting a definitive movement from the autarkic-type self-sufficient existence to that of being a full-fledged party to the emerging new global order that encapsulates the instance of capitalist hegemony. We view the changing development paradigm of India (as well as that of World Bank) as basically mimicking the philosophy of the Washington Consensus.

One may visualize the Washington Consensus as a template comprising the desirable principles of a global economy, and the development industry functioning within the new global order as fulfilling the principles enshrined in the template. Many of the seemingly variegated and often seemingly conflicting discussions on globalization end up confirming the template of the Washington Consensus. In a typical Foucauldian fashion, we may say that these constitute a system of dispersion that nevertheless coalesces to produce a regime of truth—truth sustaining the legitimacy of global capitalism.

The Washington consensus refers to the following ten objectives of policy:

- fiscal policy—controlling the budget deficit
- redirection of public expenditure toward education, health, and infrastructure investment
- tax reform—broadening the tax base and cutting marginal tax rates
- interest rates that are market determined and positive (but moderate) in real terms
- competitive exchange rates
- trade liberalization—replacement of quantitative restriction with low and uniform tariffs
- deregulation—abolishment of regulations that impede entry or restrict competition, except for those justified on the grounds of safety, environment, and consumer protection, and prudential oversight of financial institutions
- legal security for property rights
- openness to foreign direct investment
- privatization of state enterprises (World Bank 2000/2001b, 62)

The Washington Consensus is comprised of fiscal policy, monetary policy, trade policy, competitive policy, policy on legal structures, and market expansion policy, and presents a compressed portrait of an imagined global order. Joseph Stiglitz, a mainstream economist and a former CEO of the World Bank, summarizes the agenda of the Washington Consensus as follows: "A set of policies formulated between 15th and 19th streets by the IMF, U.S. Treasury, and World Bank. Countries should focus on stabilization, liberalization, privatization. It's based on a rejection of the state's activist role and the promotion of a minimalist, non-interventionist state. The analysis in the era of Reagan and Thatcher was that government was interfering with the efficiency of the economy through protectionism, government subsidies, and government ownership. Once the government 'got out of the way,' private markets would allocate resources efficiently and generate robust growth. Development would simply come" (2000). The seemingly independent policies of the different agencies—the World Bank, International Monetary Fund, World Trade Organization, International Labor Organization, and so on—as well as those of national governments and independent organizations like nongovernmental organizations (NGOs) work to sanctify the principles ingrained in the Washington Consensus. The NEP adopted in India can indeed be read as a mirror image of the Washington Consensus, reflecting the template that ensures the breakdown of its self-sufficient economy and the rise of the global economy within India. India's destiny lies in the global frame, and the NEP acknowledges that in no uncertain terms.

With India integrating itself within the circuits of the global economy, what then happens to its status as a third world society, to its Otherness? Is the phase of Orientalism not over? Despite the many other differences, is the South not being included or waiting to be included in the new global order? Is the South not getting connected into the circuits of the North and thus fast becoming a portion of the North? Does not this blurring of the North-South division make nonsense any projection of an excluded Other? In the following discussion, we contest this erasure of the Other and argue for an excluded, foreclosed space of the new global order. We argue that a country of the South like India gets disarticulated into the axes of the North and thus the emerging global order, and also into axes that break away from the sinews of the global order, as its outside. We call this outside the third world, the Other of the new global order. The development paradigm of India reflects sharply this emerging division—a new form of representation—that nevertheless is imbued with the same idea of superiority over the Other—over the third world.

We start with the predicament of Indian reformers regarding the problem of accommodating the informal sector or the Gandhian philosophy of *khadi* that clearly is based on principles that run away from those celebrated in the new global order. If the NEP is tilted toward the global economy, then what is its vision of the "renegade," "reactionary," or "backward" informal sector, the pain in the tail that covers a large body of the Indian society? We can put the problem slightly differently. Since the Indian economy had opened itself to be articulated into the emerging global order, how does global capital deal with the informal sector? Does the hegemony of global capital that is encapsulated in the new global order erase the informal sector? If not, then is it able to control, manage, and include the informal sector within its circuits, or are a segment of the informal sector and the forms of life around it able to resist incorporation into the camp of global capital and thus remain outside the global order? If the latter is true, does this excluded segment around the informal sector not constitute the camp of the third world? Does then the globe get disarticulated between the new global order and the third world, where the superiority of the former stands unquestioned? And then does the latter, that is the third world, stand as sometimes the representation of the good Other (an emotional, helpless, and submissive Other), and at other times as the bad Other (the uncivil, the barbarians) who are to be feared and kept out of the entrance gate of the civil global order?

This is then a third world that cannot be included in the circuits of global capital that dominate the new global order or be ruled through its internal principles, but that must instead somehow be managed, controlled, and kept locked. Orientalism has not disappeared but has rather changed its figuration and place. The rest of the paper uses principally the World Bank discourse of development in the context of the emerging global order to demonstrate the production of this new space of the third world and by default, the new Orientalist model. This will hopefully open up for discussion the emerging contour of a new juncture of Orientalism in India's economic history.

Orientalism in the Era of Globalization: What is the Third World?

We have already seen that the place for the Other in postindependent India was displaced into the informal sector (and agriculture as well, which we do not analyze here), which saw its integration into the Gandhian philosophy of *khadi*. So let us start with the informal sector—the site of much of the discussion of the Other in the development discourse.

Informal Sector is defined as a "very informal unit producing and distributing goods and services, and consisting largely of independent, self-employed producers in urban areas of developing countries, some of whom also employ family labour and/or a few hired workers or apprentices; which operate with very little capital, or none at all; which utilize a low level of technology and skills; which therefore operate at a low level of productivity; and which generally provide very low and irregular incomes and very unstable employment to those who work in it" (ILO 1991, 4). The informal sector is constituted by firms of "self-employed producers" or "own-account workers"; some firms "hire" laborers and others produce with "family" laborers. In class terms, the informal sector economy is comprised of a rich and large variety of class sets, from self-exploitative, feudal, and capitalist, to nonexploitative ones such as communistic and communist. We have already described the importance of the informal sector in India. This importance stretches to other countries in the South as well. As the ILO reports, "the bulk of new employment in recent years, particularly in developing and transition countries, has been in the informal economy. Most people have been going into the informal sector because they cannot find jobs or are unable to start businesses in the formal economy. In Africa, for instance, informal work accounted for almost 80 percent [of] non-agricultural employment, over 60 percent of urban employment and over 90 percent of new jobs over the past decade or so. But work in the informal economy cannot be termed 'decent' compared to *recognized, protected, secure, formal* employment" (ILO 2002, 1). We are also reminded that the informal sector holds some sway over developed societies, as well (see ILO, 2002, 24). But the crucial slip lies in the words *recognized, protected, secure, and formal,* which differentiate the informal sector in the South from those in the North.

Unlike in developed societies, an overwhelming portion of the informal sector operates in countries like India *without* any protection, recognition (especially with respect to legal, regulatory, and formal institutions, with even the trade unions remaining oblivious of this space), or security (including labor market security, employment security, job security, work security, skill reproduction security, income security, representation security, and security from the violence of local politics).

Does this mean that the informal sector does not have its own political economy? The ILO says emphatically, "The term 'informal' does not mean that there are no rules or norms regulating the activities of workers or enterprises. People engaged in informal activities have their own 'political economy'—their own informal or group rules, arrangements, institutions and structures for mutual help and trust, providing loans, organizing training, transferring technology and skills, trading and market access, enforcing obligations, etc. What we do not know is what these informal rules or norms are based on and whether or how they observe the fundamental rights of workers" (2002, 7).

The ILO's position on the informal sector and rights more or less overlaps with those of the other international institutions such as the World Bank and WTO. While ILO is confused about the nature of the political economy underlying the informal activities, this confusion immediately touches on an important subject. This is regarding the question of whether the informal sector's political economy observes rights. Why is the question of rights important to begin with in this informal domain, if the ILO does not "know" either the political economy or how the question of rights is addressed in that domain? Despite that, if the question of rights is imposed in that segment, the question remains as to whose rights are invoked, and from which ethicopolitical position they are invoked. In such a context, the (Western) rights forwarded as universally true and fundamental can only be imperial in scope and useful for rearticulating the social within that "unknown" political economy into an outside regime of power.

Globalization discourse attempts to bring the issue of rights within the informal sector. It puts on the moral garb of human rights to attempt to project the humane lacks within such informal societies, lacks that then are attempted to be subjected to the principles of some universal virtues (when they are de facto first world virtues) and its associated rules and regulations. As we shall soon show, this attempt to reign in and civilize the renegade informal sector, and the social life connected to and surrounding it, leads up to an outcome that underlies perverse processes of exploitation, marginalization, and subjugation of the informal sector (and of the constituting social life) by global capital. Furthermore, this attempt to reign in the informal sector, and the rights discourse attempting to civilize the forms of life associated with it, is targeted at a segment of the informal sector that is connected to the circuits of global capital, a segment that is hooked into the internal principles of global capital and onto which the rights discourse is considered as fair play. We call this segment of the informal sector *informal sector I. Another* segment of the informal sector opens up that remains disconnected with global capital, that is, disconnected with its networks and circuits, and where the rights discourse and the floating signifiers that structure the global production of social life remain totally oblivious of the issues of recognition, protection, and security. The presence of this segment symbolizes the surreal presence of the *fractured* moment of the globe. We call this segment of informal sector *informal sector II*. It will form the basis of defining and locating the third world. Let us discuss each in turn.

Informal Sector I

A condition for global hegemony is that the attempts to negotiate with the informal sector must simultaneously disarm any alternatives stemming from noncapitalist classes and forms of life that may carry the possibility of challenging the hegemony of global capital. In this context, the hegemonic moment lies in transforming these noncapitalist possibilities into global capital's metaphoric surplus, as if these are mere extensions of global capital, such that their destiny is to be of second-order importance to that of global capital. The other class moments will continue to socially function, but their harboring the possibility of reorganizing the economic space becomes an absurdity. Through outsourcing, subcontracting, and vertical integration, a segment of these class sets is attempted to be rearticulated to the formal sector or the circuits of global capital.

Chakrabarti and Cullenberg (2003) highlight this linkage by delving into the overdetermined relation between global capital and the informal sector in India via the celebrated concept of outsourcing and subcontracting, or the global production chain. They view outsourcing, subcontracting, and flexible specialization as a totally different text from that being sold in the corridors of civilized academic discourse. Defense of these has been attributed to innovation, transaction cost, efficiency, competition, and so on, but rarely is the aspect of Marxian exploitation invoked in this regard. By that account, the exploitation dimension remains a hidden—unrecorded—text of globalization. The multinationals or big domestic global capitalist enterprises—blue chips of world civilization or the epitome of national virtues—outsource or subcontract work to the informal sector to be produced with subhuman wages in subhuman conditions. They then put their sign (brand) on the products, only to hide behind their grandeur plants and offices when talk of working conditions in the informal sector surfaces. Informal sector enterprises, as mere appendages, feed on subhuman wages and hand over the surplus labor to the global capitalist firms. Wall Street and stock exchanges all over the world then parade the fruits of those subhuman workers as increments of values of celebrated companies, of their robustness, competitiveness, and efficiency. And investors, sharing in the spoils, celebrate the idea of the relentless march of capitalism.

Peel by peel, the fruits of the informal sector workers are appropriated and distributed. The body of surplus labor disintegrates and disappears like the unholy ashes in the holy river of Ganges. It is true that both global capital and the informal sector constitute one another, but their constitutivity gives way to a relation of increased exploitation within the informal sector as well as the intensification of the transfer of surplus labor to global capitalist enterprises. This process of exploitation is not a simple extraction of surplus labour that happens in any site, but, additionally, the special feature of this globally networked exploitative process is that it enables and is enabled by the process of marginalization via the displacement of the informal sector where, as part of a consciously designed policy, the existence of the informal sector is made into a mere appendage of global capital, as its metaphoric surplus.

Through such well-designed policies, the previously sacrosanct Gandhian philosophy of *khadi* epitomizing a different template of anticapitalist economic practice within the Indian informal sector, is now sought to be displaced into a new axes where the meaning of the informal sector is rendered intelligible only in its connection with the circuits of global capital. The good Other could never eliminate the bad Other through its accommodative policies in the previous juncture of Indian history. Now it tries to win over the bad Other to its camp through a global discourse that is threatening to swamp the very existence of the Other. One can thus also project the current Indian transition as an attempt to put the notion of the Gandhian philosophy of *khadi* under erasure.

Such a well-designed policy produces a scenario in which the informal sector becomes tied to global capital—its survival depending on the latter's benevolence. As part of that policy, the numerous subsidy protections for the informal sector from the government—some of which are ancient, going back for centuries—are exorcised or sharply reduced. The export market is usurped and handed over to big capital, wages become inhumanly low, working conditions deteriorate, families disintegrate, and the market criteria of efficiency and competition are forced to change the standpoint of production in that sector from need to profit. Competition is structured so that it is no longer international or over final products, but instead exists between the informal sector firms, each of which strives to access the gate of global capital, and it hence develops into a virtual dance of death.

It is well-known that the demand for humane working conditions, including uniform labor standards, has been part and parcel of Western countries' agenda in the WTO and in other world bodies, where the word "Western" in this context carries the moral weight of a position not simply of its governments, but also generally of the liberal position of Western civil society. In this context, we ask: does a uniform labor standard (a focal point of furious debate within and outside the WTO) mean that it is uniform at all levels?

The answer is no; it concerns only labor engaged in the global capitalist sector and does not apply to labor done in the noncapitalist sector. The same is true for other constitutive elements of humane working conditions—environmental, health, and so on. The proper metaphor for such noncapitalist sectors is that of a colony. Then, what is at issue here is a struggle between global capitalist enterprises for rights over colonies, for rights over goods produced in the informal economy at inhumanly low wages, all couched in honey-coated terms.

Despite these fall outs from such a transition, the informal sector firms will love to be tied to the global capitalist enterprises. The latter does not bother to elicit consent or faith from the former, but the informal firms do precisely that. The informal sector becomes not simply a marginalized space but also one where the meaning of marginalization turns on itself, for the process of consent implies consent to be a serf, to be tied. This does not necessarily entail an appropriation of the informal sector into global capital, even as the informal sector is hooked into the tentacles that constitute the circuits of global capital. Global capital remains what it is (the valorization of informal sector signifiers does not alter it remarkably). But global capital's floating signifiers, or its metonyms (commodity, efficiency, competition, and so on), intrude into the informal space, alter it, and put their marks on it. In other words, global capital colonizes the informal space. Materialization of the new global order turns the informal space into its colony, and the competition is the struggle over colonies.

Such informal sector enterprises, constituting the domain of informal sector I, are then a conceptual space of noncapitalist and (nonglobal) capitalist class enterprises that get locked into the circuits of global capital. We call this complex of informal sectors, circuits of global capital, and the social life connected to it the *camp* of global capital. From a class perspective, the new global order can indeed be deconstructed as the camp of global capital (and into the excluded third world, to which we will come to later on).

On the other hand, and quite paradoxically, we have witnessed how a segment of the antiglobalization movement has focused its attention on the rights absent within the informal sector. Does this critique of the absence of rights within the informal sector contain the whole of the informal sector? No, it refers to the informal sector connected to the circuits of global capital. Why is this the case? Why is it that the gaze of the antiglobalization movement has turned toward one segment of the informal sector at the expense of the rest? It is now well documented that the current phase of globalization is turning part of the industrial North into its graveyard. Drawn by the higher rate of exploitation and profit in the South, capitalist enterprises in the North, which are not otherwise global, start functioning as such, and existing global capitalist enterprises redraw and remap their global circuits of capital. Consequently, the different units constituting the variegated circuits of global capital in the North start relocating themselves to the South (principally in Asia and Eastern Europe). Thus, units in the North connected to global capitalist enterprise close down, jobs disappear, and communities that grew up around those units are destroyed.

Many people in the North locate the blame for this predicament not on capitalism and its materializing global form, but rather on either globalization per se, or on the informal sector in the South that is able to deliver higher rates of exploitation and profits to global capital. The attention of the North has consequently shifted to this segment of the informal sector connected to the circuits of global capital. Right wingers simply blame the entire South for it and call for a nationalistic solution, while liberals more subtly start using the rights discourse to highlight the aspect of security, protection, and recognition that is deemed to be absent in the informal sector, enabling global capitalist enterprises to extract higher profits. The latter de facto option also underwrites a nationalistic discourse since it is based on the desire to protect the so-called "declining" industrial North. Consequently, global pressures on the environment, labor, patent, and product standards are being fiercely argued for and forced into this segment of the informal sector. The object is to, as they say, level the playing field, that is, level the playing field through the imperial discourse of rights that would reconfigure the informal sector into the global regime of power that underwrites the dominance of global capital.

The seemingly economic impulse of global capital, containing the aspect of outsourcing, subcontracting, vertical integration, and flexible specialization, overflows with different moments of colonization in the South and creates massive disjointedness in the North, producing clashing opinions regarding globalization and the South. These present us with the possibility of a North-South clash, or what some call a dialogue between them. Much of the struggles articulated in the streets of Seattle, Genoa, and Cancun during summits and other forums are testimony to the intense contradictions within the camp of global capital. But these are *not* struggles that in any way address the concern of the forms of life outside the circuits of global capital. The forms of life of another camp—another camp outside the camp of global capital, a state of exception, the Other—must be kept out of the process of forming a new global order and yet included in the global regime of power through its control and management. This camp embodies a territory whose psychic life is so distant, so different, so dangerous, and so costly to dismantle that the regime does not want to put down or obliterate that territory, but rather wants to keep it at arm's length even as it controls it. We name this camp—the Other—as the third world. Moreover, the existence and fixing of this (b)order of the Other helps in defining the moment of difference and superiority for the new global order. One starts getting a glimpse of the new Orientalist moment in the era of globalization. Let us explore in detail the terrain of the third world to further concretize the new Orient.

Informal Sector II

We have already pointed out that the world's attention has turned to informal sector I partly due to its connection with the circuits of global capital. The antiglobalization struggles as well as various rights organizations (relating to human rights, children's rights, gender rights, environmental rights, and so on) have brought many issues pertaining to informal sector I to the forefront. This has in turn detracted attention from the rest of the informal sector (dominated by noncapitalist class sets), which remains disconnected with the circuits of global capital. We call this segment informal sector II.

Unlike developed societies, large parts of the informal sector in the third world remain consumption- or need-oriented rather than profit- or accumulation-oriented (Sanyal 1993; Sanyal 2001; Chakrabarti 2001; Chakrabarti and Cullenberg 2003; Chaudhury 2001). The American dream that so much animates the vast milieu of the informal sector in developed societies is simply not present here. If one adds the virtual absence of protection, security, and recognition, then a different space breaking away from the circuit of global capital starts emerging. What emerges is a space that is disconnected from the camp of global capital and the discourse of life connected to it, and it is a different camp altogether. The multitude in this space is also very unlike the rest: it is immobile and invisible, and not resembling the smart and sophisticated diasporas, hybrid and cosmopolitan, so much celebrated in the third world imaginary of the North or West. This is then a space that is never part of global negotiations, outside the—if we may borrow a term from Gayatri Spivak Chakrabarty—empire-nation exchange. We call this space the third world, and we call its multitude and the institutions that comprise its political economy and forms of life as the camp the third world.

The third world is thus conceptually a space that is not and cannot be hosted by global capital or its multilayered and variegated circuits. However, the point remains that the reconfigured third world we are referring to—the invisible and immobile multitude living on the basis of need in a nonglobal market environment within informal sector II—while existing outside the circuits of global capital, gets constituted by the dynamics of global capital. The third world does not have full autonomy, but instead only relative autonomy. As global capital mutates, and with it, its circuits expand their scope, the reconfiguration and relocation of the third world becomes a never-ending process. Thus, while the third world is not hosted by global capital, the latter continues to overdetermine the other and hence makes the (b)order of global capital or the third world dynamic open to spatial (re)articulation. The third world then exhibits the feature of ergodicity: what is third world in one instance may not be so in the other, and what was within the camp of global capital may slip into the camp of the third world in a different temporal or spatial moment.

Our notion of the global order thus breaks away from both the center-periphery model and the expanse of a singular global order embodying the flow of the circuits of capital into the all-encompassing production of bourgeois social life. Instead, we disaggregate the new global order into a complex product of the camp of global capital, constituting the circuits of global capital and its margin, informal sector I, connected to it and the camp of the third world, yet disconnected from the circuits of global capital. The *camp* is a reminder of the fundamental fracture that has befallen the new global order, of its failure to submit all forms of life to *its* empowering process of reterritorialization and deterritorialization.

This segment of informal sector II, and of life therein, is conceived by the mainstream development discourse as inefficient, an ancient safety valve of underdeveloped societies. This is because informal sector II nurtures unproductive labor in the inefficient nonmarket space, whose society's goal is not often production-driven, but instead consumption- or need-oriented, and whose multitude is immobile and increasingly invisible (for they are driven away from the camps of global capital). This sector is conceived of as social residual, which global capital must manage (through, say the World Bank), but can never consider as part of global capital. While global capital lives through the flexible, mobile, and expansive production of social life, the immobile, invisible third world lives and functions on the basis of *need*. Not only does this mutation of global capital continuously constitute the (b)order of this nonglobal space but, to a significant degree, its internal transition is also brought about through the direct intervention of the need-based development discourse of the World Bank, ILO, United Nations Development Programme, and so on, which challenges and more often kills these societies' own notions of need.

The multitude in the third world thus lives on the contradictory site of its own contingent need based on socially necessary desire and necessity, and the politics of the universal need, objectified by the mainstream development discourse that comes down on it from above and outside. When the global institutions enter into the third world, with its special need–focused discourse of development, the process of subjugation is drastically felt in the domain of the shared environment that constitutes the life within the third world. The transition of the third world is not a simple process of transition of fundamental classes therein but, additionally, often is focused on bringing about a dramatic transformation of the shared environment—the conditions of existence of the existing non-capitalist enterprises, of the forms of life surrounding it.

Why must the international agencies intervene into the camp of the third world when they have been effectively foreclosed from the camp of global capital? International agencies striving for the global management of spaces seek to reign in the disarticulated terrain, even as some of the moments of disarticulation might be their own making. One of the standard methods of reigning in the dislocated world, that at the same time favors the expansion of the variegating interstices of exploitation, has been through the so-called structural adjustment program (SAP) pioneered by the IMF and strongly philosophized by the Washington Consensus. The World Bank and the development industry as a whole have dubbed the SAP as sound macroeconomic management. Some countries have voluntarily adopted SAPs and some countries have been forced to do so, while others like India are adopting them gradually as part of the NEP. The cost of the transition involved with the SAP, however, cannot be ignored.

There is a growing understanding on the part of international agencies that a global transition to a market dominated economy following the SAP can turn out to be highly unstable. The SAP and the process of globalization contain measures that may throw a large section of the population outside the camp of global capital and into the heart of the third world. The SAP may also contain policies that may turn existing third world forms of life upside down by, for example, connecting farming land into the global cities or transforming it into super fast highways, disconnecting dwellings and noncapitalist enterprises (disconnected with global capital) from the vicinity and visibility of the camp of global capital, thereby presenting global capital with its comfort zone. While we find that the management of the globalization process to create a global order founded on (global) market principle underwrites an attempt to forge a camp of global capital, it might produce situations that could threaten the very livelihood and life of a vast segment of the people residing outside the camp of global capital, those considered most vulnerable, those living in the camp of the third world.

The regime trying to control the new global order is presented with a deadly paradox. Attempts to articulate and reign in the dislocated world through the globalization process are fraught with possibilities of even more dislocation and disarticulation. Living at the tip of such a traumatic existence, that is, new global order formation and materialization of the third world, the new global order gets torn into contradictory possibilities. While the emergence of the new global order cannot stop the materialization of the third world, since its own life form and representation as a superior civilized form greatly hinges on the latter's formation, it must confront the third world on a totally different platform. Development discourse must therefore undergo a change from its previous capital centricity to *that* which will address and resolve the trauma that threatens to terrorize the psychic life of the new global order.

The World Bank acknowledges as one of its central lessons,

> Growth does not trickle down; development must address human needs directly. (World Bank 2000, 57)
>
> Our experience has shown the need for a new, integrated conceptual framework that builds on previous knowledge but better reflects the world situation at the beginning of the 21st century—a situation where risks and opportunities are on the rise, here it is recognized that neither the state nor the market alone will provide the best solution, and where the plight of more than 1 billion poor people poses the question of how to manage risk better, not merely providing handouts after a shock has occurred. For the World Bank, this implies an even stronger need to incorporate social protection subsectors within an overall framework. It also indicates the urgency of integrating social protection with other sectors and themes at the World Bank. (World Bank 2001a, 7)

In line with a change in its approach, the World Bank has made need-focused discourse one of its central strategies. This is not to dethrone the capitalist growth objective (that remains the number one development goal of the World Bank) but, paradoxically, to protect and harmonize growth within the overall framework of expanding and deepening global penetration in the South. In the early days of this monumental transformation, the World Bank clearly understood that its holistic program must feature "market-oriented policies to support growth, together with well-targeted social programs" that addressed what it called "human development and poverty alleviation" (World Bank 1991, 36). In other words, the World Bank's development program encapsulates an attempt to combine two apparently contradictory aspects, growth and need, into a constitutive relation of complementarity.

We shall see that another aspect gets added with time: security and control, or what is called social harmony at times. One route taken by the World Bank to formalize its need focus came about with the birth of *social protection* as one its sector groups in 1996. The idea of social protection started gaining prominence in the 1980s until it was finally concretized in the form of a sector group. Social protection is defined as "public interventions that assist individuals, households, and communities to manage risk better and that provide support to the critically poor" (World Bank 2001a, 9). Social protection intersects, compensates, and reinforces social risk management and income distribution policies in its effort to link with the broader agenda of poverty discourse centering on need. "Social protection interventions constituted an integral part of the overall adjustment programs," such as SAP, so much so that "more than 80 percent of social protection lending was in the form of adjustment loans" (World Bank 2001a, 3). From its previous policy of intervening after the event has transpired, the World Bank is increasingly desirous of transforming itself into an active player that now, as part of its overall policy within the global framework, strives to break down the time zone of intervention, empowering itself to move in and out at will, imperiously picking its territory and targets, with its discourse of need.

In this context, it is important to make a distinction between survival needs and social needs. We define social needs as those needs perceived by the World Bank to have capitalist growth impact, while survival needs refer to the set of needs having no capitalist growth impact. The postglobalization and postcommunist discourse of the World Bank focuses on expanding the milieu of social needs in the so-called Southern countries. The social programs that were emphasized in the 1980s and 1990s, such as education and health care, were considered to have positive externality to growth. Subsequently, such programs of *social needs* were part of the logic of growth and interior to the gaze of global capital. The management of social need was deemed to have beneficial effects of a different kind on the circuits of global capital.

But what about the instances related to *survival needs* that do not have any apparent growth value? Such survival needs appear in the domain of the third world practices of the World Bank that we are emphasizing here. These are practices located in those social segments that remain vulnerable to what the World Bank perceives to be nonmarket life, or rudimentary market life, without any connection to the circuits of global capital procreating amid so-called extreme forms of poverty and deprivation, where class processes are neither

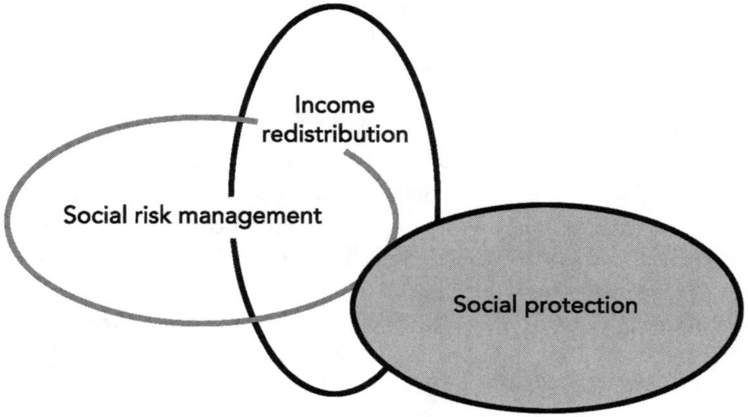

Figure 11.1 Social protection
(World Bank 2001a, 10)

driven by profit nor by accumulation motive, but rather by the consumption-perspective of need. In Figure 11.1, we can see the portion of the dark shaded area within social protection but outside the zones of social risk management and income distribution. On the truncated dark shaded area, this is what the World Bank has to say:

> Advocates of policies to combat social exclusion argue that modern social protection should not be limited to traditional forms of income support but should include measures to promote social cohesion, solidarity, and inclusion. On one hand, an income support system for the unemployed may not only enhance individual welfare by reducing vulnerability but also help to achieve social stability. On the other hand, social protection may extend well beyond mere financial and income-oriented considerations. This broader approach would include investments to support informal arrangements and upgrade the non-profit sector, strengthen the "social rights" aspects of social policy, and extend the view of social risk management to include the broader concept of "social capital." . . . Promoting social inclusion is an important objective of the World Bank. While the social, cultural, and political determinants of social inclusion may be beyond the scope of social risk management, it is essential to recognize the causes and consequences of social exclusion and to design strategies that address these issues. (World Bank 2001a, 11)

What we are seeing in the world today is the tragedy of exclusion.

> Our goal must be to reduce these disparities across and within countries, to bring more and more people into the economic mainstream, to promote equitable access to the benefits of development regardless of nationality, race or gender. The challenge of Inclusion—is the key development challenge of our time. (World Bank 2000, 13)

These quotes are an acknowledgement of the conceptual presence of excluded space and the "problem" of including these in the mainstream. They signify the acknowledgment of the excluded as the foreclosed, as a residual that cannot be included into the camp of global capital. However, at the same time, the need to support and upgrade the nonprofit sector and its associated informal arrangements (including the class processes) reflects the attempt to intervene and control the excluded space. This recent turn of the World Bank is revolutionary and reflects an understanding on the part of the regime of global order of the need to reconstitute its domain of power following the process of globalization. Consequently, the content of need discourse in the arena of global capital that aspires to bring spaces and multitude within its logic cannot be conceptually the same as the discourse of need aspiring to control and subdue this excluded space that is governed by different forms of life. We give the materialization of need from the latter discourse of the World Bank another name: survival need.

Previously such survival needs and growth logics were considered inimical to each other—the former was a deposit of an archaic age that ultimately needed to be battered down so that the growth logic could proceed freely. There was an optimism that growth pioneered by the logic of capital accumulation could integrate the need-focused (traditional) sector and absorb the reserve army of the unemployed or unproductive labor force (see Lewis 1954; Hariss and Todaro 1970). Since the 1970s, it was increasingly felt that battering down the territory of the so-called archaic time and its multitude's incorporation was deeply problematic, and a huge reserve army would remain unaccounted for within the capitalist symbolic order. Moreover, with the iron discipline of the global economy built on competition and flexibility, and the market expanding with unprecedented speed and scope, it was soon realized that the reserve army was not only not accounted for by the global economy but also that the global economy enhanced the problem of the reserve army.

As cities (re)form with unprecedented pace into global cities, as global capital seek entry into hitherto uncharted territories inside the villages and jungles and with the diasporas, and as hybrids and cosmopolitans become the smokescreen of so-called third world culture, the camp of the third world is partly displaced from its present state, and partly driven away from the camp of global capital and placed on a siege. Through continuous dislocations and reconfigurations, a third world space contrastingly and challengingly inhabited by an immobile and invisible population continues to materialize on the margin of the camp of global capital. The question of survival needs thus acquires extraordinary significance in the newly emerging global order. The foreclosed third world could no longer be left alone since its (b)order is very much a result of the expansive or changing global capitalism. Such changing forms of global capitalism carry the possibility of producing chaos and disharmony, an extreme security problem, in another plane. Questioning global capitalism from this plane—that is, from the third world—would amount to questioning the very peace of the new global order, which must be prevented at all cost. This underwrites the extreme anxiety over the possible explosion of the multitude occupying the third world space. James Wolfensohn says, "A balanced and holistic understanding of the causes and effects of poverty can lead to reforms that promote inclusion, economic growth that reaches the poor, and social development—these are key to *sustainable peace*. . . . Our job will be to help countries harness the trends . . . to promote growth, poverty reduction and *social harmony*" (World Bank 2000; 2001b, 7–8).

While we had to take recourse to the World Bank's exposition to support our theoretical rendition of the third world as an excluded space from the camp of global capital, we read the presence of excluded space in World Bank's discourse as an acceptance by the regime of the new global order of the category of the third world. This conceptual category stands metaphorically for informality, nonprofit and nonaccumulative motive, without recognition, protection, voice, representation, and security, with its unique political economy that functions from consumption or need perspective and is comprised of forms of life having no respect for Northern or Western fundamental rights. Through such differencing that protracts the contour of the new Orient, the existence of the external Other of the new global order is inaugurated. This Other is the World Bank's (and the regime of global power's) reminder to itself of the impossibility of a new global order, a reminder of the fundamental fracture that has befallen the latter, and thus effectively serves as a means of posing the Other and enacting its superiority over it.

We have already indicated that this ongoing process of Othering is simultaneously splitting the Other into a bad Other (explosive, violent, unpredictable, and so on) and a good Other (emotional, passive, helpless, and so on). One can indeed read the current geopolitical turmoil in terms of rethinking the mechanisms of dealing with the newly materializing Orient in the era of globalization, of again trying to rethink how to save the good Other from the bad Other. There could be many ways of rethinking the strategies of intervening in the domain of the Other, and the need-focused development discourse is a powerful one. One should read the transformation of the development discourse vis-à-vis the third world that we have elaborated in light of this newly emerging civilizing ethics of intervention. That is, one should read the emerging development paradigm in terms of the new Orientalist model.

At one level, the new development discourse seeks to distort and displace these societies' own forms of life, their own political economy, into the terrain of the new global order. At another level, the intervention is humble enough to recognize the conceptual existence of the third world—the foreclosed pristine outside—as a constant materialization of another space following the dynamic transformation of the new global order, and as that which cannot be immediately incorporated into its camp. Like the new global order, the (b)order of the camp of the third world is also placed in a ceaseless state of change: one, externally, through the constant and continuing materialization of the new global order that (re)creates its own (b)order and thus that of the third world; and the other, internally, through the direct intervention in its political economy a la World Bank discourse of need.

The new development paradigm is a balancing act to maintain social harmony and the superiority of the new global order such that global capital can function smoothly and its circuits expand in scope. To see development discourse simply as need management or as singularly motoring the logic of the market is to miss the story of how global capital expands its hegemony beyond its camp, into the Other, in order to manage, control, and pacify it. The need-based discourse of development works in both areas: within the camp of global capital, staying with the informal sector connected to it with the intention of suitably reconfiguring the forms of life flowing from it *into* social life favorable to its reproduction; and outside the circuits of global capital, staying with the disconnected informal sector and controlling its life form to subdue its subversive potentials and maintain social harmony. In recent times, the focus of need-based development discourse has been shifting more and more toward this latter, nonglobal space. While need-based discourse may very well be liberating in Amartya Sen's account, the buzzword the eavesdropper hears and sees in the corridors and texts of the World Bank is security, control, and social harmony, and the unending fear and anxiety of the marching footsteps of Mao's children.

Conclusion

The third world emerges as a paradoxical site that, even when attempted to be subdued by the global order's regime of power through the development discourse of need, has a relative autonomy, as well (signaled by its own forms of life and political economy). This relative autonomy telescopes processes of subjectivities and subject formations, that is, of the multitude experiencing forms of life visibly distinct from those professed by the global order and practiced within its camp. The third world is then a tension-ridden space that lives in the throes of subjugation and freedom, forever presenting the global order with possibilities of something that is outside, and threatening to defy and crack open its (b)order. The global order is "besieged" by the camp of the third world. The materialization of the new global order is overdetermined by the materialization of its Other, the third world. The relevant development paradigm for analyzing India's transition to a free market, global economy is thus not that produced by the mainstream economists who are attempting to erase the moment of the Other, but rather one that uses a complexly overdetermined, multilayered network of development practices to procreate the Other in the name of the third world, announcing in the process the very materialization of the (b)order of the new global order and its superiority.

Notes

1. This chapter takes off from Chakrabarti and Cullenberg (2003) and an ongoing book project by Anjan Chakrabarti, Stephen Cullenberg and Anup Dhar.
2. Arturo Escobar (1993) remains an important exception. Escobar does talk about the possibility of integrating Orientalism into the dominant economic project through the discourse of development. His valuable insights are integrated into our analysis, though we remain skeptical about his treatment of the economy. For Escobar, the economy remains un(der)theorized, detached from class, and protracted to the name "capitalism," with its unchanging motif of capital accumulation as an inexorable process of history allied to capitalism (see Gibson-Graham 2001; Sanyal 2001). Thus, while Escobar gives us the important insight of associating Orientalism with the economy, the absence of an undeconstructed notion of economy makes the analysis somewhat incomplete, especially when dealing with the changing face of the economy itself in the era of globalization (with its associated difficulty brought about through the blurring of the East-West and North-South dichotomy). However, despite these skepticisms, overall, we remain deeply influenced by the openings provided by Escobar, and we definitely share his concerns regarding the "politics" of the so-called depoliticized discourse of development.
3. See Resnick and Wolff (1987) for a detailed analysis of the class equation. Also see Ruccio, Resnick, and Wolff (1991).
4. If we include the state capitalist enterprises into the circuit of global capital, then the conception of global capitalist hegemony will also hold true with certain modifications. Even if not all global capitalist enterprises are private, we do believe that our emphasis on global capitalist enterprise as being private is justified in the current scenario of the globalization discourse that celebrates the private at the expense of the state form of capital.

5. *Khadi* means indigenous cloth. It is a symbol for a cottage-based economic system that is characterized by labor intensive, village- (and family-) based production and marketing processes.

References

Ahluwalia, I. J., and I. M. D. Little, eds. 1998. *India's economic reforms and development: Essays for Manmohan Singh*. Oxford University Press: New Delhi.

Bhagwati, J., and T. N. Srinivasan. 1993. *India's economic reforms*. New Delhi: Ministry of Finance, Economic Division.

Bhagwati, J. 1993. *India in transition: Freeing the economy*. Oxford: Clarendon Press.

Chakrabarti, A. 1996. *Transition and development in India: A critique and reformulation*. PhD diss., University of California, Riverside.

———. 2001. Class and need: Towards a post-modern development economics. *Margins* 1, no. 2 (August).

———. 2003. Aftermath of Iraq: What should be a radical Marxist project? *The Other Voice*, May.

Chakrabarti, A., and A. Dhar. 2002. The nodal possibility of entry point: Theorizing the end of capitalism. Working Paper: Department of Economics, Calcutta University. Presented at the conference "Subjects of Economy," University of Massachusetts, Amherst, November 2002.

Chakrabarti, A., and S. Cullenberg. 2001. Development and class transition in India: A new perspective. I*n Re/presenting class: Essays in postmodern Marxism*, ed. Kathy Gibson, Julie Graham, Stephen Resnick, and Richard Wolff. Durham, NC: Duke University Press.

———. 2003. *Transition and development in India*. New York: Routledge.

Chakravarty, S. 1987. *Development planning: The Indian experience*. Oxford: Clarendon.

Chatterjee, P. 1986. *Nationalist thought and colonial world: A derivative discourse*. London: Zed.

Chaudhury, A. 1994. On colonial hegemony: Toward a critique of brown orientalism. *Rethinking Marxism* 7 (4): 44–58.

———. 2001. Western Marxists' commodity fetishism: Looking for an exit. *Margins* 1 (2): 56–73.

Chaudhury, A., and A. Chakrabarti. 2000. The market economy and Marxist economists: Through the lens of a housewife. *Rethinking Marxism* 12 (2): 81–103.

Chaudhury, A., D. Das, and A. Chakrabarti. 2000. *Margin of margin: Profile of an unrepentant postcolonial collaborator*. Calcutta: Anustup.

Cullenberg, S. 1992. Socialism's burden: Toward a "thin" definition of socialism. *Rethinking Marxism* 5 (2): 64–83.

Escobar, A. 1995. *Encountering development: The making and unmaking of the third world*. Princeton, NJ: Princeton University Press.

Gabriel, S. 1990. Ancients: A Marxian theory of exploitation. *Rethinking Marxism* 3 (1): 85–106.

Gandhi, M. K. 1958. *The collected works of Mahatma Gandhi.* 90 vols. New Delhi: Publications Division.

Gibson-Graham, J. K. 1996. *The end of capitalism (as we knew it): A feminist critique of political economy.* London: Blackwell.

———. 2003. Globalization under interrogation: An ethics of the local. *Rethinking Marxism* 15 (1): 3–7.

Gibson-Graham, J. K., Stephen Resnick, and Richard Wolff, eds. 2000. *Class and its others.* Minneapolis: University of Minnesota Press.

———. 2001. *Re/presenting class: Essays in postmodern Marxism.* Durham, NC: Duke University Press.

Gibson-Graham, J. K. and D. Ruccio. 2001. "After" development: Re-imagining economy and class. *Margins* 1 (2): 158–81.

Government of India, Ministry of Finance. 2000. *Economic survey 1999–2000.* New Delhi: Ministry of Finance, Economic Division.

———. 2001. *Economic survey 2000–2001.* New Delhi: Ministry of Finance, Economic Division.

Hardt, M., and A. Negri. 2000. *Empire.* Cambridge, MA: Harvard University Press.

Harris, J., and M. Todaro. 1970. Migration, unemployment and development: A two-sector analysis. *American Economic Review* 40:126–42.

Jalan, B. 1991. *India's economic crisis: The way ahead.* New Delhi: Oxford University Press.

Joshi, V., and I. M. D. Little. 1996. *India's economic reforms 1991–2001.* New Delhi: Oxford University Press.

ILO. 1991. ILO: The dilemma of the informal sector, report of the director-general. International Labour Conference, 78th session, Geneva.

———. 2002. *ILO: International labour conference, decent work and the informal economy.* Geneva: ILO.

Killick, T. 1995. *IMF programmes in developing countries.* London: Routledge.

Lewis, W. A. 1954. Economic development with unlimited supplies of labour. *Manchester School* 28:139–91.

Nehru, J. 1954. *Jawaharlal Nehru's Speeches.* Vol 2. New Delhi: Publications Division.

Resnick, S. A., and R. D. Wolff. 1987. *Knowledge and class: A Marxist critique of political economy.* Chicago: University of Chicago Press.

———. 2001. Empire and class analysis. *Rethinking Marxism* 13 (3–4): 61–69.

———. 2003. *Class theory and history: Capitalism and communism in the USSR.* New York: Routledge.

Ruccio, D., S. Resnick, and R. Wolff. 1990. Class beyond the nation-state. *Review of Radical Political Economics* 22 (1): 14–27.

Sachs, J. D., A. Varshney, and N. Bajpai, eds. 1999. Introd. to *In India in the era of economic reforms.* New Delhi: Oxford University Press.

Sanyal, K. K. 1988. Accumulation, poverty and state in third world capital/pre-capital complex. *Economic and Political Weekly: Review of Political Economy* 23 (5): 27–30.

———. 1993. Capital, primitive accumulation, and the third world: From annihilation to appropriation. *Rethinking Marxism* 6, no. 3 (Fall): 117–30.

———. 2001. Rethinking development: Beyond the narrative of transition. *Margins* 1 (2): 35–57.

Stiglitz, J. E. 2000. Interview by Lucy Kosimar. *The Progressive*, June.

World Bank. 1991. World Bank report 1991. Oxford: Oxford University Press for the World Bank.

———. 2000. *Partnerships for development.* Washington: Creative Communications Group for the World Bank; Oxford: Oxford University Press for the World Bank.

———. 2001a. *Social protection sector strategy: From safety net to springboard.* Oxford: The World Bank Group.

———. 2001b. *World Bank report 2000/2001: Attacking poverty.* Oxford: Oxford University Press for the World Bank.

World Bank. 2002. World Bank Development Report. *Building institutions for markets, the World Bank*, 171–79. Oxford: Oxford University Press for the World Bank.

About the Authors

Steven Gould Axelrod is professor of English at the University of California, Riverside. He is the author of *Robert Lowell: Life and Art* (Princeton University Press, 1978) and *Sylvia Plath: The Wound and the Cure of Words* (Johns Hopkins University Press, 1990). He is the coeditor, with Camille Roman and Thomas Travisano, of *The New Anthology of American Poetry*, volumes 1 and 2 (Rutgers, 2003 and 2005). He has also edited or coedited books on Robert Lowell, Wallace Stevens, and William Carlos Williams, and he has published articles on a wide range of American poets.

Anjan Chakrabarti is reader at the University of Calcutta. He is coauthor with Stephen Cullenberg of *Transition and Development in India* (Routledge, 2003).

Stephen Cullenberg is dean of the College of Humanities, Arts and Social Sciences, and professor of economics at the University of California, Riverside. He is coauthor with Anjan Chakrabarti of *Transition and Development in India* (Routledge, 2003).

Anup Dhar is a research fellow in women's studies at the Asiatic Society, Calcutta.

Emory Elliott is university professor and distinguished professor of English at the University of California, Riverside, and the director of the Center for Ideas and Society. From 1972 to 1989, he was on the faculty of Princeton University, where he chaired the English Department and American Studies. His books include *Power and the Pulpit in Puritan New England, Revolutionary Writers: Literature and Authority in the New Republic*, and *The Literature of Puritan New England.* He is the editor of *The Columbia Literary History of the United States, The Columbia History of the American Novel, The Prentice Hall Anthology of American Literature*, and *Aesthetics in a Multicultural Age.* He is president of the American Studies Association.

Margaret Gray is assistant professor of political science at Adelphi University. Gray's work on Latino and labor politics focuses on immigration, race, ethnicity, and transnationalism. She has published academic and policy pieces. She guest edited, along with Carlos Decena, a special issue for the journal *Social Text* titled *The Border Next Door: New York Migraciones* about recent Latino immigrants in New

York state. Gray has a decade's worth of experience working for nonprofits on economic justice issues.

Dr. Frances S. Hasso is associate professor of gender and women's studies and sociology at Oberlin College. She recently published *Resistance, Repression, and Gender Politics in Occupied Palestine and Jordan* (Syracuse, 2005). The essay published in this volume is part of a book project on emerging sexual practices and marital contracts among Sunni Muslims in Egypt and the United Arab Emirates, family law, and the relationship of all of the above to national and transnational governments.

Grace Kyungwon Hong is assistant professor in the Department of Asian American Studies and the Women's Studies Program at the University of California at Los Angeles. She is the author of *The Ruptures of American Capital: Women of Color, Feminism, and the Culture of Immigrant Labor* (University of Minnesota Press, 2006).

Tiffany Ana Lopez is associate professor of English at the University of California, Riverside. She is editor of the anthology *Growing Up Chicana/o* (William Morrow, 1993) and author of *The Alchemy of Blood: Violence as Critical Discourse in U.S. Latina/o Writing* (Duke University Press, forthcoming). Her publications include the following: "Emotional Contraband: Prison as Metaphor and Meaning in U.S. Latina Drama" in *Captive Audiences: Prison and Captivity in Contemporary Theater* (Routledge, 2003), and "Critical Witnessing in Latina/o and African American Prison Narratives" in *Pros and Cons: Essays on Prison Literature in the United States* (McFarland, 2005). She is currently working on a project about Latina and Latino prison writing.

Toby Miller is professor of English, sociology, and women's studies at the University of California, Riverside. He is the author and editor of over twenty books, the most recent of which is *Cultural Citizenship* (Temple, 2007). He edits the journals *Social Identities* and *Television & New Media.*

Jasmine Payne is a doctoral candidate in English at the University of California, Riverside.

Patricia Ploesch is a doctoral candidate in English at the University of California, Riverside.

Karen Pyke is associate professor of sociology at the University of California, Riverside. As a feminist scholar, she is interested in gender, race, and class inequalities, interpersonal power dynamics, and the reproduction of inequality. Her current research examines internalized racial and gendered oppression, the construction of identity, and family dynamics in the interview accounts of over four hundred second-generation Korean and Vietnamese Americans.

Dylan Rodriguez is an associate professor at the University of California, Riverside, where he began teaching in 2001. His essay-length writings have appeared in such scholarly journals as *Radical History Review, Social Identities: Journal for the Study of Race, Nation, and Culture, The Review of Education, Pedagogy, and Cultural Studies, Social Justice: a Journal of Crime, Conflict, & World Order, and Genre: Forms* *of Discourse and Culture*. Rodriguez's first book, *Forced Passages: Imprisoned Radical Intellectuals and the U.S. Prison Regime* was published in 2006 by the University of Minnesota Press.

Jenny Sharpe teaches at the University of California at Los Angeles. She is the author of *Allegories of Empire: The Figure of Woman in the Colonial Text* (1993) and *Ghosts of Slavery: A Literary Archeology of Black Women's Lives* (2002), and is currently working on a book-length study of gender, globalization, and transnational cultures.

Cynthia Young is an associate professor in the Department of English and director of the African and African Diaspora Studies Program at Boston College. She has published articles on labor rights, Quentin Tarantino, and the influence of the Cuban Revolution on black intellectuals. Her book *Soul Power: Culture, Radicalism and the Formation of a U.S. Third World Left* was published by Duke University Press in 2006.

Index